Understanding Disability

A Lifespan Approach

Sage Sourcebooks for
SSHS
the Human Services
35

Peggy Quinn

SAGE Publications
International Educational and Professional Publisher
Thousand Oaks London New Delhi

For information:

SAGE Publications, Inc.
2455 Teller Road
Thousand Oaks, California 91320
E-mail: order@sagepub.com

SAGE Publications Ltd.
6 Bonhill Street
London EC2A 4PU
United Kingdom

SAGE Publications India Pvt. Ltd.
M-32 Market
Greater Kailash I
New Delhi 110 048 India

Printed in the United States of America

Library of Congress Cataloging-in-Publication Data

Quinn, Peggy.
   Understanding disability: a lifespan approach / by Peggy Quinn
      p. cm. — (Sage sourcebooks for the human services; vol. 35)
   Includes bibliographical references and index.
   ISBN 0-7619-0526-X (cloth: acid-free paper). —
ISBN 0-7619-0527-8 (pbk.: acid-free paper)
   1. Handicapped children—Development. 2. Handicapped—
Rehabilitation. 3. Developmental psychology. I. Title.
II. Series.
RJ137.Q46   1997
362.4—dc21   97-4852

This book is printed on acid-free paper.

98 99 00 01 02 03 10 9 8 7 6 5 4 3 2

Acquiring Editor:	Jim Nageotte
Editorial Assistant:	Kathleen Derby
Production Editor:	Sherrise M. Purdum
Production Assistant:	Denise Santoyo
Typesetter/Designer:	Janelle LeMaster
Indexer:	Juniee Oneida
Print Buyer:	Anna Chin

CONTENTS

PREFACE

This book is designed as a supplemental text for Human Behavior in the Social Environment courses in Social Work and for Lifespan Human Development courses in Family Studies, Sociology, or Psychology. Its purpose is to provide information on people with disabilities at each of the major life stages.

During the mid-1900s, many people who had disabilities either died at a young age or were virtually hidden from public view in their homes or in institutions. Advocacy efforts by people with disabilities and their families have led to massive reforms in education and in public access. Now, with improvements in medical care and educational and training techniques, and in access to housing, transportation and employment, people who have disabilities tend to experience much the same life expectancy as their peers. They are involved in the same jobs, recreational pursuits, and family crises as the rest of society. This greater integration into mainstream society means that professionals working with families will encounter even larger numbers of clients who have disabilities. It is important to have some knowledge and understanding about their lives.

The basic tenet of the book is that all people have strengths and abilities and all individuals experience development throughout their lives. By understanding the expected developmental progress of individuals with disabilities, social workers and other family professionals will be able to make better plans, provide more appropriate assistance, and serve as links to an ever-expanding pool of resources.

ACKNOWLEDGMENTS

To *Karen, Diane, Danny, Pat,* and *Paul*
who provided my initial education in child development.

To *Emma* and *Clair* who continue to test
and to build my knowledge about children.

To all those who thoughtfully and carefully reviewed and corrected
this work:

Nita Anderson, BS

John Haenes, MSSW

Melba Anderson, BS

Karen Daly, MSSW, MPA

Jennifer Rankin, BA

Ann Rankin, MSW

Daniel Kocurek, MD

Barbara McCloskey, Pharm.D.

Special thanks go to *Jim Nageotte*, my editor at Sage and to *Charles
Garvin*, coeditor of the Social Work series. Their professionalism and
support were indispensable in bringing this book from idea to reality.

INTRODUCTION

This book is about people who have disabilities and their progress through the life span. Though the Council on Social Work Education requires inclusion of course content on disability studies, little information is available to supplement the data typically included in courses such as Human Behavior in the Social Environment or Human Development (Rubenfeld & Schwartz, 1996). The purpose of this book is to present information regarding "normal" development through the life span for those whose progress may not match typical or expected trajectories. This knowledge can, then, assist social workers and other professionals in a variety of settings as they work with people with disabilities throughout their lives.

The first part of this Introduction presents the developmental perspective that serves as the theoretical base for the book. The second section addresses the concept of family. For most people, their families serve as a major source of support. Because the concept of family and the concept of disability vary widely depending on a person's cultural and religious background, some information is offered regarding the effect of different cultural ideas about disability. The last family-related issue is the effect of gender on the assignment of tasks and roles.

Understanding some of the historical views of disability is critical in being able to analyze the reasoning behind laws, policies, and programs that have, at least theoretically, been designed to assist people with disabilities. The third section, therefore, summarizes some ideas about disability, its causes, and its effects. Following that is a brief discussion about some of the policies and programs that affect the lives of people with disabilities. The final section provides a discussion of some of the roles social workers play.

Terminology used in this book follows the "people first" standpoint. Every individual is a complex mixture of characteristics. One attribute cannot describe the entire person but accentuating problems and deficits can create a subtle negative web of expectations about that individual (Saleebey, 1992). Language such as "retarded person" or "confined to a wheelchair" focuses on only one aspect of the person, possibly obscuring the person's true characteristics. The language of choice for this book, then, primarily denotes the person, with the attribute being de-emphasized (e. g., people with disabilities, person with mental retardation) (Humes, Szymanski, & Hohenshil, 1995). No person is only a Texan, or a redhead, a scholar or a wheelchair user. "People first" terminology acknowledges this fact.

To support awareness of the fact that disabilities occur in women and in men, pronouns referring to gender are alternated by chapter. Not all infants are girls, nor are all toddlers boys. Nevertheless, this mechanism avoids the cumbersome "she or he" without relying on the "universal male."

DEVELOPMENTAL PERSPECTIVE

The developmental perspective is based on the work of Jean Piaget and Henry Werner. Piaget (Piaget & Inhelder, 1969) describes the child's progress from concrete learning based on her own body to the acquisition and use of abstract concepts. Each developmental stage relies on knowledge and skills acquired in prior phases. Werner (1990) emphasizes that individuals can develop resilience to counteract the effects of vulnerability. The person also has a better chance of overcoming biological or psychological risk factors if counterbalancing protective factors are present and supported.

The foundation of the developmental perspective is that as the individual develops, body systems grow and differentiate. At the same time, the person's increasing cognitive capacities are used to organize knowledge and acquire new and more complex skills (Hodapp & Zigler, 1990). A developmental perspective also focuses on the interaction between the person with a disability and the environment. The expectation is that this interaction is bidirectional

The developmental perspective has, therefore, been selected as the most appropriate context in which to learn about the effects of disability at various stages of life. The emphasis is on assessing capacities as well as weaknesses, and then on manipulating the environment to support the individual's strengths. It is important to recognize that, in sustaining maximum development, assistance and services should enable the person to continue moving at her or his own pace toward goals that are appropriate for that individual's unique combination of abilities and differences. Most people with disabilities have a long life expectancy and follow the same developmental sequence as others. The expected timetable for completing various developmental tasks may differ, however, and some people will mark success in the life stages in an atypical manner. Using the timetables in traditional developmental theories may focus attention on a person's limitations, leaving little room for celebration of the developmental markers that are reached, albeit sometimes in a different manner. For instance, Erikson (1963), with his emphasis on bladder and bowel continence as the primary indicator of competence, ignores those who are highly competent in managing their lives without traditional "continence" (Owen, 1985).

Another consideration in the development of people who have disabilities is that the very presence of the disability can influence their perception of self and the world around them. The stereotypical expectation by some professionals, as well as the general public, is that everyone experiences life and the environment in the same way. It is vital for social workers and other professionals to recognize that the individual's body and its functioning, as well as personal experience of the world, heavily influence how the person views life.

FAMILY AND DISABILITY

For most people, developmental progress from birth to death occurs, at least in part, within the context of family. The beliefs, resources, strengths, and limitations of that family color its members' perceptions of the causes and results of disability, their relationship with the person who has a disability, and their management of interactions with the wider social and physical environment in which the family is embedded. One of the most striking events for a family is being informed that their child has a disability.

Diagnosis of the Disability

As discussed further in Chapter 2, the diagnosis of a disability is one of the most difficult events most families encounter. This may happen prior to a child's birth, soon after birth or, in the event of accident or illness, when the person is grown. The diagnosis of a disability can be traumatic for a family. Many professionals expect the family's reaction to be one of sadness, depression, or denial (Olshansky, 1962), but the research on which this expectation is based was conducted over 30 years ago. It is important for social workers to recognize the wide variety of responses a family may have to the disability of one of its members.

Families differ in their reactions to disability and in their coping styles. Whereas some may feel sad or depressed, other families appear to experience no negative effects and their adaptation seems quite satisfactory (Leyser, 1994).

In comparison to the situation only a few years ago, many resources are currently available for the person with the disability and for the family. People with disabilities are visible in politics, business, and the media, encouraging parents to visualize their children as successful, independent adults (Kingsley & Levitz, 1994). Depression and sadness need not be the expected response to learning that a family member has a disability, but when professionals anticipate such response, they will usually find it.

Adaptation

The family's success in adjusting to the presence of a person with a disability will depend in part on its ability to adapt internally and externally. Roles and tasks will be negotiated, boundaries will be adjusted, and external systems will be affected as the family becomes involved with a variety of service agencies, parent groups, school systems, and training programs (Crnic, 1990). It is unlikely that the family will reach a long-term, stable state of adaptation. Instead, a more realistic goal is an ongoing adjustment to the changing needs of its members and the constantly varying demands of bureaucracies that purportedly serve the family.

Cultural Competence and Family Professionals

A family's functioning results from the interaction of their beliefs, their resources, and the unique manner in which they respond to mundane and critical events in their lives. Some of the areas in which families manifest diverse views include parenting styles, beliefs about causes and consequences of disability, concerns about seeking help, and relationships with medical or social service personnel. It is vital for social workers, and others who work with families of people with disabilities, to be culturally sensitive and to strive for cultural competence. This means having some understanding of general patterns of belief and behavior that characterize some racial and ethnic groups. It also implies being aware of various religious convictions that may dramatically influence a family's response to the disability of one of their members and their subsequent interactions with institutions such as hospitals, schools, and other bureaucracies.

In working with families, many social workers and rehabilitation professionals assume that other people share their cultural views regarding concepts such as appearance, functional ability, success, and death. This rather ethnocentric view may not be appropriate. In reality, the only way to clearly understand the views of the family is to ask. Honesty about one's own lack of knowledge of the family's backgrounds, beliefs, and values can invite open communication (May, 1991).

New research is emerging on various cultures and their beliefs. Given the influx of new immigrant groups into many areas of the United States, social workers would do well to investigate the literature and, even more important, seek the assistance and support of people from these various cultures. If the worker approaches the family of a person with a disability with the attitude that they have different but equally valued cultural beliefs, the chances of a productive relationship are greatly increased. Among other concepts, the worker needs to understand the family's social traditions, philosophies, technological and financial resources, and ways of resolving conflict (Kagawa-Singer, 1994).

Clear communication and clarification of the family's views on the origin, meaning, and consequences of the disability may prevent the worker's labeling them as noncompliant or neglectful. Though the stance of the family may be viewed by outsiders as irrational or even harmful, it probably has a strong base in the cultural and community belief system. In some cases, the very labeling of the disability may be the source of difficulty for the family. If they do not agree that the person is "disturbed," "retarded," or "disabled" they may see no reason to enroll in special programs, spend time on painful therapeutic exercises, or attend assessment and monitoring meetings (Kagawa-Singer, 1994). If the person is functioning adequately within the family and the community, it makes little sense for the family to spend scarce resources such as time and money to correct what they see as nonexistent difficulties.

Understanding a family's beliefs and concerns about disability, health care, and involvement in bureaucratic systems is vital in order to involve the family in an assessment of its strengths and weaknesses and in developing appropriate interventions. If the family is not included when the therapeutic regime is established, they may have little reason to support and administer one more set of activities imposed by people who may not be viewed as having their best interests at heart (Alston & Turner, 1994).

Within each family, certain roles and rituals persist. Assistance or instruction that violates these traditional behaviors will not be accepted or followed willingly. The social worker must investigate carefully to understand what the family does, how they accomplish their goals, and what their needs are. The socioeconomic and educational level of the parents and their geographic and cultural location will influence their behavior, their choices, and the limits on both of these.

If a family has rituals to help make sense of the world and to solidify its place in that world, it may be important to help them find ways to include the person with a disability in those rituals. Remembering that the person with a disability, as well as all the other family members, will be continually developing, they may need this assistance at a variety of developmental stages. Various modes of including a person into a Thanksgiving dinner or birthday celebration will be different when the person is a child, a young adult, or an elder.

Family myths and stories are an important factor in the family's understanding of itself and its history (Sameroff & Fiese, 1990). The person with a disability needs to be part of these stories and to be able to relate them as well.

Religion

Some cultures regard disability as a punishment or a result of evil spirits or witchcraft (Atkinson & Hackett, 1995) and, therefore, the disability may be viewed as retribution for some sins of the person, the family, or even the community. The intervention of a social worker may be regarded as superfluous or even as a challenge to God. On the other hand, the child with a disability may be seen as a gift from a God who is confident that the parents are capable of caring for this special person

(Kagawa-Singer, 1994). In this kind of case, the parents will not seek or welcome intervention to ameliorate the disability or its consequences.

Gender

Since the advent of the Industrial Age, the role of caretaker has generally been assigned to women. As the provision of care for people with disabilities has moved from the institution to the community and family, an unspoken expectation is that much of this care will be provided by women—unpaid and with no provision for retirement, health care, or other benefits (Quinn, 1996). This role affects the ability of women to participate in the paid workforce and therefore frequently reduces a woman's power in the family and in the community. One consequence of the assignment of caretaking roles to women has been the erection of perceived barriers to men's participation in certain aspects of the family's interaction. These traditional views are being challenged, however, by the rising employment rates of women and increased involvement of men in the lives of their children.

MODELS OF DISABILITY

The medical model of disability is grounded, at least in part, on Parson's (1951) "illness model" in which he describes the criteria for being excused from certain expectations based on one's illness. Under this model, the sick person is released from some social obligations and receives special treatment, provided there is evidence of active efforts to get well. Unquestioning compliance with the orders and regimens prescribed by medical professionals is another component of the sick role (Parsons, 1958). This view may be appropriate for someone with an illness or acute injury. Those with permanent disabilities or chronic illness, however, will probably not "get well." Most people with disabilities will simply stabilize, adapt, and manage their lives. They will not be "cured."

In general, interventions based on this medical model are intended to cure the conditions or provide an elaborate system of care. They focus on modifying the person, assuming that any difficulties lie in the individual's deviation from "normal," rather than in the lack of accommodation within the environment (Finkelstein, 1991).

The social model of disability has emerged from research conducted largely by people who have disabilities (Swain, Finkelstein, French, & Oliver, 1993). This model contends that even though a person with a disability may function differently from some other people, the problems the person encounters do not result entirely from the nature of the disability (Quinn, 1995). The barriers result, at least in part, from unfounded stereotypes and prejudices toward those with disabilities (Funk, 1987). Such attitudes can reinforce an expectation of deviance, incompetence, and poor health (Gartner & Joe, 1987) that may limit social, vocational, and recreational participation. As the person who has a disability recognizes and acknowledges the numerous barriers erected by society, feelings of depression, passivity, or hopelessness may emerge, and these may be interpreted by outsiders as a lack of motivation and adjustment.

A social model of disability sees the problem as located within society. Rather than attempting to change or fix the person with the disability, the focus should be on the removal or amelioration of social and environmental barriers to full social, physical, career, and religious participation (French, 1993).

The idea of a total societal accommodation to the presence of disability is not a new one. Nora Groce tells of the social and linguistic adaptations used by residents of Martha's Vineyard from the 17th to the early 20th century. The island population contained a large number of people with a hereditary form of profound deafness. Most of the hearing people of the island became bilingual in sign and in verbal language to be able to communicate effectively. Because people with and without hearing impairments were able to communicate, neither group was regarded as being handicapped (Scheer & Groce, 1988).

In the field of disability research, most writers today recognize that the problems and barriers are not in the individual who has a disability but in the environment that erects barriers to participation. The social model of disability requires that society address barriers to inclusion rather than spending money on segregation of this population (Finkelstein, 1991).

LAWS AND POLICIES

One of the outcomes of a society's views on disability is the array of laws and policies designed to provide programs, funding, or other assistance. The United States has no disability policy (Berkowitz, 1987). Instead, it has an array of disjointed and often conflicting laws and programs. If there were a national disability policy, it would be evident in consistency across programs in regard to qualifications for service, and across benefits to eliminate gaps in the provision of essential assistance.

To qualify for Vocational Rehabilitation, for example, a person must demonstrate some potential either for employment or for substantial improvement of quality of life. On the other hand, receipt of Social Security Disability Income requires evidence that a person can engage in no substantial gainful activity.

It is highly unlikely that most social workers will have a comprehensive and accurate understanding of the vast array of laws and programs related to disability. It is important, however, to have at least a cursory awareness of some of the major legislation and the benefits that are available. Appendix C contains a brief summary of some of the major legislation related to disability.

SOCIAL WORK ROLES

Social workers are trained to assess the person and the situation, taking care to start where the client is. This requires understanding the view people with disabilities have of themselves, their limitations, and their potential (Smith & Smith, 1991). Knowledge of various developmental life tasks and mechanisms for promoting successful completion of these tasks is also necessary (Kaplan, 1982). Using the strengths approach in working with people who have disabilities leads the social worker to examine the interrelationships of the individual's particular abilities and disabilities, the family, the community, the geographical and cultural setting, and the attitude of the community toward those with disabilities (Saleebey, 1992). It is essential to consider the whole person in the environment where she or he actually functions. Social workers, aware of various cultural and religious tenets, can advocate for the inclusion of these beliefs—along with components such as housing, transportation, medical care, and vocational training—into the plans that are established. Such a focus on differing client beliefs promotes the traditional social work value of client self-determination (Congress & Lyons, 1992).

Case Manager

In implementing policies and providing services to people with disabilities, social workers carry out a wide variety of roles. Some serve as case managers in settings such as early intervention programs, schools, managed care entities, nursing homes, residential treatment centers, rehabilitation centers, or hospitals. In this role, the social workers act as liaisons between families, people with disabilities, and the professionals assigned to provide services. This may mean translating medical terms, tracking down elusive benefits or equipment, and collaborating with other professionals. One of the pitfalls of the case manager's role is the tendency to define the client's need according to what is available within the established system rather than stretching boundaries and possibly challenging current arrangements to obtain what is truly needed (Kuehn, 1995).

Collaborator

Provision of services requires collaboration with many other professionals. Within the health care field, this includes occupational therapists who assist the person in managing daily activities and in adapting the environment to allow maximum independence and activity. Physical therapists focus on increasing range of motion, strength, and endurance. Speech pathologists work on language skills but also assess and treat chewing, swallowing, or eating difficulties. Medical doctors, nurse practitioners, and physician assistants provide diagnoses, medications, and other needed treatment.

Advocate

Though a social worker may have a firm identity as a direct service worker, after being confronted with conflicting rules and regulations between programs, with shortage of necessary services, and continually shrinking funding sources, the roles of advocate, community activist, or political consultant do not seem quite as foreign. To explain the needs of clients or the impossibility of negotiating the system to obtain benefits, the social worker will need to be available to legislators, regulators, and funding sources (Smart & Smart, 1995). *Ignoring the macro aspects of social work is not an option for the responsible and ethical worker.*

Home Visitor

The role of home visitor emerges from a long tradition, dating back to the Charity Organization Societies. This role has been re-emphasized in Family Preservation programs and is an important component of services to people of all ages who have disabilities.

Resource Locator

The field of disability services features many accessible resources and many that are nearly invisible. An important task of the social worker is constant vigilance regarding potential sources of information, technology, funding, or other valuable assets. Parent support groups, groups arranged around particular disabilities, accessible transportation or leisure activities, little known funding sources, and libraries or Internet sites are some of the treasures the worker may accumulate for the future. Appendix A lists some national organizations related to particular disabilities and also identifies support groups that are active in many areas.

SUMMARY

Developmental Perspective

- Development is innate
- To reach maximum developmental levels, a person's unique abilities and timing should be supported

Issues in Working with Families

- Recognize and value the family's cultural and ethnic background
- Identify and respect religious beliefs and customs
- Realize that the family's views of the causes and consequences of disability can affect their willingness to participate in prescribed activities and programs
- Develop an extensive and current base of resources to provide support for the person with the disability and the family

Models of Disability

- In the medical model, change efforts focus on either curing or caring for the individual
- The social model identifies the environment as the focal point for change

Social Work Roles

- Serving as case managers
- Collaborating with other professionals
- Advocating for policy changes
- Home visiting
- Finding and developing resources

PART I

Infants and Children

"Normal," "typical," or "expected" development during childhood includes events and experiences that significantly affect the functioning and behavior of the person as an adult. A variety of developmental models have been presented over the past few decades. Piaget (Piaget & Inhelder, 1969) saw the child's cognitive abilities progressing from concrete understanding to a grasp of more abstract ideas and theories. Erikson (1963) proposed eight stages of development and noted that the crisis in each stage would have to be resolved for the individual to proceed to the next period successfully. To support and encourage a child's progress, it is important that parents and other caregivers understand normal or expected development. There is little evidence, however, that most people have this knowledge.

Despite the enormous amount of information available regarding child development, no theoretical model of development has been standardized for children with early onset disability. A problem arises when young children with disabilities are evaluated using only typical child development models such as those from Erikson and Piaget. The results of such evaluations inevitably focus on the deficits of the children and on the ways in which they are unable to meet expected developmental norms (Rubenfeld & Schwartz, 1996).

For parents of children with disabilities, information regarding their child's development is essential. They need to understand how the child grows physically, socially, and cognitively, and how to support and encourage maximum progress. It may be easier to feel motivated about various therapeutic regimes suggested by physicians and others if parents realize that such activities can promote the child's physical and cognitive development even during infancy. Without an understanding of expected development, it will be very difficult for parents to know how to help their child in moving toward suitable goals, or to seek appropriate assistance when the child needs it (Palkovitz & Wolfe, 1987).

DIAGNOSIS OF THE DISABILITY

One of the most important events for the family is learning about the child's disability (Harris, 1987). This may occur prior to birth, at birth, or even several years later. Parents tend to express greater dissatisfaction regarding how they were informed of the child's disability than with almost any other interactions regarding their children (Russell, 1991).

The diagnosis of a handicapping condition is a stressful event that may leave parents feeling overwhelmed and uncertain about what they should do (Krauss, 1987). It is a shock to hear their child labeled, even if they pressed for the diagnosis after noting a problem (Featherstone, 1971). At the time of the diagnosis, parents need a chance to hear and absorb the information about the child and then come back and discuss it further once they have assimilated the idea (Russell, 1991). Parents repeatedly stress that they want to be told the truth as far as it is known, as soon as feasible (Harris, 1987). They may, however, be unable to absorb and comprehend all the information at one time.

The amount and type of information that parents receive soon after the child's diagnosis can be overwhelming. It is important that someone be prepared to provide the information repeatedly and in a variety of formats so the parents can understand it and can refer back to it as needed. Most physicians do not have the training to deal with the parents' feelings, concerns, and fears, nor do they have time to repeat information or to express it in different formats to ensure that the parents understand. Working with the parents to interpret the physician's comments is an important role for the social worker or other professional.

It is normal for the parents to feel overwhelmed, shocked, and sad. They may mourn and even berate themselves as though something they could have done would have prevented the disability. They need to be supported in acknowledging these feelings. They will probably be tired, frustrated, and feel trapped and tied down at least some of the time. At other times they may feel stupid and confused (Buscaglia, 1983). All of these are normal feelings and parents should not be blamed for feeling them or for expressing them.

Based on some literature, intense and unremitting grief is an expected reaction to the birth of a child with a disability (Yura, 1987). This perspective notes that mourning for the loss of the anticipated, perfect child is not an encapsulated experience. The parent cannot experience the loss, mourn it, and then move to another part of life. The child is still present and the sorrow may be ongoing (Salsgiver, 1996). On anniversaries of special events or at the passing of an expected developmental goal, parents may be reminded again of their child's difference, and feelings of sadness can erupt once more (Davis, 1987).

Most of the research on families' responses to disability has focused on this "tragedy" model (Salsgiver, 1996). Because parents are expected to grieve for the loss of the "perfect child" (Olshansky, 1962), the professionals involved may push the family toward a particular mode of grieving (Powers, 1993). Parents who do not follow the prescribed course of grieving may be viewed as denying the reality of the child's disability.

The research on which this "grief model" is based has serious methodological flaws. First, children with a wide variety of disabilities have been included in the studies, ignoring the differential effects of particular disabilities. In addition, studies have not generally incorporated a comparison group. Therefore, if the family has any negative experiences, these are presumed to be a result of the child's disability (Salsgiver, 1996).

The belief that having a child with a disability is a problem leads to the use of instruments to measure pathology when studying these families. Families of children with disabilities may experience stress, but this may not indicate dysfunction, nor does it necessarily indicate a need for therapeutic intervention (Glidden, 1995).

The stage model of adaptation to the grief of having a child with a disability may have assisted parents and professionals to acknowledge the normality of reactions such as anger toward the child or toward professionals dealing with the family. The universality of such a grief reaction is, however, being questioned (Spiker, 1990). Parents may experience shock when they learn that their child has a disability, but the availability of better information, of visible role models with disabilities, and of parent support groups can mitigate the despair and fear that are the expected components of the traditional grief model.

A nurse working with families in Australia is challenging the grief/crisis model. Penny Kearney's (1993) research indicates that parents may be accurately realistic about the child's disability and still have high hopes for him and great satisfaction with his progress. In other studies, Singer et al.(1993) reported that parents saw their children as fun, kind, loving and cheering. They felt their children had introduced them to new information about disability, mental retardation, and to other people with disabilities (Singer et al., 1993).

Even after they have adjusted to the presence of a child with a disability, parents must continue to adapt to an environment that does not understand their situation. Parents consistently report their dissatisfaction in interacting with medical personnel. When the child's disability is first disclosed, there is seldom an appropriate level of emotional sensitivity. This deficit continues as parents must constantly educate medical professionals regarding the disability, the special needs of the child, and the limitations of various therapeutic regimes (Spiker, 1990).

FAMILY AND DISABILITY

Leo Buscaglia (1983) provides some reassurance to parents as he reminds them that "No parent is perfect, but no child demands perfection. In the early stages of learning the requirements of their unique role, the parents will feel irritations, anxieties, and fears" (p. 30).

People are seldom really ready to become parents. Parents whose child has a disability are not superhuman creatures who suddenly gain the ability to cope with strange and confusing feelings and situations. Parents who have been informed that their child has a disability may feel overwhelmed and depressed. They are not in a physical or mental state to make decisions or plans. It is important that they receive support and information in a quantity and form they can manage. It may be helpful for them to talk with parents of a child with a similar disability. On the other hand, they may need some time to adjust to their situation before they are ready for such discussions.

The transition to parenthood is difficult for most families. With a child who has a disability, it is even more difficult to know what a "good parent" is and how one functions successfully (Krauss, 1987). Leo Buscaglia (1983) points out that parents should be reminded of their child's needs for cuddling, rocking, babbling, and exploring—the very same needs that all children have. Without such reminders, the parents may find that these normal needs are obscured by the child's physical pain, specific diets, frequent doctors' visits, and special medications and treatments.

SUPPORT FOR PARENTS

The most important factor in parental adjustment to having a child with a disability is the availability of parent support groups. These groups provide education for the new parent and for the community. They also gather and distribute research results and other information to the various medical professionals who are involved with their children. In addition, the group members serve as models in managing the medical aspects and the behavioral components of the disability. Most research has focused on the mother and her interactions with, and responses to, the child. In general, the father has been ignored (Bailey, Blasco, & Simeonsson, 1992). Parent groups, however, offer a place for fathers to be involved as well. They can talk to other fathers, observe how they work with their children, and feel supported in their roles (May, 1991).

All parents may not participate in parent support groups and there may be a variety of reasons for this. The age of the parents, their income and educational level, as well as the severity of the child's condition are a few factors. Distance from the meeting sites, transportation availability, and the presence of siblings can also affect participation. Language barriers, or cultural mandates prohibiting the discussion of family matters such as a child's disability may also limit the family's involvement.

VARIATIONS IN CHILD REARING

Families have a wide variety of styles in raising children. Geography, ethnic or racial heritage, religion, and socioeconomic level are all factors in determining parenting styles. The presence of a child with a disability can add even more diversity. It is important to understand the family's view of the goals of child rearing and their ideas about the impact of the disability. If the disability is seen as a punishment from God, shame and guilt may be an issue. If the family focuses on raising children who are well behaved and compliant, their choices about activities and disciplinary structure will differ from those of families who strive to instill independence and decision-making skills. The social worker needs to be aware of local customs and expectations as well as those that the family espouses.

GENDER AND FAMILY INTERACTION

Most research about families has focused on mother-child interactions and only recently have interactions between the father and the child been considered (Sameroff & Fiese, 1990). Within the larger society, the roles men play in their families have changed dramatically during the last few generations. More women are involved full-time in the labor force, thus reducing the time and energy they can give to family. Men are expected to fill in the gaps but without the socially ingrained knowledge about child rearing that women have supposedly received throughout their lives. Fathers who have children with disabilities confront these same situations, plus they must reconcile their concerns about the disability and their uncertainty about the role they should play. Given this societal background, for the benefit of the child and of the whole family, the expectation that fathers want to be involved in the lives of their children must be a given as social workers and other professionals design interventions or care plans (May, 1991).

To support their involvement, it is vital that fathers be included in discussions about their children from the moment the disability is diagnosed. Otherwise, the subtle expectation will persist that mothers are the ones who know about and care for their children. There are a number of ways to engage fathers: Calls to the home can be arranged when the father is likely to be home, information in records and plans should be written for both parents, and so on. If the father does not live in the home, arrangements should be made to supply him with information, taking into consideration the mother's wishes as well (May, 1991).

One limit to fathers' involvement is that services for children with disabilities are generally offered during the workday. Men may not feel comfortable leaving work for doctor's appointments or early intervention meetings, and this can push their wives into the role of "expert" about the child and his needs. The result is that the father is left with a much smaller base of information regarding his child. Without some support and assistance, he may find that most of the decisions being made are out of his control because they involve knowledge he does not have. Men need encouragement to be engaged in their children's lives. The benefits to the entire family are enormous (May, 1991).

Fathers need help in learning appropriate interactions with their children. It is important that they be competent in understanding the child's communication efforts. In addition, they must acquire skills in using adaptive equipment or in becoming an advocate for the child (May, 1991). It is also important that fathers have information and support so they can answer questions of coworkers, relatives, or even strangers who may stare and make comments.

Parent support groups have traditionally provided a network of social contacts and medical information but are often composed primarily of women. The few men who do attend may feel quite uncomfortable and out of place. Some parent groups, however, have focused on providing opportunities for fathers to be involved. Such involvement has been shown to reduce stress and sadness, improve self-esteem, and support more equal sharing of family tasks. Their participation gives men confidence in their parenting abilities while providing a chance to develop relationships with other men who are in similar situations. When designing support programs for men, it is important that they be based on needs and concerns identified by the fathers themselves, rather than on issues the "professionals" deem important or necessary (May, 1991). Variations in men's preferences for support and interaction may reflect their cultural, ethnic, and socioeconomic backgrounds. A variety of mechanisms can be used to ensure that these men have access to information in formats that are helpful and useful. One example would be having videotapes and videotape recorders available for fathers to check out and take home. This enables them to learn about medical procedures, care techniques, child development, or other issues in a setting that is comfortable and familiar (May, 1991).

RESOURCES

Social work with families of children with disabilities has been an important intervention for more than 40 years. The social worker needs to examine the family's strengths and its needs. Information should be gathered about the organization of the family and its income level, the health of the parents and the role each family member plays. In addition, the social worker should investigate just how much overload the parents can manage and what are the unresolved conflicts regarding having a child with a disability in the family. Cultural forces that are operating within the family should be identified as should the constructive attitudes and strengths of its members. The answers to these questions will help in determining what services and assistance would be helpful (White, 1955). It is essential that any treatment plan be developed with the family members. If they disagree with the regime, or if they do not have the financial or emotional resources to carry it out, the likelihood of their following through is greatly reduced (Eicher & Batshaw, 1993).

One task of the social worker is assisting the family in understanding and accepting the realities of the child's disability and prognosis (White, 1955). Parents may need help in understanding the limits of therapeutic interventions and surgery. They may hope for a cure while the surgeon or therapist may have some improvement as a goal (White, 1955).

The first section of the book focuses on the child's development from birth to adolescence. Each chapter begins with a summary of some basic information about expected physical, social, and cognitive development during that particular period. Following that is a description of some of the differences that may be encountered by children with four disabilities: Down syndrome, visual impairment, cerebral palsy, and spina bifida. As mentioned in the Introduction, the use of female and male pronouns is alternated by chapter.

It is essential that parents, social workers, and other professionals be aware of the particular barriers a child may encounter, as well as some of the techniques, resources, and equipment that can be used to support each child in reaching appropriate developmental goals.

Chapter 1

INFANCY
Birth to Six Months

Emma had surgery when she was only 2 days old and was fed through a tube for several days after. Even in the neonatal intensive care unit, her parents were encouraged to hold and cuddle her while the formula was being dripped into the tube. This allowed her to have a sense of warmth and security along with the feeling of a full tummy, just as if she had been sucking on a bottle or breast.

The first 6 months of a child's life involve considerable adjustment to the environment as well as a tremendous amount of physical growth and change. The 1-month-old sleeps most of the time, waking only to eat. The 6-month-old, however, is interacting with her environment and the people in it while focusing great amounts of energy on learning about and using her own body.

EXPECTED PHYSICAL DEVELOPMENT

Development is multifaceted. At any given time, a child is developing in many areas, progressing slowly in mastering some tasks and rapidly in others. Social workers and other professionals need a basic understanding of development to assess a child's progress and to recommend sources for assistance or adaptations.

First Three Months

The newborn lacks the ability to control her arms and legs and is concentrating on the development of visual acuity. Visually stimulating mobiles (those that are visible to the child, not just to adults), small fabric pictures (in black and white) attached to the crib sides, and people who talk and make faces supply intriguing entertainment.

Many of an infant's earliest interactions with the environment are based on reflexes—responses that are present at birth. A touch on the cheek will trigger the *rooting reflex.* She turns her head toward the touch and begins a snuffling search for the nipple. The nipple, a finger, or any other object inserted in the child's mouth will result in a vigorous example of the *sucking reflex.*

The *startle, or Moro, reflex* consists of convulsively jerking the body and then throwing arms and legs out before rapidly drawing them in again. Because this reflex is stimulated by a loud noise or a sudden sense of falling, it is usually followed by vociferous crying.

The *tonic-neck reflex* is also evident in the infant. When lying on her tummy with her right cheek touching the bed, her right arm and leg are extended and her left arm and leg are flexed. Moving her head so that the other cheek touches the bed leads to a change in the arm and leg positions as well (White, 1975).

The *palmar, or grasp, reflex* is exhibited when an object such as a rattle is placed in the child's hand. Her fingers immediately close around the rattle with a surprisingly strong grip. She is unable, however, to release the toy at will. Drawing your finger down the inside of the child's foot demonstrates the *plantar reflex.* Her toes first spread and then curl.

By 6 weeks, the child can hold up her head more steadily and may succeed in getting her fist in her mouth regularly. She is gaining coordination and strength. Arm and leg waving provides exercise as does holding up her head for longer periods of time. As her ability to focus her eyes develops, the child can follow objects moving across her visual field. In addition, watching her own fingers is a fascinating pastime.

Four to Six Months

During this time, the child sleeps less and is much more active. She learns to raise her torso, begins to turn from her tummy to her back, and works on turning from back to stomach. Reaching for objects, checking textures, and waving her arms and legs provide exercise, increase her circulation, and help her learn about her body and her environment. Discovery of her fingers, and especially her toes, leads to hours of entertainment. The ability to grasp a rattle or toy extends play activities even further. It will be several months, however, before she learns the advanced skill of releasing the toy at will.

At about 4 ½ months she begins to reach for objects within her visual range. Toys that make noise and have interesting textures are preferred by the child. Rattles, balls, activity boxes, bells, mobiles, squeeze toys, textured surfaces, teething toys, and blocks are all suitable possibilities for this age child (Pratt, 1989). Playing with these toys teaches the child about cause and effect. She learns to squeeze a toy to make noise or to shake the rattle to see the colored pieces move. These activities also promote the development of hand-eye coordination and improved control of her hands and arms.

TYPICAL SOCIAL DEVELOPMENT

During her first weeks, most of the infant's time is spent sleeping. When awake most children enjoy being cuddled and rocked. Within hours after birth, the newborn may make purposeful eye contact and mimic others' mouth movements. Her concentration is limited to a few seconds at a time, but these early interactions can be an important source of bonding with caregivers and others. Even for the newborn, such social interaction is an important component of development. First, she smiles, and the adult smiles in return, reinforcing her efforts (White, 1975).

Between 6 weeks and 3 months, the infant's social skills improve, and personality characteristics become evident as she indicates what is pleasurable and what is not. She smiles more and begins to chuckle when tickled (Batshaw, 1993). She may also shriek in delight on seeing a familiar face. As she increases her saliva production, she adds bubbles to vocalization in a precursor to language development (White, 1975). Early babbling and vocalizing serve as one screening mechanism used by speech therapists to determine whether the child is physiologically capable of making consonant and vowel sounds necessary for language production.

EXPECTED COGNITIVE DEVELOPMENT

Various theorists have developed lists of achievements or tasks appropriate for the child between 1 and 6 months. Erikson expects the child
to learn to trust, which involves allowing her mother out of sight without
becoming too upset or angry (Erikson, 1963). If the parents consistently
respond to the child's crying or fussing, she gains confidence that her
needs will be met. This base of confidence supports the child in learning
to control and calm herself.

The infant is constantly taking in information, learning about herself
and her place in her surroundings. Jean Piaget regards this period as
concrete and centered on the child's own body; the child sees the world
as an extension of herself and explores and manipulates her own body
to investigate the environment (Piaget & Inhelder, 1969).

SUMMARY OF TASKS

- Progress from random physical movements based on reflexes to pur-
  poseful actions such as rolling over and moving about to explore the
  environment
- Initiate reaching for objects and then grasping and investigating them
- Develop a sense of trust, knowing that the environment will respond
- Use eye contact and smiles to promote social interaction
- Begin babbling, blowing bubbles, and other verbalizations preparatory to
  developing spoken language

INFANTS WITH DISABILITIES

The birth of a child with a disability is a surprise for most families. It
is important to remind the family that almost all parents of newborns
have concerns about parenthood, whether the infant has a disability or
not. A new baby means change and adaptation for the parents as well as
the infant. It is common during the baby's first few weeks for most
parents to wonder if parenthood was a mistake. Parents of children with
a disability, however, might not give themselves permission to experience these feelings. Because their baby is so vulnerable and so in need
of all the affection and care they can give, it seems inconceivable to have

anything but overwhelming love and concern. Anything less might indicate they somehow were not "good enough" parents for this baby. It is important to help parents give themselves permission to wish the baby away, without feeling overwhelmingly guilty. It may help the parents to realize that this wishing is a normal reaction for parents of all children at some point (Rynders & Horrobin, 1996).

Though most parents manage the interactions with their child comfortably, some issues related to the child's disability may become apparent fairly early. Some problems are inherent to the disability and its effects. For example, if the infant has muscle spasms, this may cause difficulty in activities such as feeding and cuddling (Sutkin, 1984). Dealing with a tiny child who has a disability may be frightening and uncomfortable for the adults in her life. They may be hesitant to treat this child as they would other infants. They could feel intimidated about trying to play with her, roll her about, or tickle her (Buscaglia, 1983).

Another concern for parents may be locating a pediatrician who is comfortable and competent in dealing with children who have disabilities. Pediatricians tend to prefer to treat children who have acute, curable diseases rather than those whose condition or disability is a lifelong actuality (Darling, 1991). Contact with other parents of children with disabilities allows parents to locate needed medical personnel. (See Appendix A for a list of resources.)

Babies who have disabilities will usually progress through all of the anticipated developmental stages and accomplish most of the expected tasks. The timetable for these children, however, may be quite different. They may be well within "normal" times for some tasks, ahead on some, and behind on others. Depending on the disability and its overall effect, there are some developmental markers that will not be attained, at least not in the traditional manner.

It is vital for social workers and other professionals to have a sense of what these children *can* accomplish and where they can be expected to succeed. The focus of many assessments and interventions, to which the child and her parents are subjected, is to identify problems and deficiencies. Professionals and family members also need to understand and identify the many areas in which developmental markers are being reached, either unaided or with some environmental adaptations. These successes should be noted and celebrated by all concerned.

Throughout this book, four disabilities will be highlighted: Down syndrome, visual impairment, cerebral palsy, and spina bifida. These were chosen because they represent the four categories of disability that qualify a child for inclusion in early intervention programs. Involvement in these programs is one of the mechanisms by which the child and the family are brought into contact with social workers and other professionals.

Down Syndrome

An infant who is born with Down syndrome can be expected to live into middle or late adulthood, but this is a relatively new phenomenon. As recently as 30 years ago, parents of an infant with Down syndrome were encouraged to place the child in an institution. She was not expected to survive past childhood, nor to ever function at more than an infantile level. Today, with advances in knowledge about physical and cognitive development, accompanied by early intervention services and appropriately designed educational programs, parents can realistically anticipate that their baby will live a long and healthy life.

Down syndrome is a result of a chromosomal disorder that causes physical and cognitive differences. Most children with Down syndrome have 47 rather than 46 chromosomes—an extra 21st chromosome, leading to the term *trisomy 21* (Selikowitz, 1990). Other children with Down syndrome have a translocation in which an extra piece of chromosome 21 attaches itself to another chromosome in every cell. These forms of Down syndrome reflect a chromosomal difference; therefore every cell in the child's body is affected. Another form of Down syndrome is *mosaicism,* a condition in which only some of the cells have 47 chromosomes, with the remainder having 46 (Sugden, 1990). Because only certain cells are involved, the child's physical features and intellectual abilities may be less affected.

Down syndrome is the most common chromosomal anomaly and the most common genetic cause of developmental disabilities, and its cause is unknown (Hayes & Batshaw, 1993). Approximately 17 in 1,000 babies, boys and girls in all racial and ethnic groups, have Down syndrome (Ventura, Martin, Mathews, & Clarke, 1996). The chances of having a child with Down syndrome increase dramatically as the mother gets older (Leck, 1994); however, 75% of these babies are born to mothers who are less than 35 years of age.

In adjusting to having a child with Down syndrome, parents must get the best information possible and seek out support from other parents.

It is much easier to sort out the feelings that are a normal part of adapting to the reality of having a baby with Down syndrome if parents talk to those who understand firsthand what they are experiencing (Rynders & Horrobin, 1996).

Parents' behavior toward their infants tends to be based on their expectations of what the child can do (Hodapp & Zigler, 1990). It is helpful, therefore, for parents to realize that children with Down syndrome progress in the same patterns as other children. Reading books on the development of children who have no disabilities can provide information on what is to be expected at each stage. A particular child may move through the phases at a somewhat slower pace but the steps are the same.

Physical Development

The most visible indication of Down syndrome is facial appearance. The infant may have a small nose with a low nasal bridge, giving her face a flatter look. Her head may be small and less rounded at the back, and her neck may be shorter with loose folds of skin at the back (Hayes & Batshaw, 1993). Her eyes may slant up at the outer corners and have an extra fold of skin (the epicanthal fold) at the inner corners. This child is, however, the result of the chromosomal contributions of both of her parents, and this will be reflected in her resemblance to family members.

Due to the possibility of hearing or visual impairments, it is important that careful screening and assessment be done during the first 6 months. A combination of small, lower set ears and small ear passages can lead to frequent ear infections and fluid build up. This increased fluid dampens the transmission of sound and other auditory stimuli, reducing important brain stimulation. Because some children tend toward strabismus, or crossed eyes, early vision checks should be conducted for corrections to be made surgically or therapeutically, if necessary (Stray-Gunderson, 1986). Lack of visual and auditory stimuli in the early months can limit socialization and cognitive growth. If problems are detected, adaptations can be introduced to support continued appropriate developmental progress.

A child who is born with Down syndrome may experience physical problems. Approximately 10% to 12% have intestinal malformations; blockage in the esophagus, small intestine, large intestine, or rectum are most common (Sugden, 1990). These can usually be corrected with surgery, which is customarily done shortly after birth in order for the child to absorb nutrients from food (Hayes & Batshaw, 1993).

More than 40% of infants with Down syndrome have heart defects. These may be evident at birth or may not be detected for several months or even years (Kozma, 1986). If necessary, heart problems may be addressed immediately, or surgery may be postponed until the child is older and stronger (Hayes & Batshaw, 1993).

Thyroid problems, which are fairly prevalent as well, can be detected through blood tests and can be treated. It is important that these problems be identified before they cause serious developmental delays or other complications. This screening should be repeated every year (Kozma, 1986).

Hypotonia, or low muscle tone, is also fairly common in infants with Down syndrome (Hayes & Batshaw, 1993). This influences all the muscles of the body, including the heart. Good and consistent physical therapy is important in promoting proper muscle tone to maximize development, enabling the infant to roll over, crawl, and walk at or near typical ages (Stray-Gunderson, 1986). Excessive joint flexibility may accompany the low muscle tone, leading to difficulties in head control and in learning to sit and crawl (Hayes & Batshaw, 1993). Low tone in the muscles of the mouth can affect the infant's ability to suck and swallow. In addition, because her mouth is small and has a lower roof, her tongue may tend to protrude. With therapy, her muscle tone can be improved to prevent or reduce the tongue protrusion. She may also teethe later than other children and her teeth may erupt in a different sequence than would normally be expected.

Parents may be faced with additional decisions as medical advances provide potentially beneficial new treatments. For example, some studies have shown that children with Down syndrome can benefit from receiving human growth hormone. If this is given at 6 months, the child may have greater cranial growth and possible cognitive benefits. Given later, the injections may increase growth, thus allowing the child to be closer in size and stature to others the same age (Reilly, 1992). Several issues need to be addressed if parents are considering this treatment. At present, no longitudinal research has been conducted to determine potential long-term problems or side effects. In addition, the treatment is very expensive and unlikely to be covered by insurance. It is important that the social workers and other professionals working with the family be informed about new treatment methodologies and be prepared to help parents investigate the potential benefit or problem for their child.

Socialization

A child who has Down syndrome demonstrates typical social development during infancy. She tends to observe others carefully and respond appropriately. Her early verbalization efforts, in the form of babbling and vocalization, are indistinguishable from other infants for the first 6 months (Steffens, Oller, Lynch, & Urbano, 1992). To encourage appropriate socialization, parents and other caregivers can begin reading to the child and telling stories, as well as playing finger games and singing children's rhyming songs.

Cognitive Development

Cognitive development in infants is difficult to assess. To maximize development, a stimulating environment should be provided. The infant needs high contrast, black and white symbols or pictures on the sides of her crib, mobiles that have pictures that are visible to her, and music boxes, radios or tape recorders with a variety of musical selections (not all Brahms' Lullaby). Exposure to a diversity of settings is also important. She should be in the kitchen to see the activities, smell the odors, and hear the noises and conversation. Lying on the carpet or on the tile floor is another learning opportunity as she explores the texture and experiences the sounds and colors of the different rooms.

Summary of Tasks

Rolling	Low muscle tone may delay accomplishment of some physical activities.
Reaching	Vision problems may impede reaching. Using brightly colored, textured, noisy toys encourages activity.
Trust	This is probably a loving, cuddly baby who responds to everyone.
Eye contact and smiling	If strabismus is not a problem, eye contact and social interactions tend to be excellent.
Babbling	Outstanding babbling skills are indistinguishable from others the same age.

Infants with Down syndrome, once physical problems have been corrected, show little difference from others for the first few months. It is important to provide a stimulating environment to assist the child in reaching her full potential.

Intervention Dilemma

Emma is 5 months old and has Down syndrome. Up to this point, her development seems to be progressing appropriately. She was born with a blockage between her stomach and intestine but the surgery she had when she was 2 days old solved the problem. She has been healthy since then.

Emma's parents have been reading a great deal about Down syndrome. They have learned about treatments using human growth hormones that appear to help children with Down syndrome grow taller. The treatments also seem to increase the child's head size, theoretically allowing the brain to grow larger as well. To be effective, these treatments must be started by the time the child is 6 months old. There is no long-term data on the potential side effects or consequences of this treatment.

1. What are some of the questions the social worker should help the parents ask?
2. What are some of the ramifications if the parents have no health insurance to cover the costs of the treatments?
3. What resources should the social worker identify for the family?
4. What strategies could the family use to resolve conflict if grandparents, or other significant family members, disagree with the parents' decision?

Visual Impairment

Approximately one child in 1,000 has a visual impairment, but most of them will have at least some usable vision (Holbrook, 1996). Almost half of the children with visual impairments are born blind and another 38% lose their sight before 1 year of age (Batshaw & Perret, 1992). The label *legally blind* does not necessarily mean that the infant is completely unable to see. She may be able to see only a narrow area but the objects in that field may be quite clear. If her visual acuity is severely limited, she may have a wider field of vision but the objects she can see may be fuzzy (Sugden, 1990).

Loss of vision may result from structural problems in the infant's eye or from damage to the parts of the brain that interpret visual information. Cataracts are another cause of vision loss in infants. The lens of the eye is cloudy, obscuring some or all vision. Surgery to remove the clouded lens may be done during the child's first 3 months to allow visual input to encourage normal development (Holbrook, 1996).

Physical Development

Visual ability affects all areas of the infant's development. Vision allows her to capture a complete picture of what is occurring and where the action is taking place: What is seen provides a frame of reference for interpreting other sensory and perceptual information (Sugden, 1990). If the child cannot see what is happening, it is important to provide verbal and tactile cues about her body, her surroundings, other people who are present, and the actions she should take. For example, it is important for people to speak to the infant each time they enter the room. This helps her associate certain sounds with the presence of a person. People should be encouraged to speak before picking the child up, to prepare her for the fact that she is to be lifted. Without such a warning, the sensation of suddenly being raised in the air can be startling and she may justifiably respond by screaming and stiffening. Though this response indicates that her reflexes are in excellent shape, it is not likely to result in comfortable social interactions.

For the infant with sensory impairments, some developmental tasks may be difficult, but most markers can still be reached if she has the support and assistance of others (Patterson, 1988). Touch, for example, is an important mechanism for taking in information and can be used to bolster the infant's proprioceptive development—her ability to know where her body is in space.

Caregivers can talk as they stroke her arms and legs, or as they wipe her bottom during diaper changes. In her crib, on the floor, or wherever she is lying, she should also have toys with interesting textures and sounds.

Sounds are the infant's other source of sensory input. A sighted baby moves her head to turn her eyes toward a sound. A child with visual impairments often keeps her head very still, as if she is listening intently (Sugden, 1990). At times, this is necessary because, if she squirms, the noise of her body against the sheets or the carpet can block out other sounds (Ferrell, 1984).

Naming sounds can also augment the infant's learning. Parents and other caregivers can tell her that the clicking sound is the clock and the banging is the door closing. She will not understand all of this at first but she needs to become accustomed to voices and sounds and to learn how to relate them to her own body and its position.

During the first 2 or 3 months, the infant's motor skill development is quite adequate, possibly because so many of her activities are based on reflexes (Dunlea, 1989). Problems begin to emerge between 4 and 6 months, when the lack of visual perception reduces the child's motivation to reach for objects and move around (Sugden, 1990). If she cannot see an object, she has little reason to reach for it, and this may reduce her opportunities for exercising and strengthening her muscles. The resulting low muscle tone can impede the development of gross motor skills (Batshaw & Perret, 1992). It is important, therefore, that her toys have interesting textures, shapes, and sounds that make them appealing and easier to locate. Shaking a bell near the child's hand and then helping her reach for it can provide information about objects just out of range. Reaching is an important skill because she is less likely to creep or crawl or move around in her environment until after she has reached into it. Once she is able to hold an object and move it from hand to hand, she will begin to manipulate it to learn about its possibilities. These developmental tasks are usually accomplished within the expected time range (Sugden, 1990).

A child often learns to roll over after she accidentally flops from her tummy to her back and then works to repeat the event. In the same way, she will probably learn to crawl on the basis of her own experimentation. If she is unable to observe other children crawling or sitting up, it may slow her progress somewhat. Parents or therapists can physically move her arms, legs, and body through the stages of rolling over, crawling, and sitting erect to ensure that she continues to master the appropriate developmental tasks. It is also important that her caregivers play with her, rolling her over and moving her arms and legs around to give her a sense of her body's position.

Socialization

Just as with other infants, the child with low or no vision shows her response to others by snuggling close to them and making cooing sounds. Her lack of eye contact, however, may be distressing to adults who are expecting this reinforcement. The adults must learn to use the child's tactile and verbalization abilities to support and sustain intimate contact.

An important component of language development is the child's babbling. The sounds she makes stimulate her to continue making noise and moving around. The next step, imitating the sounds of those around her, typically occurs within the same age range as for sighted children. In fact, "expressive jabbering" with its intonation and pacing changes may even occur earlier than would be expected for sighted children (Dunlea, 1989).

Cognitive Development

Using a variety of forms of input such as talking to the child, touching her, and moving her body allows her to learn through all of her senses. She needs opportunities to create associations between objects and their names, and between sounds or touches and various experiences.

A problem for the infant with visual impairments is the "Good Fairy Syndrome": Things just happen out of thin air (Holbrook, 1996). It is important, therefore, to assist her in associating various occurrences with sounds or words or actions. When someone is about to change her, they can touch her tummy or use particular words. Similar techniques can be used for feeding. Providing a routine allows the infant to associate the sound of the microwave warming the bottle, or some particular words preceding breast-feeding, with the sensation of sucking and of a warm, full tummy (Ferrell, 1984).

Summary of Tasks

Rolling	Some help may be needed until she realizes she can roll by herself.
Reaching	This is a difficult skill to learn, but progress can be encouraged with a voice or a noisy toy.
Trust	The help she receives in understanding and acting on her environment supports her progress in developing trust.
Eye contact and smiling	Adaptation: Use touch and words to supplement eye contact; smiling may be somewhat slow.
Babble	Excellent skills and right on time.

Special assistance may be required for the infant to develop her proprioceptive senses. She must be able to balance herself, determine when she is upright, and know where her limbs are in reference to the rest of her body.

Cerebral Palsy

The term *cerebral palsy* refers to faulty development or damage to motor areas of the brain, causing a disruption of the brain's ability to control movement and posture (Eicher & Batshaw, 1993). This may result from problems during intrauterine development, from brain injury at birth, or from trauma due to an accident prior to age 16 (Stanley & Blair, 1994). Approximately 4,500 infants and babies are diagnosed each year (Taylor, 1993). Causes include infections such as rubella during pregnancy, severe and untreated jaundice in the infant, lack of oxygen during or following birth, Rh incompatibility, and stroke (Taylor, 1993).

Symptoms can range from severe to mild. The adult with cerebral palsy may be nonverbal and unable to care for herself, or she may experience only a clumsiness of gait. By definition, cerebral palsy is not progressive; the symptoms may vary over time but they do not worsen, and almost all children with cerebral palsy live to adulthood (Eicher & Batshaw, 1993).

The three types of cerebral palsy are spastic, athetoid and ataxic. *Spasticity* refers to the inability of muscles to relax (Miller & Bachrach, 1995). It may be indicated by jerky, explosive movements due to permanently increased muscle tone (Sugden, 1990). This is also known as pyramidal cerebral palsy, referring to the pyramidal tract of the brain that has been damaged (Kurtz, 1992). *Athetosis* is the inability to control the muscle's movement (Miller & Bachrach, 1995). *Athetoid cerebral palsy* is characterized by slow, writhing, uncontrollable movements. If her face is affected, this may cause grimacing and drooling, and she may have difficulty coordinating the muscles needed for speaking. *Ataxic cerebral palsy* affects balance and coordination (Sugden, 1990). She may have a wide-based, unsteady gait and may have difficulty with movements involved in buttoning or writing (Eicher & Batshaw, 1993).

Not all areas of the body are equally affected by cerebral palsy. The severity of involvement is indicated by two terms: *-plegia refers to paralysis and -paresis* means weakness. The term *hemi-* indicates that one side of the body is affected. *Para-* denotes difficulties in both legs, and *quadra-* or *tetra-* means that all limbs are affected. Therefore, spastic hemiplegia refers to lack of control in the leg and arm of one side. Spastic paraplegia refers to spasticity in the legs, and spastic quadriplegia means that both legs and both arms are involved (Eicher & Batshaw, 1993). Double hemiplegia indicates that the entire body is affected but the arms may be more involved than the legs (Gersh, 1991).

A large number of children with cerebral palsy also have strabismus, or crossed eyes. If this is not treated, the child compensates for the double vision by using only one eye, resulting in poor vision in the neglected eye and difficulties in judging distance due to the loss of binocular vision.

Though congenital cerebral palsy is present at birth, it may not be detected for several months because initially the baby may appear to be progressing normally (Scherzer, 1990). Parents are often the first to recognize the signs of problems in the child but may have difficulty in convincing others. Diagnosis of cerebral palsy relies on a careful assessment of the child's developmental progress. The physician or therapist will need information about the timing of various milestones such as smiling, head control, and grasping, as well as data about any difficulties in chewing or sucking (Scherzer, 1990). In some cases, the actual identification of cerebral palsy is a relief to parents who have known that something was wrong but had no diagnosis to support their concerns (Cogher, Savage, & Smith, 1992). Once the diagnosis is confirmed, the family can begin to understand the child's disability and to plan realistically for the future.

Physical Development

Depending on the type of cerebral palsy and on the affected areas of the infant's body, it is important to hold and position her correctly for maximum support and mobility. An occupational therapist can instruct the parents and other caregivers in therapeutic handling techniques that can be used throughout daily routines of playing, feeding, bathing, and dressing. This allows the child to experience and learn from the sensations of normal movement and the parents to feel success and satisfaction in their role as caregivers (Kurtz & Scull, 1993).

Some therapeutic interventions are designed to prevent postural abnormalities and improve motor control (Kurtz & Scull, 1993). The goal of a positioning program, for example, is to help the infant maintain a flexed, symmetrical posture with her arms and legs oriented toward the middle of her body. Parents can position her flat on the bed or lying on her side using rolled towels. In addition, she should be exposed to a variety of sights, sounds, and textures to encourage her development (Kurtz & Scull, 1993).

Some of the symptoms of cerebral palsy can cause difficulties in feeding, digesting, and eliminating food. Because lack of proper nutrition can lead to other serious problems, medical intervention is essential if the infant is having difficulty in eating or retaining food (Gersh, 1991).

Between 3 and 6 months, the infant is expected to gain control over her body, preparing for crawling and walking later in the year. An infant with difficulty controlling her head movement may have trouble rolling over, sitting alone, and making eye contact (Cogher et al., 1992). If she has difficulty in moving, she may not be able to grasp and hold toys and other objects unless they are placed in her hand. Without assistance, she may miss the opportunity to learn through manipulation and exploration of the toys (Coley & Procter, 1989).

An area that may be problematic is that of bathing. If the infant tends to have some involuntary muscle movements or poor head control, bathing may be more frightening than enjoyable. A sponge wedge in the tub can provide support and stability for the child and reassurance for the parents (Cogher et al., 1992).

Socialization

An infant typically stimulates interaction with the adults in her environment. Even in her first few weeks, she tends to react to a human face, searching it and responding with strong eye contact. For the infant with cerebral palsy, this social interaction may be more difficult. An action as small as a smile can trigger a dramatic physical response, causing her body to stiffen and her eyes to roll back. The interaction with the adult is thus interrupted by the loss of eye contact (Cogher et al., 1992). Poor eye control may cause difficulty in making and maintaining eye contact with others, again reducing the opportunity for interaction. Other social building blocks include rocking and cuddling. If the infant's muscle tone is extremely rigid, these activities can be more difficult to manage (Cogher et al., 1992).

Social workers and other professionals can assist parents and other adults to learn ways to manage the infant so she experiences the essential cuddling, rocking, singing, and gazing. Parents need to be encouraged to sing songs and do finger games as part of the ongoing social interaction. Once again, the positioning of the child has a major influence on what she can see and on how her body can move. This requires the assistance of occupational therapists or other professionals until parents can begin to interpret these instructions according to the child's individual needs (Cogher et al., 1992).

Providing visually stimulating pictures, mobiles, and toys and then talking about these with the child is important even in the early months. Reading books can offer an opportunity for cuddling, introduction of sounds, and directing of her visual attention.

Cognitive Development

Even an infant needs to begin to comprehend cause and effect. For most children, one association is between nursing and a warm, full feeling in their stomachs. If an infant must be tube fed, she does not need to suck on the breast or bottle to experience this sensation. The tube, however, will probably be removed at some point and, without some intervention, she may not associate the effort of sucking with satisfying her hunger. To assist in establishing this connection, parents can make a habit of holding and cuddling the infant during feedings to provide a sense of warmth and caring as her tummy begins to feel full (Cowan, 1991). She can also be encouraged to suck on her fist during the feeding, thus connecting a sensation of fullness with movement and activity of her mouth.

Movement is not inherently pleasant for some children with cerebral palsy. It may instead be painful or frightening. For such a child, exploration of the environment may not come naturally and easily (Cogher et al., 1992). It is important that she be assisted in touching objects and moving about to gain knowledge of her surroundings and of her own body. A child will typically learn about her environment by putting things in her mouth. She may need help from others to carry out this type of investigation. In this and other efforts, it is important that she be assisted in exploring with the unique abilities that she possesses.

Parents and other caregivers must also observe the infant closely to encourage her beginning efforts at communication and interaction. It may be that a slight movement of a clinched fist is her only means of indicating which toy she would like to examine. It is important that these initial attempts at communication receive attention and response from others in her environment (Cogher et al., 1992).

Though the infant's crib may seem the safest place, she needs to experience a variety of settings (Cogher et al., 1992). Noises, smells, and even temperatures are different in the kitchen or the living room. She should also be included in many of the family's activities even before it is evident that she has an understanding of what is happening.

Summary of Tasks

Reach	Adaptation: Watch for indications of reaching and offer help to encourage her progress.
Rolling	Excessive muscle tone or spasticity may impede her ability to move about purposefully.
Trust	Proper positioning can encourage social interactions.
Eye contact and smiling	Lack of eye control, or severe spasticity, may make it more difficult to maintain appropriate eye contact.
Babble	On time in making sounds.

Occupational and physical therapists can help establish routines and develop techniques for positioning to ensure that the infant reaches her maximum developmental potential.

Spina Bifida

Neural tube defects (NTDs) are congenital malformations of the vertebrae and spinal cord (Charney, 1992). In the United States, spina bifida is one of the most common and most serious birth defects, occurring in approximately 1 in 1,000 births (Hobdell, 1995). It is the major cause of paraplegia in young children.

Spina bifida means open spine or spine in two parts and results from a failure of the spine's vertebral arches to fuse completely (Shurtleff, Luchy, Nyberg, Benedetti, & Mack, 1994). Soon after birth, surgery may be required to close the spinal canal to prevent infection of the spinal cord or the brain. *Spina bifida occulta* is the most common and least severe type of spina bifida. An abnormal opening is present in the spine, but the spinal cord and nerves are usually not damaged and neural functioning is not affected. The only indication of the abnormality may be a dimple on the skin at the site of the vertebral opening; the person may not even be aware of the condition (Lewis, 1987). *Spina bifida aperta* means that the spinal cord is open, with no skin or bone covering for protection. *Spina bifida cystica* refers to a fluid filled sac, called a *myelomeningocele,* which protrudes through the gap in the spine (Rekate, 1990a). This sac contains part of the spinal cord and the attached nerve tissue, leaving them vulnerable to injury and infection (Lewis, 1987). Both spina bifida aperta and spina bifida cystica expose the spinal cord to possible injury because of the lack of protection usually provided by the overlying bone, skin, and ligaments.

The location of the spinal lesion is the major determinant of the extent of physical problems. If the lesion is in the sacral area, down in the very low back, most of the muscles needed for ambulation will probably be spared but some bowel and bladder dysfunction may be present (Rekate, 1990b). A lumbar level lesion, generally below the ribs, may result in paralysis of the ankles and some weakness in the knees and hips, requiring the use of braces and crutches (Rekate, 1990b). Foot and ankle deformities may also be present.

Scoliosis, or curvature of the spine is a common problem in children with spina bifida. If required, this may be treated with therapy, an orthotic device, or the insertion of pins into the spine to hold it in place. Some children will also have rib abnormalities, most of which will cause no difficulties and require no treatment (Rekate, 1990b). Kyphosis is another possible problem. This is an abnormal forward curvature in the spine causing a hump in the back and may be associated with rib abnormalities (Charney, 1992).

A child who has a myelomeningocele may also have a congenital abnormality of the brain called a Chiari malformation in which the lower portion of the brain is displaced down into the spinal column instead of remaining within the skull (Tarby, 1990). This malformation can interfere with the circulation of cerebrospinal fluid between the brain and the spinal column and can result in enlargement of the brain called hydrocephalus. Between 70% and 90% of those with spina bifida have hydrocephalus, commonly called "water on the brain," which can lead to retardation (Charney, 1992). This may necessitate installation of a shunt to drain the excess fluid. The shunt is a small plastic catheter inserted into the brain and run under the skin behind the ear and down the neck into the abdominal cavity (Charney, 1992). From time to time, hospitalization may be required for shunt replacement or for further surgery on the spinal cord (Johnson, 1988).

A thorough neurological assessment of the newborn is essential. Spina bifida is a static condition rather than a progressive one. An accurate evaluation of the infant, therefore, should offer a reasonable prediction of the child's motor potential throughout life (Rekate, 1990b). This means that if the child, at any time in life, is not living up to this potential, an assessment should be done to determine what is wrong, because the problem can generally be corrected.

Family members will find themselves continually educating all the professionals who are working with their child. This means forwarding copies of newspaper articles and other publications as well as ensuring that every person working with the child receives the results of all assessments and examinations (Peterson, Rauen, Brown, & Cole, 1994).

Professionals working with families of children with spina bifida need to help the family develop a positive—yet realistic—view of the future. The family, as well as all medical, social, and educational professionals who will work with them, need to be educated about the physical and developmental needs of the child and the importance of setting realistic goals for the child and family (Peterson et al., 1994).

Physical Development

Parents of a child with spina bifida or myelomeningocele, will be required to understand the child's physical condition as well as all the treatments that are used. For example, they need to know about shunting, which is designed to relieve the pressure of hydrocephalus, and about any possible complications arising from this procedure (Peterson et al., 1994). Parents also need to be aware of latex allergy, which is common in these children. They must be able to recognize the symptoms and to minimize the child's exposure to latex rubber (Peterson et al., 1994).

Another major concern for the infant with spina bifida is decubital ulcers, often called bedsores. If she is not physically active, continued pressure of her body on the bed or other surfaces can cause skin breakdown. Caregivers should check the child daily so that any problems may be dealt with before they become serious (Charney, 1992).

Proper positioning of the infant encourages appropriate development. To prevent deformity or contraction of her legs, the child may be placed flat on the bed with a pad between her legs, keeping her hips in the proper position. This and other techniques are designed to ensure that her muscles and joints develop properly, allowing her to reach typical developmental milestones such as sitting, standing, and walking (Pomatto, 1990).

The child with a myelomeningocele may be delayed in rolling over and sitting up. As she begins to move about, if she has little or no sensation in her legs she may use her arms to propel herself, commando-style, across the floor. If she has a sacral or lower level lesion, she may manage to crawl on all fours (Charney, 1992).

It is vital that family members clearly understand the instructions they are to follow regarding all the various areas of care. Given the stress many people experience when in a doctor's office, even information that seems clear at the time may not be recalled accurately when it is needed. Professionals working with the family should provide information in as many formats as possible. Parents need written material, verbal discussions, and videos that can be reviewed at home. They should also be encouraged to call with questions whenever necessary.

The family's linkage with early intervention or other programs provides them with information on the child's condition and expected progress. In addition, the early intervention team members will develop an appropriate program to help the family provide activities that encourage the child to move about and explore the environment as independently as possible (Peterson et al., 1994).

Socialization

The presence of the myelomeningocele, or the scars from surgery, may be intimidating to parents and other caregivers. The infant, however, still needs to be touched, cuddled, and rocked. She also needs conversations—even if they are one-sided—singing, finger games, and stories.

As she begins to make sounds, she needs to have her babbling imitated by those around her. In this way, she realizes that she has an influence on her environment.

As soon as she is physically capable, she should accompany her parents and others on outings to the grocery store or the local library. She and her parents need to learn how to deal with the outside world, responding when necessary to questions about her condition.

Cognitive Development

The development of an understanding of cause and effect is important for the child with spina bifida just as it is for all other children. If she hits a toy and it moves, she has made something happen. Repetition of this action reinforces her power and ability. She needs to see black and white figures in her crib, and mobiles over her bed to stimulate her visual development. She also needs to meet a variety of people in a number of settings such as malls and parks.

For an infant with difficulties in mobility, it may be difficult to accomplish some of the developmental tasks associated with infancy (Patterson, 1988). She may need help in moving toward toys in order to manipulate them and learn about their various properties. Appropriate braces or supports can enable her to sit alone, providing a new view of the world and its possibilities.

Summary of Tasks

Rolling	Depending on the level of the lesion and the severity of the paralysis, rolling may be on time or slightly delayed.
Reaching	If no visual problems are present, reaching is probably on time.
Trust	Frequent or painful surgical procedures and treatments may slow the development of trust.
Eye contact and smiling	Proper positioning and support encourage timely progress.
Babbling	Right on time.

Caregivers need to learn about shunts and latex allergies, to prevent complications and encourage developmental progress. The child will need to be touched, rolled about, and generally stimulated to help develop muscle control, strength, and balance.

CHAPTER SUMMARY

During her first 6 months, the infant is expected to grow in size and weight, to progress in learning to control her body, and to develop social skills that allow her to interact with others to get her needs met. A child who has a disability may have additional issues to manage. Surgery or braces may be necessary and frequent therapy sessions may consume much of her time and that of her parents. The particular symptoms of her disability (low vision, spasticity, or low muscle tone) may also present difficulties.

Despite these potential problems, an infant with a disability will complete many of the expected developmental tasks. Her timing may be a little slow in some areas, and adaptations may be needed to reach some markers, but with appropriate support and encouragement, her progress will be very similar to that of any other infant.

DISCUSSION QUESTIONS

1. Popular literature frequently features "miracle treatments" that will "cure" a child of her disability. Identify some sources of information the social worker could use in helping parents decide whether or not to give the child treatments that might possibly spur growth and development.
2. What are some recent laws or policies that will affect benefits and services for children with disabilities?

Chapter 2

TODDLER
Six Months to Two Years

> Jeff is beginning to investigate his environment. He is reaching out for the music box that plays incessantly and is learning to retain his grip on the fuzzy bear whose nose he loves to chew. Because his vision is very limited, Jeff tends to use his sense of taste as he examines his world. Now that he is more mobile, his parents must watch carefully to keep him from using this mechanism to test the characteristics of their dog's tail.

By 6 months of age, a child is expected to have gained some control over his body and begun to focus on interactions with his environment and those in it. He will actively strive for mobility, progressing from crawling to walking, to explore the various settings in which he finds himself. He eagerly searches the faces, voices, and gestures of others to understand what they are saying and what they want of him. His personality shows itself both in charming ways and in typical 2-year-old tantrums. Using his increasing physical abilities and social skills, he becomes an active participant in his world.

EXPECTED PHYSICAL DEVELOPMENT

Increased gross motor control allows a toddler to become much more mobile between 6 months and 1 year of age. Most children progress from rolling over to scrunching their knees under their tummies and rocking back and forth. The next phase involves forward and backward lurching that may or may not result in his moving in the intended direction. Gradually, he progresses to consistent crawling movements toward desired objects.

At about 6 to 9 months, the child masters leaning back to one hip from a crawling position, which allows him to sit independently. The next tasks are pulling up on objects, then taking steps while holding on to furniture or people, and finally, standing and walking independently. As he begins to walk, toys that can be pushed will help him improve balance and mobility. By 18 months, he gains confidence in his ability to walk and even run. He will still have a wide stance to support his uncertain balance. Another consequence of the efforts to maintain stability is his signature "kidney bean" appearance—a bowed back and a protruding stomach.

Fine motor skills are developing during this period as well. At 6 months, the child is able to grasp toys and is generally capable of releasing them at will. There are a variety of toys on the market that can be attached to his crib or playpen to encourage activity. These toys make noise, rotate colors, or otherwise provide reinforcement when the child is able to hit them. Once he can sit independently, he can grasp a toy, examine it visually, check out its taste and texture, shake it, and then toss it on the ground for someone to retrieve. He can also bang two toys together, demonstrating new skills in making things happen.

When he is first able to hold objects, he will use his palm and all his fingers. Later he will refine the ability to use his fingers independently. At this point, an important developmental task is learning how to put objects into a bucket or cup. Next comes the ability to stack objects. Threading beads on a string, snapping blocks together, and coloring or drawing are other steps in cultivating fine motor skills.

Learning to eat independently also involves dexterity. Early finger foods may include items such as cookies or toast slices that are easy to grasp. As his fine motor control improves, he will be able to handle smaller items such as peas or pasta. Gradually, his desire to imitate others will lead him to use a spoon or fork.

To prepare for games and sports, it is important for a toddler to learn to throw and catch balls of different sizes. As he improves in his walking skills, he should also master kicking a ball.

SOCIALIZATION

Learning to communicate is a fundamental task for a toddler. He progresses from nonverbal gestures to multiple-word sentences during his first 2 years. Waving "bye-bye" is an early communication accomplishment. Initially, a child may wave with his fingers pointed toward his own body rather than toward the other person because this is what he sees when someone waves at him. Pointing and gesturing are other communication tools that serve as precursors to spoken language.

The infant's babbling and bubble blowing give way to the mimicking of sounds. Language, or spontaneous articulation, appears at about 6 to 12 months. The child is fascinated with the sounds he can make. At first these are random noises, but by the end of the first year, he uses pacing, intonation, and inflection to mimic the conversations he hears around him. Around his first birthday, the child begins to associate the sounds he is making with the appropriate objects or concepts, and language formally begins. As he improves in his ability to reproduce sounds, he enters the stage of echolalia, repeating the sound of the last word another person has said. "Go outside," for example, reverberates as "ousside?"

Between the first and second year, he is able to communicate effectively by using "telegraphic speech." One word, accompanied by gestures, can convey large amounts of information. The word *eat,* for example, when coupled with a gesture toward the microwave indicates that he is hungry. The progression to two-word sentences occurs at about 2 years. With the addition of a second word, the child can accomplish amazing feats of manipulation. "Go car," or "Eat now" produce responses from the environment that are usually sufficient to encourage him in further exploration of the wonders of speech. His pronunciation may be fairly unique during this period, and it may be that only those familiar with him can provide accurate interpretations.

The refinement of communication skills is basic to the development of social competence. A child must observe and listen to understand when he should speak, listen, or follow a command. This learning takes place in a variety of settings such as the home, shopping centers, church, or playground.

In addition to learning to communicate, a toddler masters other social skills. As an infant, his play activities focused first on his own hands and toes and then on whatever objects he could grasp. By the age of 1, he might play near others but not usually with them. The 2-year-old, however, progresses toward real interactive play with his peers. He also begins to learn how to share toys and take turns. In addition to peer contact, the toddler should be involved in relationships with people outside the family to encourage appropriate social interaction.

COGNITIVE DEVELOPMENT

The development of cognitive skills is demonstrated in most of the toddler's activities. Learning to move about independently and beginning to communicate needs and wishes are contingent on the ability to process ideas. To support cognitive development, educational professionals suggest that he be exposed to a wide range of concepts and objects as part of his prereading program. Zoos, farms, stores, and libraries are important resources. Children need to be introduced to books at a very early age. In addition to having stories read to them, they should have books of their own, preferably small, cardboard-paged books with bright simple pictures. By the age of 2, a child can "read" his own books by pointing to pictures, mimicking actions, and identifying characters in the stories.

Another part of cognitive development involves learning the names of objects. The 2-year-old can point to tummy, eyes, toes, doll, dog, and other people when someone says the name. In most cases, the child can also independently name many objects and people.

One suggestion to support this learning is a "names" book. Photographs of objects and people in the child's life can be glued on cardboard pages. The name of the person or object should be printed on the page using upper and lower case letters like the printing style taught in most schools. In this way, he becomes accustomed to the names as they will be encountered when he begins reading. Another important resource for prereading skills is the television program *Sesame Street,* which teaches letters and numbers in an enjoyable format (Oelwein, 1995).

In addition to all his other tasks, a toddler is learning about cause and effect. By 8 months, he will move a towel or blanket to search for a toy hidden underneath. A few months later, he may pull a rug or blanket on which a toy is sitting to bring it within reach.

From birth to 2 years, a child's play activities are characterized by exploring and manipulating objects, himself, and others to learn about the sensory characteristics and the basic actions of objects in his environment (Pratt, 1989). Appropriate toys for this kind of learning include balls, blocks, push and pull toys, pop-up toys, pots and pans, sand and water toys, hammers and peg boards to pound, dress-up clothes and hats, and musical instruments such as bells, tambourines, keyboards and drums. Simple puzzles and other toys that can be taken apart and put together are also suitable.

SUMMARY OF TASKS

The toddler is expected to increase his abilities to explore and interact with his environment and those who populate it. Toward this end, he will usually

- Progress from crawling to walking
- Increase fine motor control
- Develop communication skills: make himself understood and understand others
- Begin social interactions with peers—sharing, taking turns, and playing near or with others
- Expand his base of knowledge by participating in a variety of experiences

CHILDREN WITH DISABILITIES

The toddler's task is to develop autonomy and self-control by exploring and interacting with his environment. If he has a disability, his physical or sensory deficits, or the overprotectiveness of parents and other adults, may limit his ability to accomplish this task (Patterson, 1988).

Supporting the developmental progress of a child who has a disability is just as important as for other children. He needs to experience movement, sounds, smells, textures and tastes, as well as interactions with other children and with adults. Adaptations in the environment, or in toys and equipment, can support the child's exploration of his world and his progress toward maximum use of his abilities.

Physical Development

A major task for the toddler is developing a means of moving about in his environment. Most children will learn to crawl, sit erect, stand and walk. If the child is not able to crawl, he can still move about by using a scooterboard, which allows him to lie on his stomach and propel himself about, using his hands or his feet (Coley & Procter, 1989). Sitting erect and scooting backward provides another approach to mobility for the child who cannot crawl. He sits upright, uses his hands to lift his buttocks just a little off the floor, and then scoots backward. He may use this procedure to move up or down stairs as well. Another mobility aid is a caster cart, which allows the child to move about while seated. This can extend his play range considerably and ensure that he does not miss important cognitive stimulation and social interactions with his peers (Coley & Procter, 1989).

These variations on traditional mobility are sufficient to allow the toddler to participate in activities with others who are also playing on the floor. When play activities of his peers move to a desk or table, however, he needs to be able to join them. A stroller or a wheelchair can enable him to engage in games or tasks at a table and can also provide a means to keep up when his playmates move to other settings.

Social Development

In addition to improving his mobility, another of the toddler's tasks is to interact with others and develop a repertoire of socially acceptable behaviors. This learning process involves experimenting with a variety of activities to determine which ones are approved and which will get him into trouble.

Some of his behaviors will probably seem cute at first. Blowing bubbles in his milk or smashing peas on the table are funny for a few minutes. If these elicit laughter or other signs of reinforcement, he will assume that this is permissible behavior. It is virtually impossible for a toddler to discriminate accurately between social situations in which a particular behavior is allowed and those in which it is not. Consistently discouraging inappropriate activities, therefore, makes life simpler for parents and child.

Various authorities on child behavior may offer a range of suggestions on behavioral training. Discouraging behavior through time-out is often recommended as a disciplinary technique. It is important, however, that the child not feel intimidated by this. Time-out can be taken in the same room, using a specific location that reduces stimuli. For example, the child can be taken to a chair that faces the wall or a corner. The time needs to be brief; 2 to 3 minutes is a lifetime for a toddler. A kitchen timer can remind parents of how long the time-out has been in effect and can help the child to know when the time is up. The object of discipline is not to punish the child but to assist him in learning to manage his behavior.

Toward the end of the toddler phase, a child begins to express his food preferences firmly. Though this may not be a totally positive experience, parents need to know that it is normal and indicates progress toward independence in self-care. It may be helpful to find ways to allow him to participate in making some choices between, for example, applesauce and yogurt, rather than just waiting until he refuses what is offered (Cogher, Savage, & Smith, 1992).

Language Development

Children learn speech from interacting with others. They move from bubbles and babbling through echolalia to intentional use of words and sentences. In some cases, due to illness or surgery, a child may have experienced limited interactions with others. In such a situation, he may need conversation and verbal stimulation even more than other children (Buscaglia, 1983).

Some children exhibit a delay in acquiring speech. Because speech is such an important aspect of social and cognitive development, early intervention team members or other professionals may suggest the introduction of sign language, to ensure that the child has some means of expression until his formal verbal language becomes sufficient. Parents and family members may object strenuously to the introduction of sign language, fearing that this indicates the child will not use verbal language. On the contrary, very young children seem to be quite capable of acquiring skills in both verbal and sign language (Miller, Leddy, Miolo, & Sedey, 1995). For them, this is not a sign of failure, it is one more way to communicate.

Cognitive Development

In addition to learning to communicate with his environment and to be an actor in it, the toddler is gaining knowledge about himself, his abilities, and the properties of his world. At 6 months, he tastes any object he can get in his mouth. This is his primary method of determining its characteristics. If his grasp is weak or underdeveloped, he may need assistance in putting something in his mouth. Between the ages of 1 and 2, he is expected to become more sophisticated in his learning efforts. He will carefully examine texture, color, and shape, and finally, he attempts to determine exactly what the object can do. He will drop it, toss it or hit it with his hand or another object. No matter what his physical abilities or limitations are, he still needs to engage in these important learning opportunities. Creativity, careful observation of what he can do and what he appears to want to do, as well as consultation with other parents and professionals, will allow parents to support the child's efforts and stimulate his cognitive progress.

If a child is hospitalized during his early years, his opportunities for exploring the environment can be greatly restricted. Even at home, he may be confined to special beds, braces, or chairs designed to keep him safe. It is at least as important for this child as for those who do not have disabilities to sense and explore his world. He needs to feel and smell grass and touch dirt as well as watch bugs and birds and dogs. A balance must be struck between keeping him clean and safe, while still allowing the exploration of his environment that is essential to learning (Buscaglia, 1983).

Evidence of progress in cognitive development may be found in many areas. He begins to make decisions such as whether to wear the blue shirt or the striped one. He also states his wishes and intentions, sometimes in the form of a tantrum. He can begin to use his knowledge by helping to pick up toys as they are named and by following directions to bring an object to his parents or to put something in the trash bin.

Family and Disability

One area of family interaction that the child will affect is that of social activities. Having a toddler inevitably complicates the lives of the parents. It is difficult to gather all the necessary paraphernalia for activities such as going to the laundry, the park, or the store. If the child has a disability, the task of organizing an outing or a recreational activity can be even more complex (Featherstone, 1971). Despite the difficulties innate in social outings, families need interactions with people in their community. Research studies and conversations with parents consistently indicate that parental social networks or support groups are essential for the parents' psychological well-being, and for the acquisition of accurate and helpful information on child development, medical advances, and parenting techniques (Crnic, 1990).

Many families of children with disabilities have no reference points for developmental milestones (Krauss, 1987). They may not know any other families with children who have the same disabilities. Despite this lack of knowledge, the family may be called on to provide information about their child to professionals working with him. Doctors, therapists, and teachers may have even less knowledge than the parents about the disability, its effects, and the resources available for managing it. Some of these professionals may be familiar with "normal" developmental progress and some may know about medical and therapeutic interventions, but very few will be able to support the family in anticipating and celebrating appropriate developmental progress for their particular child. For that kind of support, a well trained and informed social worker is needed.

Parents may find it helpful to attend support groups or advocacy groups that are focused on a particular disability (Schilling, 1988). Though many services are available for children, it is up to the parents to gain enough knowledge and confidence to advocate for their children to ensure that they actually receive needed benefits. Contact with other parents, particularly those who are experienced in negotiating the health and educational systems, can be an enormous help (Smith & Smith, 1991).

A variety of issues interact to influence a child's development. The family's educational and economic status, as well as their experiences with disability, will affect how they understand and manage the child's disability. Social workers must be sensitive to the parents and their interests, fears, and beliefs. It is important that social workers understand the level of the parents' knowledge about human development as well as their beliefs about managing behavior and promoting maximum growth in social, cognitive, and physical arenas (Sameroff & Fiese, 1990).

Down Syndrome

The development of the toddler with Down syndrome may seem to slow a little compared to the progress he made as an infant. Low muscle tone and difficulties in focusing his eyes can be problematic. He continues, however, to advance in all areas of development. His social skills with other children and with adults are improving and he is probably a delight to those around him—when he is not demonstrating typical 2-year-old tantrums.

During this time period, his parents will be making important decisions about his participation in early childhood programs and child care settings. Social workers and other professionals can provide information about the various available programs and assist parents in making appropriate choices for their child.

Physical Development

A toddler who has Down syndrome follows the same physical developmental stages as any other child. His progress may be a little slower but he can be expected to reach the same milestones. Some problems that are common to a child with Down syndrome may affect his development if they are not detected and treated.

Because visual problems can slow learning or affect communication, vision checks should be performed regularly. Cataracts and strabismus (crossed eyes) are common in children with Down syndrome. Vision correction ensures that he will not overuse one eye and gradually lose function in the weaker eye. Hearing loss due to fluid build-up is also common. He may not act as if he is in pain even though an ear infection is present.

Low muscle tone may be a factor in the timing of the child's ability to sit, walk, and run. Though these skills may be slow in developing, the child can be expected to progress through the normal developmental sequence. By age 2 it is likely that he will be walking independently or at least moving toward this major step.

In 10% to 20% of children with Down syndrome, low muscle tone and flexible joints result in an increased mobility of the top two vertebrae of the spinal column called atlanto-axial instability (Selikowitz, 1990). When the instability is present, the extra bending of these vertebrae can result in spinal cord injury. Parents should avoid having the toddler engage in activities such as turning somersaults or jumping on trampolines until age 3 when an X-ray examination will determine whether this problem is present. If the instability is identified, the physician will probably suggest that the child be involved in activities such as swimming that do not involve jumping or intense physical contact with others.

Social Development

Learning acceptable social behavior is a major task for the toddler, and parental consistency is a significant factor in his success. Temper tantrums are well-known among 2-year-olds, and the child with Down syndrome is no different. It is important for the parents and other caretakers to help him learn to manage his behavior, even at this young age. When he is overly tired or stimulated, for example at holiday time, he may become out of control. Shouting, "No," or striking out at adults is unacceptable behavior for the child. Shouting or striking back are no more suitable for the adults. It may be necessary to remove the child from the situation for a few minutes and talk to him, perhaps singing songs or telling stories until he can regain his composure. This helps him understand that inappropriate behavior will not be tolerated, and that he can learn to control himself.

Cognitive Development

A child who has Down syndrome is, by definition, considered developmentally delayed. This means that he is expected to lag behind his cohorts, especially in areas of cognitive development. This lag tends to become more evident as he ages. The newborn child with Down syndrome shows few cognitive differences from his peers, but by his first birthday, he may be noticeably slower. The development of concrete concepts appears easier than comprehension of more abstract ideas. He may be able to point to his toes and tummy and will probably indicate his understanding of favorite stories by imitating gestures or sounds. Rhyming songs and finger games allow him to demonstrate memory as he joins in on the movements and probably on the ending sounds. It is important for his parents and other caregivers to continue providing him with a variety of experiences and the opportunity to display his expanding knowledge base.

Summary of Tasks

Mobility	He can be expected to creep by 1 year and to walk by age 2.
Fine motor skills	Putting items in a cup and stringing large beads demonstrate these skills.
Communication	Verbal communication may be supplemented with sign language.

Social interaction	He listens well and enjoys imitating actions and sounds.
Knowledge base	When someone points to objects and body parts, he can name them.

Visual Impairment

Little research is available on toddlers with visual impairments (Dunlea, 1989). In most developmental areas, their progress follows the same trajectory as other children. One major difference is that, for a child who has very limited vision, facial expressions and gestures must be verbally described, and actions such as throwing a ball or riding a tricycle must be physically demonstrated. It is important that each child's needs be individually determined because even among children who are identified as totally blind, there is great variation in usable vision. Most are able to distinguish light and dark (Holbrook, 1996). Contrary to popular myth, limitations in visual ability do not automatically create superior auditory or tactile aptitude. These senses are simply used more efficiently when vision is not an option (Dunlea, 1989). To understand what the child can do and what to expect for the future, it is very helpful for the family of a child with visual impairments to know an adult with low or no vision (Fewell, 1986).

Physical Development

During the first 2 years, a child is expected to progress from lying in one spot to crawling, sitting, and walking. To some extent, this physical progress is dependent on his maintaining good muscle tone that, in turn, is contingent on his moving about and exercising all of his muscles. As mentioned in the chapter on infancy, a child with a visual impairment may tend to lie quite still to be able to hear what is happening. Encouraging him to begin moving about involves offering stimulation which he finds inviting (Sugden, 1990). A familiar voice, a toy that rattles or jingles, or other auditory stimuli can be used to attract his attention and encourage him to reach out and move toward the object. These sounds need to be ongoing rather than intermittent to give the child the opportunity to locate them and move toward them. When he glances at an object, the sighted child can maintain visual contact until he chooses to glance away. Sounds, however, tend to be intermittent rather than continual and the child may not be aware that the object making the sound continues to be present even when the sound is not audible (Lewis, 1987).

During his first year, it may be helpful to have someone move his arms and legs to demonstrate the mechanics of crawling and of shifting into a sitting position. As he progresses to walking, parents can facilitate his self-initiated mobility efforts by setting up areas around the house with objects he can explore (Sugden, 1990).

Word games and songs involving gestures can also encourage involvement and movement. Once the actions have been demonstrated, he may still need some assistance in bringing his hands together (bringing his hands to midline) so that he can participate successfully (Sugden, 1990).

It is important that the child's unique visual abilities be identified and used. If he has difficulty in very bright or very dim conditions, the lighting can be adjusted to provide the optimal situation so that he can move around, examine objects and, in general, have a successful interaction with his environment.

Social Development

Visual impairments do not lead to language deficits, though the child's language may be different in the first few years (Fewell, 1986). He may experience a mild delay in beginning to say words but tends to acquire his first 50 words soon afterward. After this initial stage, his progress parallels that of sighted children, mastering two- and three-word phrases and beginning to name objects and follow simple directions (Holbrook, 1996).

As he develops speech, a blind child relies on his ability to hear and imitate sounds because he cannot see the facial expressions and mouth movements that accompany articulation (Dunlea, 1989). Involving him in games and songs makes him aware of how important verbal communication is. Nursery rhymes that include clapping or rocking offer a very effective means for attracting and maintaining the child's attention as well as providing him with tools for socializing with his peers. Knowing the songs and the accompanying gestures for "Itsy Bitsy Spider" or "I'm a Little Teapot" can assist him as he initiates interactions with other children (Dunlea, 1989).

As with his sighted peers, this 2-year-old will encourage social interaction by playing games with adults, repeating actions that elicit laughter from others, and imitating household activities such as sweeping or folding laundry (Holbrook, 1996).

Cognitive Development

The toddler needs a variety of experiences to relate to the concepts he is learning. He needs to play in the grass, hold a worm, pour water, and cut cookies. He can be encouraged to be aware of the smells, sounds, and textures of various activities. All of this provides the essential base of experience on which reading and other learning activities depend (Holbrook, 1996).

The toddler with a visual impairment uses his sense of hearing to determine distance or direction of objects. Though this helps him manage communication and mobility, it does not give concrete information about objects that are unfamiliar. To be able to name and understand the properties of various phenomena in his environment, a child must know about visually based characteristics such as shape, size, and movement (Dunlea, 1989). The child without visual impairment watches to see what people and objects can do and thus learns more about them. A child with low or no vision needs to hold, bounce, taste, and manipulate objects to identify their properties and their uses. This can present problems with distant objects such as mountains, or fragile items like soap bubbles (Dunlea, 1989). It can also lead to delays in developing some sensorimotor schemes and some abstract concepts (Fewell, 1986).

The sighted child is able to watch the direction of his caregiver's gaze for clues to the meaning of requests and commands. The toddler with a visual impairment can be given verbal cues and tactile indicators such as a touch on his arm or his head to help him interpret what is said to him.

Summary of Tasks

Mobility	Noises and voices encourage crawling; walking can be expected by age 2.
Fine motor skills	Improving skills are demonstrated as he strings beads, stacks toys, and feeds himself.
Communication	He has a good vocabulary and is learning appropriate use of gestures and facial expressions.
Social interaction	Songs and finger games encourage peer and adult interaction.
Knowledge base	Touching and manipulating objects allow him to learn about their characteristics.

Heredity and Disability

Jeff is 18 months old and, like his mother, has a visual impairment. His father, who is sighted, has some serious concerns about his ability to deal with another person in the household who has a visual impairment. He also worries about the quality of life that Jeff will have. Having lived with a visual impairment for most of her life, Sara, Jeff's mother, sees no insurmountable problems for the family or for Jeff. In fact, Sara wants to have another child, even though there is a strong chance the child would have a visual impairment.

1. As a social worker, what are your feelings about visual impairment?
2. What is your response to the idea that a family with several generations of hereditary blindness wants to have more children?
3. What steps would you take to help this family?

Cerebral Palsy

The diagnosis of cerebral palsy may not occur until after the child is a year old. It is not unusual for parents to be the first to note that the child is not developing as expected. Some indicators are: not crawling by 8 months, not sitting by 10 months, or not walking until after 18 months (Anderson, 1991).

By definition, cerebral palsy is not a progressive disability, but the symptoms may differ at various developmental stages. The child's progress will be dependent on the extent of the disability. He may have difficulty holding up his head, sucking, chewing, or successfully reaching for a toy. Another child may experience spasms involving his whole body when he moves his head or even when he smiles at someone. Children with less severe involvement may have normal intelligence and accomplish most developmental goals at an expected time. It is important that parents receive accurate and useful information about the effects of cerebral palsy on their child. The assessment and screening conducted by early intervention professionals can provide this essential data.

The family of a child with cerebral palsy may be bombarded with suggestions from a bevy of experts. The occupational therapist will encourage activities to develop hand control and sensory response. The speech therapist wants the child to play language games, and the physical therapist has a list of exercises to be done each day. Parents must develop the ability to determine what is best for their child or they will be so overwhelmed by all the good suggestions that they will not be able to support and assist him in appropriate ways (Anderson, 1991).

Physical Development

The toddler with cerebral palsy needs to be encouraged to move about and to experience his world. Roughhousing with him (while keeping in mind the motion and positioning information given by the occupational therapist) is an important means of helping him become aware of tactile and kinetic sensations—how his body feels when it moves, changes position, or contacts different textures and surfaces (Anderson, 1991).

Mobility is an important component of gross motor development. The toddler's early efforts at mobility usually involve scooting and rolling. This enables him to move around, though he may not go in exactly the direction he intended. To enjoy and learn from play, he needs to be able to make his way to the toy or activity and still have enough energy to play once he is in position. If he can crawl, he can move more effectively and efficiently toward the desired location. If mobility limitations prevent crawling, adaptive equipment such as a scooterboard can allow him to travel more easily across the floor using whatever arm or leg movement he can manage (Coley & Procter, 1989). There is some concern that supplying mobility aids will reduce a child's motivation to develop independent mobility. On the other hand, it can be argued that the sheer pleasure of participating in play and other activities will support progress toward mobility rather than suppress it (Cogher et al., 1992).

Around 12 months, many children begin pulling up on furniture and taking their first steps. Some children with cerebral palsy lack sufficient equilibrium and righting responses to be able to maintain upright posture. They may also be unable to stop themselves once they lose balance and start to fall (Cogher et al., 1992). Protective equipment may be recommended to reduce concern about injury and allow the child to continue his development.

As a toddler becomes more active, he will have mishaps. Bruises, scrapes, and even broken bones are possible. Parents may have difficulty allowing participation in activities that might result in injury. Reassurance may be needed to remind parents that the child needs to play with toys and peers in ways that stretch his abilities and push him toward further accomplishments, even if this means falling off the crawl board or ending up at the bottom of a pile of children. Once again, balance between safety and progress must be assessed, and the parents must be supported in their decisions.

Play is an essential component of development, providing the child with information about his own body, the qualities of the environment, and the possibilities of the objects in it. He bangs, tastes, shakes, and drops objects to learn their properties, and at the same time, he becomes aware of his capacity to manipulate his body and his environment. Play is, therefore, fundamental in the development of cognitive, social, and physical skills as well as in the establishment of a sense of self-esteem. Most parents know the importance of play, but if they feel overwhelmed with carrying out therapeutic and feeding regimens, play may be accorded a fairly low priority.

In play, as in other areas of the toddler's progress, his unique abilities and potential must be assessed accurately to determine what assistance he may need. For a child with severe motor difficulties, positioning for play activities is extremely important. The posture he instinctively chooses may not be the most beneficial in terms of long-term development. The adult, therefore, needs to help him into the appropriate position and then place toys so he can manipulate them and experiment with their possibilities (Cogher et al., 1992).

To receive maximum benefits from play, the toddler needs toys that are age appropriate and can be manipulated and enjoyed. For a child with severe motor problems, the toys that are most enjoyable may be those for infants, such as rattles and activity boxes. Continued use of infant toys, however, reinforces the perception of the child as a baby. For maximum benefit, toys should be chosen for their potential to expand the child's knowledge of his social and physical world (Cogher et al., 1992). Dolls, cups, telephones, and other objects that represent the toddler's real world are suitable as toys. These allow him to manipulate his environment and imitate the behaviors of those around him.

Between 6 months and 1 year, many children are able to sit alone. Being in a sitting position frees the child's hands to hold and manipulate toys and other objects. If he is not able to sit alone, pillows or special chairs can provide needed support to ensure that he does not miss this important stage.

As the child develops, his toys must change as well, supporting his desire to pretend and to create. He may need some specially adapted toys to make play easier but many items that are commonly available are suitable as well. For example, fat crayons are easier to grip, and taping the paper to the table can decrease the budding artist's frustration. Blocks that stick together easily can facilitate his construction efforts. Again, therapists and other parents have a wealth of ideas and suggestions and probably a treasure chest of toys that other children have outgrown.

For the 2-year-old, running, jumping, and rolling activities promote development of gross motor skills. If he has limited mobility, some of these experiences will be severely curtailed unless appropriate equipment is supplied early. Again, assessment must be made of the child's abilities and needs so that posture is correct, muscle development is supported, and progress is encouraged (Coley & Procter, 1989).

Another task for the toddler is to learn to feed himself. This involves coordinating his hands, mouth, and eyes, plus balancing his body. This child, like most toddlers, will get most of the food on his face, the chair, and the floor, at least until he develops some control. To encourage self-feeding, the child's seating must be appropriate and comfortable with sufficient support to allow him to use his hands freely. In addition, he needs to be able to make eye contact with the others at the table and to observe their interactions (Cogher et al., 1992).

One aspect of eating is to learn about the properties of food—a task usually accomplished through experimentation. He may pour the milk on the table just to see what happens, or he may carefully mash the peas while studying their texture. This messy play helps him learn about the characteristics of the food, the limits of parental tolerance for this behavior, and his own physical ability to control his body (Cogher et al., 1992).

Socialization

Because family meals are such an important component of socialization, the child's mealtime should coincide with that of other family members at least some of the time (Steadham, 1994). Working with the therapists, parents can develop a regimen that meets the child's nutritional requirements, supports his progress toward socially appropriate behavior at meals, and yet does not contribute to increased stress at mealtimes.

A major decision facing parents of the toddler involves placement into a play group or preschool. Learning to share and to take turns are important tasks for this age group and are appropriately learned among peers. The question is whether *peers* means age-mates or children who have similar disabilities. Some early intervention program may offer separate classes whereas others place children in more mainstream settings. It may be helpful for parents to discuss these options with social workers and other professionals and also with other parents who have had similar experiences.

Cognitive Development

One of the tasks of a toddler is learning to make decisions, thus identifying himself as an independent person—separate from others in his life. Early decision making can be as simple as choosing apple or orange juice, or the red or blue shirt, or which story to read at bedtime (Cowan, 1991).

In addition to beginning to make decisions, the toddler also needs a sense of mastery over his environment. Even if he has limited success with any kind of physical manipulation of toys, it is vital that he perceive himself as having some control over his surroundings. Computers may provide an answer. Equipment is now available that responds to eye blinks, eye direction, breath puffs, or head movements. Whatever part of his body the child can consistently control can be used to operate the computer. Parents, and the professionals who work with them, may be apprehensive about selecting computers, but the book, *Computer Resources for People With Disabilities,* (Alliance for Technology Access, 1996) is an excellent source of information and ideas. Using computers, the toddler can begin to learn about cause and effect and develop control over at least some areas of his world.

Summary of Tasks

Mobility	Mobility and ambulation skills are improving, supplemented by scooterboards, caster carts, or wheelchairs if needed.
Fine motor control	Skills in self-feeding and toy manipulation are developing; adaptive equipment and toys are available if needed.
Communication	If necessary, he can use speech boards, sign language, or computers to supplement speech.
Social interaction	He is learning appropriate social skills and behaviors in play groups with disabled and nondisabled peers.

| Knowledge base | Exposure to a wide variety of settings and activities supports his growing knowledge base. |

Spina Bifida

A toddler with spina bifida may have experienced surgery and hospitalization to insert a shunt or to repair the lesion. Restrictions designed to keep him safe and to avoid infections may have reduced his opportunities to interact with others and to explore his environment. Despite this, with some support and encouragement, he can be expected to improve his mobility skills and his ability to interact with others and to exert control on his surroundings.

Physical Development

The toddler's physical accomplishments provide a base for his social and cognitive development. Thus, it is important to encourage him to accomplish physical tasks as far as possible, using braces, splints, mobility devices, or other adaptive equipment as they are needed.

At about 6 to 8 months, most children will begin to sit up. If the level of the lesion prevents independent sitting, an orthotic device, such as a brace or splint, may be needed (Mayfield, 1990). From a sitting position, he can manipulate objects and learn about their properties. He also sees the world from a very different perspective and can participate in social interactions more easily.

Crawling is another important activity in terms of physical, social, and cognitive development. Even if the child has a high-level myelomeningocele and therefore little muscular control of his legs, it is important that activities such as crawling be encouraged. He may devise his own method of propelling himself by rolling or by using his forearms and elbows to move about commando-style. To reduce the possibility of rug burns and to speed up his travel, he may also use a wheeled scooterboard to pull himself across the floor with his hands (Pomatto, 1990).

It is appropriate to assume that any child with spina bifida, if he is not severely mentally retarded or does not have gross spasticity, will be able to walk (Mayfield, 1990). After his first birthday, he should be encouraged to stand and move about even if this necessitates the use of bracing or an orthotic device. Walking is important for mobility and it also serves as a foundation for social interactions and for language, self-help, and cognitive development (Mayfield, 1990).

Socialization

As the toddler progresses in his abilities to sit and to move about, he needs to interact with peers and with adults who are not his customary caretakers. Participation in parents' day out and early intervention programs enables him to develop his social skills within his peer group. Learning to share and to take turns, in addition to improving his communication abilities, are important tasks for this life stage.

If the toddler must use braces or special equipment, his parents will find themselves describing his disability and the accommodations they are making. It is important that they become adept at conveying this information because they will face these questions in each new situation.

Cognitive Development

Unless he is limited in his ability to move about by being confined to a playpen or a bed, the toddler will explore, manipulate, and examine everything in his surroundings. Even if braces, splints, or mobility devices are necessary, he will find ways to reach objects of interest, especially if his parents think they've put these objects safely out of his grasp.

He needs to be encouraged to taste and bang and throw toys to learn what they can do. Managing to control at least some parts of his world is also essential. He will drop his spoon from his high chair tray to see if it falls, if it bounces when it hits the floor, and if some adult will jump up to retrieve it. When he repeats this exercise, he demonstrates his understanding of cause and effect and also experiences the thrill of manipulating someone much more powerful.

Reading books, going to the library, the shopping mall, the zoo and the playground provide the toddler with visual and tactile data that he will need as he develops his vocabulary and his understanding of a variety of concepts. He can also begin to demonstrate his ability to follow instructions and to help with household chores such as putting an item in the trash or folding washcloths.

Summary of Tasks

Mobility   Mobility and ambulation are improving with scooterboards, braces, or crutches used for ambulation.

Fine motor control	He is learning to feed himself and his fine motor skills are developing.
Communication	Speech development is probably on time and is supported by his growing base of concepts and knowledge.
Social interactions	Braces, or other equipment, may need to be explained as he meets other people.
Knowledge base	Continued exposure to many settings is important in developing concepts.

CHAPTER SUMMARY

Developmental progress during the toddler period serves as a foundation for the child's continued physical, social, and cognitive growth. Sitting, standing, and moving about are necessary for appropriate social interactions and for exploring and manipulating the environment. Parents can use a variety of adaptive equipment and the advice of social workers, other professionals, and parents with similar experiences in helping the child to accomplish the tasks of the toddler stage.

DISCUSSION QUESTIONS

1. If the family does not trust the medical or social service system, yet you as the social worker feel that the child requires services, how can you reconcile your professional knowledge and the family's right to self-determination?
2. What are some steps you can take now to build a base of referrals and resources for working with families of children with disabilities?

Chapter 3

PRESCHOOL
Two to Five Years

The fact that Janie has spina bifida did not relieve her parents of the opportunity to experience a 4-year-olds' tantrums. She was quite adept at managing her braces and crutches and at manipulating those around her. When she stumbled getting into the car one day, her mother stood, waiting for her to get up. Janie's demands for help drew the attention of others in the parking lot and it was all her mother could do to remain calm, not giving in to the glares of the other adults nor to Janie's tantrum.

The major task for the preschool child is preparing for school. This requires developing physical abilities such as holding a pencil, throwing a ball, and sitting still. She also is expected to listen, to follow directions, and to relate to authority figures.

EXPECTED PHYSICAL DEVELOPMENT

The preschooler is not experiencing the rapid growth of the infant, but she is still growing taller and gaining some weight. Her fine motor skills are improving and she demonstrates these as she eats with a spoon or fork, holds a crayon or pencil with her fingers rather than her whole hand, ties her shoes, and buttons her clothes. She is learning to cut with scissors and to draw objects that may be recognizable by others. Making items of clay, painting with a brush or with fingerpaints, and creating elaborate structures of blocks are further evidence of her growing abilities.

By the time she enters school, she is expected to be able kick, throw and catch a ball, to stand alternately on each foot, and ride a tricycle. She needs to be able to move from one setting to another and to engage in the games and activities of her peers.

Auditory processing is another skill the preschooler is developing. She must be able to hear and follow instructions and to express herself so others can understand. Many tasks will require appropriate visual processing and perception as well.

SOCIALIZATION

Being able to sit still and pay attention are vital skills for the preschooler to master. She must also develop the ability to relate to other children at an appropriate emotional level, not too shy nor too aggressive. Being able to work in groups and to relate to authority figures are important to successful performance in school (Stephens & Pratt, 1989).

Learning and exhibiting socially appropriate behavior are other tasks for the preschooler. Some professionals will suggest a behavioral management approach in encouraging suitable behaviors and inhibiting undesirable conduct. This can be a very successful approach, but parents need to be reminded that until the child is nearing her teens, she needs immediate reinforcement for appropriate behavior. For example, it is ineffective to wait till bedtime to put stars on the chart for accomplishing dressing goals in the morning. If the reward is a star, it must be presented immediately on the completion of the task.

An important long-term skill that begins at this developmental stage is the ability to manage her own life. Even a preschooler can be responsible for brushing her teeth, putting her pajamas away, and helping to fold laundry. As she learns to put dishes in the sink or dishwasher and to set the table, she is creating a base of knowledge that will be essential to independent and successful living when she is an adult.

COGNITIVE DEVELOPMENT

As she nears school age, the preschooler focuses on intellectual as well as physical development. She can imagine scenarios and pretend to be a heroic figure. She also begins to think about what she will be when she grows up (Cowan, 1991). Her use of symbols and abstract thinking continues to improve, but because her processing is so concrete, she lacks gray areas in her thinking. Things are either good or bad; nothing is in between.

Her ability to link cause and effect may also be a little tenuous. A child will often feel extremely powerful, not yet understanding the limits of her abilities. If she wishes something bad would happen, and it does, she may feel responsible. An adult might understand that the child had nothing to do with the outcome, but it may be very difficult for the child to make that kind of distinction. It is important to explain things to a child at this age, recognizing that she will not understand all of it but, with repetition, will improve her grasp of the situation. It is difficult to know how to answer questions such as, "Where do babies come from?" "Why did you and daddy get a divorce?" and "Where did Grandpa go when he died?" Caregivers need to consider the child's ability to understand their responses, but most important, they need to answer honestly and directly. The questions will arise again and the answers can be refined as the child matures.

To fully understand the stories she will read and the words she will learn, the preschooler needs a body of knowledge acquired through a variety of experiences. These may include riding in a car, a train, a bus, or a buggy as well as visiting a zoo and possibly touching several different animals. Going to a library or bookstore and "reading" many books is helpful, as is the experience of shopping for groceries, clothes, and household items.

Decision making is another skill that the preschooler needs to master. She can begin with age-appropriate choices such as the shirt she will wear or whether she'll have pudding or yogurt for dessert. The complexity and the importance of her decisions will increase as she matures, but it is vital that she begin to develop these skills before she enters formal school settings. As she realizes that the choices she makes are important and valued by those around her, she gains in self-esteem and in understanding that she has some ability to control her environment. Without this knowledge base, she may allow herself to be pushed into making poor choices that can cause problems for her and for others.

CHILDREN WITH DISABILITIES

The tasks for a preschooler with a disability parallel those of other children. She learns to manage and control her body and to handle daily self-care. She also becomes more adept at social interaction with peers and with adults.

Physical Development

Some expected activities and skills may be more difficult for a child who has a disability. Adaptations and accommodations, however, can enable many children to participate in most activities. For example, adaptations to a tricycle can allow a child to ride it using only her hands. Special seating can enable her to propel the tricycle even though her muscle control is limited. Successfully riding a tricycle is an important age-appropriate task that can give the preschooler and her parents a strong sense of accomplishment (Anderson, 1991).

Outdoor activities are important for all children. Some adaptation may be necessary but many activities are readily available. Lying in the grass, smelling the flowers, and watching the bugs can provide an enormous amount of information and stimulation (Anderson, 1991). Being carried in a backpack or being pushed in a stroller can allow a change of scenery.

Becoming toilet trained is a major marker in a child's development. Theorists regard it as important in the development of self-management. For some children, however, reaching this milestone may be slowed or disallowed because of the disability (Patterson, 1988). Even if traditional toilet training is not a possibility, a program of catheterization and bowel management can be developed that allows the child to remain clean and dry most of the day.

Children with developmental disabilities tend to have problems in visual function more often than children without such disabilities (Menacker, 1993). Two of the most common problems are amblyopia and strabismus, or crossed eyes. Amblyopia is also known as "lazy eye" and indicates that the child is using one eye while the other may be atrophying. Treatment usually consists of patching the good eye to force the child to use the weaker one. Strabismus is frequently treated with glasses or surgery (Burke, 1991).

Socialization

Peer interactions and relationships with adults other than customary caretakers are fundamental to the preschooler's social progress. She must learn to maintain an appropriate emotional balance—neither throwing temper tantrums when thwarted nor being too timid in interactions with others (Cogher, Savage, & Smith, 1992). In encouraging their child to engage in interactions, parents may force her to move more quickly than is comfortable for her. On the other hand, some parents may tend to be overprotective, fearing that the child's feelings could be hurt if her contact with other children is not totally successful.

There is a tendency for parents to regard their child's behavior as a reflection on their abilities as caregivers. If she throws tantrums or shyly hides from strangers, her parents may be concerned about how others view them and their child. When the child was very young, the parents worried about her physical well-being, but now that she is a preschooler and experiencing more of the outside world, they worry more about her behavior in public (Darling, 1991).

A preschooler is expected to plan and carry out activities such as building a house of blocks or setting a tea party for the dolls and teddy bears. If her parents provide too much assistance, anticipating her intentions and correcting her mistakes, she may not learn how to make plans and reach goals (Sutkin, 1984). Discipline is another major concern for parents of a preschooler. In their efforts to support the child and help her build a positive self-image, they may fail to set suitable limits and fail to expect appropriate behavior (Patterson, 1988).

It is very easy for parents and other caretakers to get in the habit of training children in poor behavior and then being quite upset when the child demonstrates the results in a public setting. Some consistency is necessary for the child to understand what is acceptable and when. It may be cute when the little one runs away as the parent tries to get her settled for a nap. That same running behavior near a street can be tragic, but there is no way for a child this young to make that distinction.

The language adults use is also important. They need to be specific about what they request and be sure the child can actually understand the instructions. Telling the child to "Stay where I can see you" is useless. She has no idea what the other person can see. On the other hand, "Stay where you can see me" is understandable and gives a command she can actually follow.

During the second year, the child may begin to imitate actions that she has observed, such as stamping her foot in anger as the playmate had done (Piaget & Inhelder, 1969). Another important activity is symbolic play. This involves acting out scenarios such as lying on the floor with her eyes closed, pretending to nap, or feeding the toy bear. Drawing and "writing" are other activities that demonstrate cognitive progress. By 2½, the child may have progressed from scribbling to intentionally drawing images.

Deciding whether to enroll the child in a school or play group with other children who have disabilities or with nondisabled children is a serious concern for parents. Participation in a group of children with disabilities may reduce the possibility of rejection or negative reaction. Parents may fear that the child, who is active and mobile at home, could be injured when interacting with more energetic and physically active peers (Cogher et al., 1992). This may be a difficult decision. The parents need to feel comfortable that they have made a good choice on the basis of their concerns, their knowledge of the child's abilities and needs, and the information from early-intervention program professionals.

Teachers and child care workers may perceive an assertive child as disruptive or manipulative, whereas her parents may see this as an excellent step in the child's learning to manage her life and her environment.

> "Your child has become very manipulative," was the firm message delivered by an obviously disapproving preschool teacher. The mother sat quietly for a moment. If the teacher could have seen inside the mom's heart, she would have seen a quarterback spiking the ball after a touchdown along with major cheering. (Albrecht, 1995, p. 94)

An issue that confronts many parents is compliance with all the rules, regulations, suggestions, and therapeutic regimes recommended or demanded by the professionals who work with the child. Helen Featherstone, mother of a child with a disability, poignantly illustrated this problem several decades ago, and the issues do not seem to have changed. She described the child's daily routine of physical therapy, school, and transportation to medical and other professionals. All of these activities had to be integrated into the usual routine of feeding, loving, and talking to the child, while managing the rest of the family's needs. At one point, a nurse suggested that Helen begin brushing her son's teeth with an electric toothbrush each day for 15 minutes. This would prevent encroachment of the gums, which was a possible side effect of his medications. Helen's response was, "Now you tell me that I should spend 15 minutes every day on something that Jody will hate, an activity that will not help him to walk or even defecate, but one that is directed at the health of his gums. This activity is not for a finite time, but forever." Then she asked where she could possibly find that time. "Because there is no time in my life that hasn't been spoken for, and for every 15-minute activity that is added, one has to be taken away." (Featherstone, 1971, p. 78).

As Featherstone's comments indicate, parents may feel overwhelmed trying to follow all the recommendations from all of the professionals who enter the child's life as formal educational services begin. The social worker might suggest that the parents compile a list of all the goals and activities that have been suggested or mandated and then show the list to each of the professionals involved. The parents can then ask the professionals for their assistance in prioritizing the activities and grouping those that can help to accomplish multiple goals (Holbrook, 1996).

Cognitive Development

The cognitive tasks for the preschooler with a disability parallel those for all other children. She is learning to make choices and decisions. She is expanding her understanding of concepts and ideas and using this new knowledge as she expresses herself to others and as she plays alone and with her peers. She is also participating in the chores of the household by picking up toys, folding towels, or helping with yard work or car washing.

During the preschool period, as she and her peers begin to notice differences and to understand social roles, the child with a disability may become aware that she has some distinctive characteristics and abilities. This is the time to explain to her, at a level that she can understand, about how she is special. She and her parents will also need to develop an explanation of her situation that is comfortable to them and provides adequate information for neighbors, teachers, or folks they encounter in the grocery store. This is just one step in the ongoing educational process in which the child and the family will engage throughout her life.

Summary

Parents of preschoolers expect to reach a period during which they have a sense of relief that the child has gained some independence in feeding, mobility, toileting, and verbalizing her feelings and needs

(Fewell, 1986). If she has a disability, her parents may fear that this respite period will never arrive. Talking with other parents can provide reassurance that most children will indeed accomplish many of these activities on their own.

A very important resource for children with disabilities is the presence of grandparents. Grandparents may be able to offer the adoring kind of love that parents, involved in discipline and limit setting, rarely can. To keep grandparents informed, parents can be encouraged to share the reading materials they have received as well as medical information about the child. Parents can also ask their parents for suggestions on parenting techniques. Most important, parents can keep the grandparents informed about all the child's accomplishments (Holbrook, 1996). The social worker might remind the parents that grandparents and others can be included in designing and discussing the individualized family service plan (IFSP) for the child under 3 years or the individualized educational program (IEP) for the child over 3 years (Balkman & Smith, 1995).

SUMMARY OF TASKS

- Improve fine motor skills, such as coloring, drawing, and tying shoes
- Learn ball handling, tricycle riding, and other game skills
- Develop toileting and hygiene skills
- Hear, understand, and respond to requests and commands
- Interact appropriately with peers and authority figures
- Expand vocabulary and comprehension of a variety of concepts
- Engage in appropriate decision making

Down Syndrome

Families of children with Down syndrome seem to be distinct from families of children with other disabilities. One factor may be that Down syndrome is usually identifiable at birth, so parents know what they are facing and what the prognosis is. This early identification also provides the opportunity for parents to become involved in early-intervention programs and parent networks that can provide information, support, and encouragement (Crnic, 1990).

Research indicates that children with Down syndrome follow the same developmental trajectory as other children. Their timing may differ but the basic progression is identical. This information is helpful for parents and for professionals because it means that the vast amount of knowledge available regarding normal development is applicable to these children as well (Hodapp & Zigler, 1990).

Physical Development

A child who has Down syndrome tends to lag behind others in her physical development. She may begin to walk at 2 years instead of at 1. Encouragement may be necessary to help her accomplish tasks such as opening bottles, stringing beads, and going up and down stairs.

She may also have a tendency toward increased joint flexibility. The ligaments in some joints are loose and allow quite a bit of motion. An area in which this can be problematic is called atlantoaxial instability. The first neck vertebra, the atlas, resembles a bony ring. The axis, the second vertebra, has a bony peg that fits into the ring of the atlas. The joint between these vertebrae is the atlantoaxial joint. For some people with Down syndrome, there is extra flexibility between the peg and the ring, and this can create pressure on the spinal cord (Rynders & Horrobin, 1996). To determine if a child has this condition, X rays should be taken at about 3 years of age. If the child does have this extra flexibility, she should avoid activities such as tumbling, trampolining, diving, and some contact sports.

If the child has low muscle tone, she may also have a lower activity level, which can result in overweight. She should be encouraged to participate in games and then in sports to increase muscle tone and burn calories. Games and toys can also help in developing her fine motor skills as well as assisting her to learn about rules and about playing with others.

Social Development

A large number of studies has been conducted on cognition, language, and learning in children with Down syndrome. Research into the development of peer relations of these children, however, has not kept pace. As early as 1866, John Down identified four personality characteristics in children with Down syndrome. Other researchers in the early 1900s noted similar attributes; the children were thought to be cheerful, good-natured, and submissive to authority (Serafica, 1990). Over the next few decades, researchers simply accepted this positive social stereotype as a given.

In reality, there is as much personality variation among children with Down syndrome as among any other groups. A child may enjoy mimicking others, and this can be problematic if those she imitates demonstrate less than desirable activities and attitudes. Perhaps as part of her efforts to communicate, a child with Down syndrome will watch the faces of others closely. This is flattering to most people, and they will tend to regard her as sociable and attentive.

Peer relationships are an important component of a child's socialization. In playing with her peers, she refines her language skills, learns to take turns, and improves her self control. For a child with Down syndrome, however, these relationships may not be as productive if most of her peers also have developmental delays. If both children in an interaction are lagging in the development of social skills, the tendency to mimic others may not lead to an improvement in the abilities of either child.

Verbal communications are not as easily developed in a child with Down syndrome. Some research indicates that she can understand concepts and follow directions long before she is able to clearly articulate her ideas (Miller, Leddy, Miolo, & Sedey, 1995). When she does begin to speak, her vocabulary skills are likely to improve more rapidly than her proper use of grammar and syntax. Sign language may continue to be an appropriate option to enable her to express herself during this period. Otherwise, if she knows what others are saying and knows what she wants to say but is unable to articulate the words, she may feel and express intense frustration. In one study, children were asked to identify a word printed on a flash card. Those who knew sign language were observed signing the word while still struggling to speak it, indicating that they knew the word even if they had difficulty in articulating it (Buckley, 1995).

The option of special classes versus mainstreaming continues as an issue. If the child plays only with her peers who have developmental delays, she may not be stimulated to improve her social skills. If she is in groups of children without delays, her lower language levels may confuse and dismay them. If her physical appearance indicates that she is their peer and yet her language skills are lagging, the other children may not know how to maintain the interaction (Serafica, 1990). It may require the assistance of an adult to help the children learn how to support each other and make each child in the group feel like an important contributor.

The ongoing development of self-help skills continues for the preschooler. She can brush her teeth, bathe herself (with supervision and help for the hard to reach spots), and dress herself. She can also help with household tasks. These skills are essential for her future success as an independent adult. It is also very good for her self-esteem to be seen as a contributing member of the family and of her class at school.

Cognitive Development

A "names" book that is individually constructed for the child is one way to promote reading readiness. It can contain photos of people and objects that are important to the child, including siblings, parents and grandparents, the car, special toys, and pets. Each picture should be clearly labeled in printed letters using capital and lower case letters to look like the printed words she will encounter in school.

Decision making provides another opportunity for exercising her developing cognitive skills. She can choose her shirt, her snack, or which book to read at bedtime. This helps her demonstrate her strengths and abilities to herself and to others.

Summary of Tasks

Improve fine motor skills	Progress in self-feeding, bead-stringing, and coloring are evidence of her improving abilities.
Learn game skills	Skills are improving and may be stimulated by play with peers.
Develop toileting and hygiene	Peer pressure and parental encouragement support acquisition of these skills.
Interact with peers and with authority figures	Socially appropriate behaviors should be expected and need to be reinforced.
Expand vocabulary	Sight reading may promote speech; sign language can supplement verbal speech.
Increase decision making	Choosing snacks or clothes is good practice.

Visual Impairment

Most preschoolers with visual impairment will be tested and assigned a diagnosis. One possible designation is *legal blindness,* a term used by a variety of agencies. The determination of legal blindness is based on the amount of detail a person can see at a particular distance (visual acuity) and how wide the area of vision is (visual field) (Moore, 1995).

If visual acuity of the better eye is 20/200 or less, the person is classified as legally blind. Even if visual acuity is 20/20, if the visual field is 20 degrees or less the person is probably also identified as being legally blind. This label, however, does not mean that the person cannot see anything at all. Though it may seem negative to label a child as legally blind, many benefits and services are restricted to those with such a diagnosis. If her vision is indeed limited, it is to her and her family's advantage to be identified as eligible for the available assistance.

The preschooler who has a visual impairment continues to mature in all areas of her life. Development is a process of learning and growing and acquiring skills in understanding one's environment, communicating with others, accomplishing self-care tasks, and moving about purposefully (Holbrook, 1996). For children with visual impairments, however, there has been surprisingly little research on what constitutes normal development.

Some difficulties face the child who has low or no vision. She may have a diminished ability to recognize faces and facial expressions and may also have problems with visually guided motor tasks. In addition, it is more difficult for her to comprehend the important features of her environment and thus to move about freely (Moore, 1995).

Physical Development

To learn and grow, children with visual impairment, just like all other children, need to run, crawl, and explore their environments. Parents and other caretakers can assist in this by providing a safe setting and some auditory cues that encourage the child to move about. Her ability to progress through important stages of motor development can be inhibited if parents or caregivers, fearing that she could be injured, limit her activities and her freedom to explore her environment (Skaggs & Hopper, 1996).

Running, jumping, walking up and down stairs, and balancing on one foot are important activities for this age group. She is also learning to stack objects, string beads, and copy geometric figures either by sight or by touch (Holbrook, 1996). In terms of physical growth, a child who has a visual impairment tends to grow steadily throughout the year, whereas children without visual impairment grow more in spurts during the spring months when there is more daylight (Skaggs & Hopper, 1996).

Toilet training is a major task for the preschooler. The signs of readiness are the same for a child with a visual impairment as for others.

She needs to be able to pull her pants up and down, stay dry through naptime, know when she is wet or soiled, and be able to communicate her need to use the bathroom (Holbrook, 1996).

Some children with visual impairment develop mannerisms that may be distressing to others. Children who tend to poke themselves in the eye may be attempting to create visual sensations. They may enjoy the feeling of contact with their eyes as well as the sense of light flashes they can trigger. A child may flap her arms or weave her head. If she spends too much time in these activities, she is reducing the opportunity to involve herself more in the external world. Working with the professionals on the early intervention team, or in discussions with other families, parents can learn ways to curb unwanted mannerisms while still supporting the child's sense of self-esteem and self-efficacy (Holbrook, 1996).

Social Development

For a preschooler, some of the social developmental markers include playing with peers, asking for help, and engaging in pretend play. Dressing independently and putting away toys are also important activities (Holbrook, 1996). Verbal communication continues to develop. The child will begin to use *I,* ask questions, and understand and use some prepositions such as under, behind, and over. By the age of 3, the child with visual impairments will be linguistically indistinguishable from her sighted peers (Dunlea, 1989).

A child with visual impairment may not be able to read the facial expressions and gestures that others use to assess communications. She must learn other cues to be able to know when to remain quiet and when to enter the conversation. In addition, she needs to be taught about gestures and encouraged to point or wave as the situation requires (Holbrook, 1996).

Her self-help skills are improving as well. She can help to put away toys, brush her teeth, and set the table. Activities such as assisting with the laundry and accompanying her parents to the grocery store also help her to understand where things come from and where they should be put when she is finished with them.

Cognitive Development

Even as a preschooler, a child is learning about her world and her place in it. It is important that she begin to exercise some control in areas in which this is appropriate. Even making small decisions, such as the television program she will watch or the brand of cereal she will eat, are important precursors to more vital decisions later in life.

Thinking, reasoning, and problem solving are other components of cognitive development (Holbrook, 1996). First, the child learns about object permanence; that is, objects and people still exist even if they are not visible, audible, or within reach. It seems easier for a child with visual impairment to develop a sense of "people permanence," realizing that Mommy and Daddy still exist even if they are not present. She can be helped to learn about object permanence if caretakers encourage her to search for a dropped object. It is also important to have consistency in the names of various objects and people so the child has a chance to learn them. Once she has grasped the idea of object permanence, the next step is to realize that objects may have more than one form. An egg can be fried or scrambled or raw, but it is still an egg (Holbrook, 1996).

Other indicators of cognitive development: matching objects, remembering past events, telling the use of objects, and sorting objects by size, color, or texture. Categorization, which involves ordering or sorting people and objects, can be problematic for a child with a visual impairment. Most children begin by arranging objects according to their physical attributes, such as color and shape. Sorting by function is the next step. If the child cannot see the similarities and differences in objects, caretakers can assist her by describing these qualities and helping her as she makes the connections (Holbrook, 1996).

Another cognitive task is understanding how the parts of an object relate to the whole (Holbrook, 1996). If the child cannot see the entire object (such as a car), she must mentally construct its image from the pieces she accumulates one at a time.

She also must learn about the totality of actions. She needs to understand that clothes are kept in a chest of drawers or a closet, that toys don't get back in the toy box by themselves, and that a banana must be peeled to get to the part that can be eaten (Holbrook, 1996). If she cannot see the various components involved in doing laundry or in cleaning the room, then each part must be demonstrated to her until she understands the entire task. As she begins to learn to drink from a cup, she may simply drop the cup when she is finished. It is necessary for someone to show her how to pick the cup up from the table and replace it there. Otherwise, because the cup appears magically from midair into her hands, she assumes that midair is the proper place for it (Groenveld, 1993).

Vision specialists can assist parents in organizing the child's books and toys so that she can locate them independently. They can also suggest chores and responsibilities that are age-appropriate (Holbrook, 1996). Continued cognitive development demands input about a variety of concepts. A child who has patted a cow and felt her breath has a better understanding of the meaning of *cow* in her books. If she has climbed on a railroad engine or floated in a boat, she has experiences to connect to the words she reads or hears. Books with audiotapes allow the child to hear and "read" at the same time. These may be available at local libraries.

Early reading experiences may include books with textured objects. The fuzzy bunny in *Pat the Bunny* makes the book easy to locate and identify. Children with low vision may enjoy brightly colored, high contrast picture books. Large, dark markers can make art work more pleasurable (Holbrook, 1996).

Decision making at an age-appropriate level is another important skill. As the child practices this ability on mundane choices such as the type of cookie she will eat or the story she will read, she is preparing for more important decisions later. This is truly a skill. It does not appear full-blown when she becomes a preteen and is required to decide whether to engage in activities her parents might not approve. Early and consistent practice of the skill of decision making is essential.

Summary of Tasks

Improve fine motor skills	She sorts and stacks textured blocks and colors with dark markers.
Learn game skills	Balls containing bells or beepers are helpful, tricycle riding comes easily.
Develop toileting and hygiene	Peer pressure and parental encouragement support acquisition of these skills.
Interact with peers and with authority figures	Consistent discipline and encouragement of socially appropriate behaviors are needed; play with sighted peers may improve some social skills.
Expand vocabulary	Vocabulary is improving, supported by exposure to a variety of objects, concepts, and experiences.
Increase decision making	Choosing snacks or clothes is good practice.

Cerebral Palsy

The developmental tasks for the child with cerebral palsy are similar to those for all other children. She is learning to manipulate and control her body, to interact with others, and to integrate new concepts and information into her current knowledge base. Accomplishing some of these tasks may be complicated by the effects of cerebral palsy.

Physical Development

A major goal of the preschooler is mobility. To accomplish this, problems such as scoliosis, contractures, or dislocations may require correction through bracing, casting, or corrective surgery. Devices such as walkers, scooters, tricycles, and wheelchairs may be necessary (Eicher & Batshaw, 1993). For problems with eating or with excessive drooling, a speech therapist may become involved as well.

As the preschooler with cerebral palsy enters a school or child care setting, therapists or teacher's assistants may provide some of the physical care the child needs. The parents, however, continue to be the primary resource for the child (Cogher et al., 1992).

To keep up with her peers, the preschooler needs to know how to draw with a marker or crayon, how to cut with scissors, and how to write her name. She will also need to master ball-handling skills so she can join in playground games. Riding a tricycle is an important ability as well. Adaptations are available that allow the tricycle to be propelled by hand, by one foot, or with other body motions.

Another task for the preschooler is toilet training. In some areas of society, the successful completion of this task is a source of great pride for the parents—especially if it is *early* (Cogher et al., 1992). Toilet training may also be a requirement for entry into some preschool classes or groups. Parents need to be aware of all of the physical, social, and cognitive clues and abilities the child must master to be continent. Parents of some children are able to catch their child squirming or giving other signs of a need to urinate. Parents of a child with cerebral palsy may not be able to see these signals due to her posture or to her involuntary movements. The help of a professional may be needed to assist the child in accomplishing this task. Some adaptation of the potty chair may be necessary to accommodate her need for support. As she becomes more proficient, it is important to ensure that she can manage her clothing to allow the level of autonomy appropriate for her age (Cogher et al., 1992).

Dressing and undressing are important skills for preschoolers. The first step in learning to dress is taking her clothes off. The child who has cerebral palsy may need assistance through proper positioning to maximize her efforts. It is helpful to begin with small steps. For example, the caregiver can pull the sock almost off and allow the child to finish the task. Then they can celebrate that success and gradually increase the difficulty of the chore. It may be necessary to purchase clothing that is specially designed for ease in dressing. Therapists and other parents can provide information about clothes and other adapted equipment that make daily life easier (Anderson, 1991).

Some children with cerebral palsy may exhibit hypertonicity, or increased muscle tone, resulting in stiff limbs that inhibit dressing. If her clothes must be changed several times a day, this can become a very difficult and distressing activity. The use of songs and body part rhymes can make dressing more pleasant. A therapist may be able to suggest positioning and movement that will make this task easier and make it possible for the child to have a greater degree of participation (Cogher et al., 1992). Learning to dress herself is important for the child's sense of self-esteem and autonomy. It also provides an opportunity to learn about her body while practicing movement and balance.

Social Development

For the child who has seldom been away from her parents, the preschool years can be stormy and difficult. The child may be clingy, have tantrums, or become withdrawn. As the early intervention team works together, using the parents' knowledge of the child's abilities and difficulties, they should be able to develop strategies to help her cope successfully with the new environments and with separation from her parents (Cogher et al., 1992).

When determining how to respond to a child's fear of separation, parents will probably encounter a different opinion from every person they question. Some say let the child cry it out. Others say respond to every call. It is probable that the child needs to feel safe and secure, aware that her needs will be met. This is a base for beginning to let her parents out of sight, trusting that they will, indeed, return and supply what she requires. A child who has experienced a variety of caregivers— parents, grandparents, baby-sitters, and others—gradually learns that her parents do return. She also learns that others can provide whatever care she needs. This kind of experiential base can make the transition to preschool or child care much easier.

It is essential that the parents feel comfortable about the setting and the timing of the child's preschool care. The team must support the parents and assist them if they seem hesitant about relinquishing her care to others whom the parents may not view as capable of providing the kind of support she needs.

During the preschool period, the child is learning to communicate her needs and wishes to others. Parents must be careful not to anticipate all her needs, thus reducing her motivation to communicate these needs herself through hand movements, eye pointing, or verbal signals (Cogher et al., 1992). It is important that the child learn that she has some control in her environment; she can make things happen intentionally.

Discipline is another major issue. Each child needs to learn to behave within the norms of her society. Ignoring the need for discipline because a child has a disability is not doing the child any favor. This can lead to behaviors that make being with her unpleasant. Rules that the family has developed to be obeyed by everyone should be applied to each member on an appropriate level. Allowing the child with a disability to engage in unacceptable behavior can create a situation that will not be helpful in the long term.

For a young child, it is especially important that discipline be immediate and appropriate—an understandable consequence of her undesirable behavior. If time-out is used, the child must be placed in time-out as soon as she misbehaves. Rewards for good behavior need to be immediate as well. A child often has difficulty associating experiences that are separated in time by more than a few minutes.

As the preschooler interacts with her peers, if she has severe limitations, she is more likely to be able to participate successfully in activities such as circle games, story telling, and sing-alongs that are less physically demanding. In this kind of situation, she is able to demonstrate her social skills to herself and to others (Miller & Bachrach, 1995).

Cognitive Development

Though speech is an important element in socialization, it is also essential in cognitive progress because language and comprehension are interactive. Children use speech both to communicate with others and to control their own behavior (Vygotsky, 1962). Therefore, if a child is unable to express herself well in verbal language, people may lower their expectations of her. In such a situation, a wide variety of computers and related equipment is available to enhance her ability to communicate (Alliance for Technology Access, 1996). For example, a child who is unable to speak may be able to control the computer by using special equipment such as a pointing device attached to a headpiece (Taylor, 1993).

A child who has limited movement capability and little verbal communication skills may still be eager to interact with others. Parents and early intervention team members need to be alert for indications of comprehension and work with her abilities.

A child may be slow in learning language and words if her experience with objects and activities is limited either by her disability or her environment. It is essential that she be exposed to a variety of experiences and settings. Interacting with several playmates who have varying levels of physical and mental abilities allows her to observe a range of behaviors. Toys that have interesting textures, sounds, and capabilities can help her explore possibilities. Even a child with severe disabilities can be positioned and assisted in the exploration of her environment.

Children want to learn just for the sake of learning (Cogher et al., 1992). For the child with cerebral palsy, attempts at learning and manipulating her environment may not be easily discernible. She needs to be exposed to a variety of opportunities to examine and to play with a range of objects. At the same time her parents and other adults should be reminded to facilitate the child's learning rather than doing things for her. If adults consistently complete tasks in which she is experiencing difficulty, she gets a message about her incompetence that affects her developing sense of self-esteem (Cogher et al., 1992). There is a fine line between forcing the child to learn (which will probably result in rebellion) and doing everything for her—giving her a negative message about her capabilities. Parents and others who spend time with her will be best able to understand her efforts and provide appropriate encouragement and assistance (Cogher et al., 1992).

Play is the work of a child and represents a task that she will approach spontaneously. If an adult intrudes to assist or correct what she is doing, the child may resist. When she is engaging in a new activity, it may be necessary for her to concentrate intensely. An adult's interference, to correct or assist her, breaks this concentration and she may justifiably become angry and frustrated. Once she is more proficient in an activity, she can be more flexible—pausing to watch others or to listen to suggestions and ask questions (Cogher et al., 1992).

Play time is her opportunity to try out actions, roles, and ideas with no risk of failure and she does not need an adult correcting her efforts. She may also integrate play into many other activities. While drinking from a cup, she may tip it over to see what happens. She may play peek-a-boo with her blanket at naptime or with her clothes while dressing (Cogher et al., 1992).

At some point during her preschool years, the child will probably undergo a standard intelligence test. For a child with cerebral palsy, one problem with such tests is that they rely on a motor response to a command. It is quite possible that the child understands the command but is unable to perform the desired action (Miller & Bachrach, 1995). Once again, the parents' knowledge of the child may be necessary to supplement the more formalized testing results.

During the preschool years, the child will practice and improve her skills in decision making. From humble beginnings such as the choice of toys in the bathtub, she progresses to decisions about which play-mates to call and which games she'd like to play. These seemingly minor choices are precursors to much more important decisions that will be required of the child during her elementary school years. She must begin to hone these skills and become comfortable in her decision-making abilities before she is faced with more difficult choices about activities which her parents might not approve.

Summary of Tasks

Improve fine motor skills	Self-feeding may require special utensils and seating.
Learn game skills	Noisy, highly textured toys are attractive; adapted tricycles encourage mobility.
Develop toileting and hygiene	Supportive seats and easy-to-remove clothing encourage independent toileting.
Interact with peers and with authority figures	Consistent discipline and encouragement of socially appropriate behaviors are needed; play with peers may improve some social skills.
Expand vocabulary	Computers or speech boards can supplement verbal abilities.
Increase decision making	Choosing snacks or clothes is good practice.

Spina Bifida

Preschoolers with spina bifida have the same needs as other children at this age. In addition, their neurological, urological, and orthopedic progress must be monitored. Some of the important developmental goals for this stage include moving toward independence and self-management in areas such as safety, nutrition, mobility, and peer interaction (Peterson, Rauen, Brown, & Cole, 1994).

As the child moves into her preschool years, the family will be involved with even greater numbers of professionals. It is important that the parents be encouraged to continue trusting their own instincts in setting developmental goals for their child and in helping the child reach these goals (Peterson et al., 1994).

Physical Development

Independent mobility is an important goal for preschoolers. If the child is not able to walk, she may still move about using aids such as scooterboards and caster carts so she can engage in floor play with other children (Coley & Procter, 1989).

Different professionals will have different opinions about the necessity of walking for a child with spina bifida. Even though she may eventually use a wheelchair for her primary means of mobility, there appear to be major benefits to having some experience with standing erect and managing at least minimal ambulation. The advantages of standing and walking are related to improvements in blood flow, urinary, renal, and bowel function and in the reduction of bone fractures (Rowley & Rose, 1991).

Skin care is another major concern for a child who has very little sensation in her lower body. Even as a preschooler, she can learn to participate in this effort. She can watch for injuries and be aware of the effects of heat and cold on her skin (Peterson et al., 1994).

Other activities of daily living are appropriately introduced during the preschool period. These include toileting, eating, bathing, and dressing (Peterson et al., 1994). Even though the child with spina bifida may not be able to manage complete independence in toilet training until 6 or 7 years, she needs to be actively involved in learning how to manage this important area. Fecal continence is especially essential for the child's sense of well-being and for her social acceptability. One step toward such continence is the introduction of a regular bowel program. This necessitates the establishment of a consistent time each morning, or every other morning, when the child is placed on the potty chair. The entire program will require from 15 minutes to an hour and is generally scheduled shortly after breakfast to take advantage of intestinal activity (Dixon & Rekate, 1990).

Though most parents don't want to begin thinking about it at this time, age-appropriate information about sexuality is a necessity, especially for the child with spina bifida. Because she is subjected to frequent physical examinations and to bowel and bladder procedures, it is important for her to understand socially appropriate norms of privacy and modesty. Such an understanding can allow her to maintain a sense of dignity and self-control (Peterson et al., 1994). In school, she may learn about "private parts" and "good touch, bad touch." She needs to understand how these warnings apply to her.

Some potential problems are specific to children with spina bifida. If a child who has a shunt appears to have staring spells, this may indicate that the shunt is not performing properly and needs to be repaired (Rekate, 1990c). Another potential problem is tethered cord. The spinal cord usually moves freely within the spinal column, being linked permanently only at the base of the brain. As the child grows, if the cord is also attached at the point of the lesion, it may become stretched between the two points. This can cause symptoms such as back and leg pain, changes in bladder tone, changes in motor or sensory level below the lesion, and unexpected incontinence when the child is on intermittent catheterization. If symptoms are severe, surgery may be required to de-tether the spinal cord (Rekate, 1990c).

Social Development

All children have a need to play with their peers. They learn social skills such as sharing and turn taking while they gain proficiency in language and nonverbal communications. The level of independence the child has gained in areas of bladder and bowel management and in mobility will influence the degree to which she will be able to associate with other children in a variety of settings (Peterson et al., 1994).

Discipline is important for all children. Parents need to assist the child in learning to manage her own behavior. In addition, parents will have to work with other caregivers to maintain some consistency in methods of discipline, whether this consists of time-out or a discussion of the undesirable behavior.

Within the home, parents must set limits and assign responsibilities for chores (Peterson et al., 1994). Even a young child can participate in picking up toys or folding laundry, establishing her as an important and contributing member of the household. If she is not held accountable for appropriate behavior and for contributions to the household management, she will have a difficult time meeting expectations at school and in other social settings.

One skill required of a child who has a disability is being able to explain her situation to others. As a preschooler, she is capable of understanding some facts about her disability. She will encounter other children and some adults who will ask about her braces or crutches, or any other adaptive equipment she uses. It is important that she be assisted in developing an explanation that is comfortable for her and that provides adequate information for others. This is just the beginning of a lifelong process in which she will be educating others.

Cognitive Development

Some children with spina bifida display impulsiveness, inattention, and difficulties with reasoning and problem solving (Peterson et al., 1994). In particular, she may have difficulties in sequencing. This can show up in areas such as taking turns or in understanding a series of steps required for some activity (Lollar, 1994). Early identification of any learning disabilities will allow parents and other caregivers to assist the child in developing appropriate mechanisms for managing attention span and for regulating her own behavior.

The preschooler's ongoing exposure to a rich diversity of experiences, playmates, and settings allows her to continue developing her vocabulary and her understanding of a variety of concepts. She needs to know where groceries are bought, how dirty clothes become clean, and who her neighbors are. Story time at the library can provide peer contact, an enjoyable introduction to reading, and a chance to check out and "read" books of her very own. Involvement in a parent's day out or early childhood program can stimulate her social skills and her desire to learn in order to keep up with her peers. She needs every opportunity to feel good about herself and to feel prepared for the big step of entering school.

The decision-making skills that the preschooler develops are an important base for choices she will encounter later. As she begins with simple choices about books to read or videos to watch, she refines her abilities to consider options and make a selection. This type of practice prepares her for decisions that will face her as she interacts with her peers and with adults outside her home.

Summary of Tasks

Improve fine motor skills	Stringing beads, stacking blocks, coloring, and self-feeding demonstrate her abilities.
Learn game skills	Mobility aids and adapted tricycles encourage play and peer interactions.
Develop toileting and hygiene	Bowel program and intermittent catheterization ensure continence.
Interact with peers and with authority figures	Consistent discipline supports her in controlling impulsive behavior; she will also learn to explain her braces or equipment to peers and adults.
Expand vocabulary	Continued exposure to a rich variety of experiences supports vocabulary development.
Increase decision making	Choosing snacks or clothes is good practice.

Discipline and Disability

Three-year-old Janie has spina bifida and uses braces and crutches for ambulation and, occasionally, as weapons. Janie's parents love her very much and hate to punish her for anything. At home, she always gets her way.

At preschool, Janie intimidates her playmates. She is not hesitant to hit another child to get her way. The teachers have made some progress in helping Janie learn new ways of handling anger and socializing with her peers. Her parents, however, do not follow through with any consistency in disciplining Janie at home.

1. What suggestions can you give the teachers regarding Janie's behavior at school?
2. What strategies would you suggest to involve the parents in developing an appropriate disciplinary structure?
3. How would you determine Janie's developmental level in order to suggest age-appropriate techniques?

CHAPTER SUMMARY

Though physical growth is not as rapid as in earlier stages, the preschooler is learning to control and manipulate her body and is improving in her gross and fine motor skills. She is also interacting with a larger group of peers and adults as she learns to share, take turns, and respond to authority.

She is making decisions, developing her self-care skills, and helping around the house. All of these activities help her prepare for school and for successful and competent adulthood.

DISCUSSION QUESTIONS

1. A major issue for parents of preschoolers with disabilities is the choice of settings for child care or for preschool. Develop a list of questions that would be helpful for parents as they consider this very important decision.
2. In working with families, if you discover gaps in service what are some of the steps you can take to advocate for needed resources? Consider legislative, private, and community levels of action.

Chapter 4

SCHOOL AGE
Six to Twelve Years

Steve is one of the most faithful supporters for his sister's soccer team. His motorized chair sports streamers in the team colors, and he always wears his team T-shirt. Though his cerebral palsy limits his articulation, he has excellent volume. A goal by one of "his" team, or a missed call by the referee, elicits an immediate response from this attentive and enthusiastic cheerleader.

Between the ages of 6 and 12, most children are actively involved in some educational system. A major event for the 6-year-old child is the transition from home or preschool to a regular academic setting. He will be required to interact with a number of peers and with many adults in positions of authority. In addition, he must sit still, listen to instructions, and learn to follow rules. Throughout this period of his life he will be learning skills that he will use for the rest of his life.

PHYSICAL DEVELOPMENT

The elementary school years are the time when a child learns to play games, develops ball-handling skills necessary in many sports, and begins to identify special qualities about himself. Learning to ride a bicycle, skate, and swim are the bases for activities that can be enjoyed throughout his life. An interest in music, drawing, reading, or handicrafts that is encouraged at this time can be the foundation for adult hobbies and for socializing with others who share those interests.

Other competencies that may not seem life changing but are important to a child include blowing bubbles with bubble gum, whistling, snapping his fingers, and playing computer games. Some of these skills may seem minimally important to adults, but their absence in later years can cause problems. It is much more difficult to learn to kick a ball, or skate, or play computer games when everyone else already has the skill mastered. These abilities are much easier to learn when one's peers are going through the same process.

Most children who are entering elementary school are able to run, jump, and climb, as well as throw, catch, and kick a ball. They can probably also write and draw with some efficiency (Sugden, 1990). During the early elementary school years, children's growth tends to slow, but by age 10 for girls and 12 or 13 for boys, the preadolescent growth spurt begins. This means that they are likely to be fatigued, have muscle and joint aches, and experience a roller-coaster of emotions. They may also demonstrate much less coordination as their legs and arms grow rapidly.

SOCIAL DEVELOPMENT

The move from home or preschool to regular classrooms requires the child to interact with his peers for long periods of time. He must also respond to all the adults who function as authorities in the school. These changes can be difficult for a child who has not had experience with groups of his peers or with adults outside his family.

Involvement in household tasks is another component of social development. A child who is regularly responsible for setting or clearing the dinner table, folding laundry, or helping with the grocery shopping learns his importance as a member of the family. He also has practice in activities that will be an important part of his daily life when he goes to college or moves away from home.

As he nears his teens, acceptance by his peers becomes the primary concern and the main criterion for many decisions. For a preteen, one of the tragedies of life is to be "different," whether this means being the only one who has to wear glasses, or the only one without braces on his teeth. Anything that differentiates a child makes him a potential target for teasing or shunning. This can be a very difficult time and the child will need support and encouragement from family and friends.

COGNITIVE DEVELOPMENT

During the elementary school years, a child's cognitive abilities develop dramatically. He is able to understand more complex ideas and his thinking progresses from understanding concrete concepts, such as color or size, to abstract processes involving morality, the human race, or social problems.

As his mental capacities change, he is capable of understanding, and will demand, more elaborate explanations of ideas. Even though he has known for many years where babies come from, he will ask again. Now he is looking for a more mature and complete explanation rather than the simple story that satisfied him at age 5. If his parents have divorced, he may ask for an explanation of what happened, even though he seemed to understand and accept the divorce when it occurred. In these and other areas, he needs more information and greater detail than he did previously.

Another quality of the child's thinking is egocentrism, which means that the child sees himself as the center of the world as he knows it. He assumes that any problem or idea can be seen in only one way—his—and he has a very difficult time understanding that someone else could possibly have a different view. In addition, he is quite sure that in any given situation, everyone is looking at him and making judgments. This perspective is gradually eroded as the child begins to understand others' views and to realize that everyone is not actually watching him all of the time (Elkind, 1978).

Within the school setting, the child is expected to perform arithmetic computations, read and understand complicated material, and engage in varying levels of abstract thinking. He will also memorize information and present it either verbally or in written form and develop skills necessary for critical thinking.

Making appropriate decisions is another task for the school aged child. If peers suggest activities his parents would not approve, he must decide whether to follow his friends or not. These situations arise more and more frequently as he nears his teens. He needs practice and support in making decisions and in accepting the consequences.

SUMMARY OF TASKS

- Develop skills in bicycling, skating, swimming and other sports
- Exhibit appropriate social skills in interactions with peers and with adults
- Demonstrate decision-making abilities
- Master increasingly complex and abstract ideas and materials
- Learn and abide by the rules of games

CHILDREN WITH DISABILITIES

A major goal of most parents is for their child to become an independent adult. The skills needed for independent living, however, do not emerge suddenly at the end of adolescence. This transfer of responsibility for the child's behavior must be instituted prior to adolescence and continued throughout the teen years. One component of this procedure involves assisting the child to develop a sense of self-responsibility. Assigning household chores can be used as one way to indicate the parents' expectations and to identify the child as a valued and contributing member of the household (Blum, Resnick, Nelson, & Germaine, 1991).

School is different from the other settings in which a child may have been involved. Even if he has participated in early intervention programs or in child care settings, his elementary school classroom will probably be larger and there will be more children. He will be expected to eat meals in the cafeteria and participate in assemblies that include all the children in the building. Possibly most frightening of all may be the fire drills that occur suddenly and unexpectedly. For a child who had learned to feel quite comfortable within his preschool, these changes may be distressing and may require some adjustment time.

Another issue for the school-age child is the widening of his world. As an infant, he was safely ensconced in a carefully controlled setting. The toddler roamed a little more freely at home, and the preschooler may have visited his friends and attended parties at a variety of locations. With his entry into "big school," he may see others riding their bicycles, or skating, or playing at a nearby park. Their ability to play outside the ever-watchful eye of an adult is expanding. His wish to extend his world may be limited by needed equipment, physical limitations, or lack of social skills. It is important that his parents and teachers assist him in stretching his boundaries so that he can join his friends as far as this is reasonable.

In terms of dealing with the public at large, a child who has a disability needs to learn about that disability and be comfortable in explaining it to others. It is generally unrealistic to expect that people will not notice if the child uses a wheelchair or has distinctive physical features. If he is comfortable in providing this information, he will be able to help those he meets to feel more at ease in interacting with him.

Physical Development

The expected physical accomplishments for children in the elementary school years involve strength, control, accuracy, and speed. For a child with a disability, accommodations or adaptations may be needed to ensure that he can participate successfully in the activities of his peer group.

The growth spurts experienced by preteens can be expensive if the child's changing size results in the need for new braces or different equipment. Pubertal changes, including weight gain, can occur very early in some children. Consultation with his physician is essential to reassure the child and his parents that what he is experiencing is normal for him.

Social Development

Play with peers is critical for the socialization of children but may be denied to those with disabilities. Having adequate opportunities for play may be limited by parental overprotection, architectural barriers, or a schedule overcrowded with therapy or medical care (Rubenfeld & Schwartz, 1996).

A major concern for the school-age child is being accepted by his peers. Illness, hospitalization, different physical appearance or speaking style, and the presence of equipment can all cause him to appear different and thus be less acceptable to peers. Parents, teachers, and others can work with the child and with his friends and classmates to emphasize his strengths and support his integration into the peer group.

Parents hope their child will eventually be able to function autonomously. They may have difficulty, however, releasing their control over his activities. To develop socially, the child must be allowed to experience failures and to learn that he can survive them. This can be very difficult for his parents (Sutkin, 1984). In reality, all children get hurt, are called names, or get chosen last for games. Learning to cope with such situations is an essential component in the developmental process. Parents should be encouraged to support their child's inclusion in as many peer-related activities as are reasonable. This allows him to learn interpersonal skills and coping strategies as he successfully negotiates a variety of experiences (Rubenfeld & Schwartz, 1996).

The acquisition of suitable social behaviors is essential for the child's successful development. He must master desirable patterns of social behavior, as well as manage to conform to societal expectations. He then must determine when each behavior and each socially established boundary is to be used (Weisgerber, 1991). Behaviors and boundaries differ by situation and by context. He must realize that an action that is permissible when playing with his peers in the local park may be totally unsuitable in church or at the grocery store.

If a child has limited physical movement capacity, this can affect his ability to develop skills in self-care and social interaction. If he doesn't move well, others may lower their social expectations of him (Fewell, 1986). Adaptations suggested by educators and other professionals can create situations in which the child can successfully engage in suitable interactions.

Other tasks for the school-age child involve learning how to play games, participate in sports, socialize with others, manage his time, and care for himself. Learning to handle money is another important skill to be mastered at this time.

He should be comfortable in bathing, grooming, and dressing himself and be able to do these tasks without much direction. As he is learning these skills, he will be slower, and at some points it will seem much easier for the parents, or other caregivers, to "do it themselves." Though this may save some stress at the time, it robs the child of the opportunity to learn these essential skills.

A school-age child is expected to produce things and to develop new skills; the usual place for these accomplishments is in school (Patterson, 1988). On the basis of his perceptions of his own abilities and on his experiences in school and other settings, he develops a sense of himself and his value. If he is unable to demonstrate the usual skills or is unable to attend school regularly, this may lead to lack of confidence, lowered self-esteem, or a sense of inferiority (Sutkin, 1984).

A child wants to be like his peers. Even if he must use special equipment or clothing, some concession can probably be made to fashion. Orthopedic shoes could be dyed. Hats, tee shirts, or jackets can have the current and popular logos. As far as possible, parents should be encouraged to provide the child with the accessories that "everybody else" has (Albrecht, 1995).

Cognitive Development

The primary task of the elementary school child is participation in some educational undertaking. Prior to school age, a child is entitled to services through early intervention programs. Once he enters school, the provisions of the IDEA (Individuals With Disabilities Education Act, PL 101-476) require that a free and appropriate education be provided in the least restrictive environment (LRE) (Albrecht, 1995). For most children this setting is the neighborhood school, but when the child has a disability, school selection can involve a number of decisions.

A fundamental question is whether the child should be "mainstreamed" (included in regular classes) or placed in special classes. Mainstreaming is becoming much more common and accepted but it is not universal, and parents need to know that not all mainstreamed programs are equal. One district, or even one neighborhood school within a district, may be superior to others. Parents must decide whether it is more important to have their child near home and interacting with children who live in the neighborhood, or for him to be enrolled in a setting that is better suited to his needs. Parents may be able to force the issue and obtain needed services and a fairly integrated curriculum for their child in the setting of their choice. If this creates a hostile atmosphere with school personnel, however, the outcomes may not be as beneficial for the child.

The decision about participation in special education is not an easy one. Enrollment may appear to stigmatize the child. On the other hand, without the label, he may not be able to receive needed services such as Braille materials, catheterization, or transportation. An advantage of special classes is that they generally feature a centralization of resources and professional expertise (Cogher, Savage, & Smith, 1992). The trend seems to be, however, to place the child in as many classes as possible with his age peers. Special services can then be added as necessary to allow him to function at his maximal level.

Before a child begins school, the IDEA requires that he be evaluated and that an individual education plan (IEP) be developed. Establishment of the IEP is intended to ensure that his unique needs will be addressed, regardless of the school district's established procedures

(Humes, Szymanski, & Hohenshil, 1995). If needed services are not readily available, they must be developed. Court rulings mandate that the school district provide services and programs outlined in the IEP. Lack of funding does not free the district from this obligation.

Prior to enrolling the child in school, the parents should send a letter to the district's special education department requesting an evaluation of him. Within 60 days, the school district must schedule an evaluation to determine the child's needs. As with all other materials related to the child, a dated copy of this letter should be kept (Albrecht, 1995).

The first step in the evaluation is a screening to determine whether the child needs services. If the need is established, an evaluation is conducted that consists of a number of diagnostic tests. These may include an assessment of social development, vision, and hearing. The law requires that the evaluation be conducted by people who are fluent in the child's primary language or mode of communication.

Once the evaluation is completed, a meeting will be held to discuss the results. This meeting must be scheduled within 60 days of the parents' initial request for the evaluation. The purpose of the meeting is to establish the IEP, which details the child's educational goals for the year, and the services the school district will supply to meet these goals. The IDEA mandates that the IEP be developed by a team that includes the child's parents, teachers, other school personnel, and any others who can provide helpful information. Social workers or other professionals should inform the parents that they may bring along any person they choose when the report on the evaluations is presented (Albrecht, 1995).

For this or any meeting, a tape recorder may be useful in helping the parents remember what was said. If a recorder is used, all participants should be asked to introduce themselves and state their role in the meeting. In case difficulties should arise later, the parent will have a record of what was said; therefore, the tape should be retained with a note as to the date and subject of the meeting.

Information should be provided in the parents' primary mode of communication. If the parents or child appear able to comprehend some English, school administrators may be tempted to avoid involving a translator or interpreter. When it is known that a translator or interpreter will be needed for these meetings, the request should be made as early as possible so arrangements can be made (Albrecht, 1995).

The social worker needs to remind the parents that if they disagree with the IEP that is developed, the form that is presented at the end of the meeting should not be signed. Such a signature indicates that they agreed with the IEP and this agreement can make changing the plan more difficult. Instead, the parents can sign a different form that states only that they attended the meeting. Any of these forms should be read carefully, and the parents should be encouraged to ask for clarification if they have any concerns. If the child's physical or educational needs change before a regular IEP meeting is scheduled, another meeting may be requested (Albrecht, 1995).

Once a determination has been made as to what programs will be provided and what equipment the school district will supply, the parents need to find out if the equipment can also be used at home on weekends, holidays, and breaks or vacations (Albrecht, 1995). Parents may point out that the child's progress can continue more smoothly if the equipment is available for ongoing practice and use.

Despite all the meetings and assessments, the primary responsibility for ensuring that the child's needs are met falls on the parents. Physicians are not generally involved with schools, and teachers have not been trained to work with the medical system. Parents, therefore, must serve as translators of complex medical information as this affects plans for their child's educational program (Koenning, Benjamin, Todaro, Warren, & Burns, 1995). A major difficulty can arise if parents assume that information offered to teachers and professionals during one academic year will be transferred to the next year's teachers and special educators. Frequently, this is not the case and the parents are left with the responsibility for ensuring that the appropriate information is in the hands of those who need it (Weisgerber, 1991).

Social Work Roles

As primary control over the child's daily activities is transferred from the parents to a school setting, the social worker may be needed to provide assistance, guidance, and coordination. For many parents, in-home visits from therapists and other professionals have furnished in-depth information and a sense of participation in the child's progress. Once the child is involved in school, many of the therapeutic services will be offered at school (Cogher et al., 1992). Parents will need to make a special effort to retain the contact and coordination with all of these services. The social worker is in a position to assist in establishing conferences or home visits that can provide information to the parents regarding the child's progress, future needs, and additional resources that may be necessary.

Parents may require assistance in determining the optimal setting for their child's education. The debate regarding mainstreaming versus inclusion is ongoing. A knowledgeable social worker can offer essential information to the parents, advocate with the educational system for the decision the parents have made, and help parents to lobby for themselves with legislators, school districts, and other systems for needed resources.

Once a child is placed in a particular school, the social worker may need to assist in locating resources for training of teachers, aides, janitors, and lunchroom workers. If personnel at this school have no experience with a child who has a disability, it may be necessary to offer not only informal consultation but also to develop more structured informational sessions or regular training classes (Cogher et al., 1992). It is important that the social worker be very supportive of the teachers and respectful of the additional time and energy they are expending for this child. The addition of extracurricular training may be perceived as an extra burden.

A critical challenge may face the social worker in serving as a coordinator between parents who are very concerned about their child, teachers who know their classrooms and material well, and therapists or other professionals who are concerned about other aspects of the child's progress. It is important that each person feel recognized and respected and that they work together for the child's best interests. Given the specialized nature of the disciplines, and the turf protection that may emerge, the social worker's coordination task may require a range of professional skills to minimize conflicts (Cogher et al., 1992).

Down Syndrome

The beginning of school may be stressful for parents and child. Parents may worry about their child's being accepted by teachers and classmates. They may feel a need to be vigilant to ensure that all of the agreements in the child's IEP regarding services and accommodations are being followed. With appropriate support, this can be an exciting time.

Physical Development

Because of low muscle tone, a child with Down syndrome may tend to be overweight. Participation in sports can help him control his weight, improve his physical coordination, maintain cardiovascular fitness, and improve his self-image (Batshaw, 1993). In most cases, he can participate in any sports in which he is interested. The problem that might prevent this is atlantoaxial instability (extra flexibility in the top two vertebrae). If this is a problem, he should be encouraged to engage in activities such as swimming, slow horseback riding, and running rather than in gymnastics or contact sports. For about 1% of children with this instability, surgery may be required to stabilize the vertebrae. Most children, however, do not experience this problem and can participate in all sports and activities that are of interest to them (Kozma, 1986).

Being able to run fast and throw hard are skills that are important to school-age children. Another component of these skills, however, is control and accuracy. A child must be able to run to the correct spot, dodging other children, and then stop. He must also be able to throw a ball, somewhat accurately, to another child so that he may participate in the games (Sugden, 1990). Encouraging him to practice these skills can increase his chances of being included in his peers' play and can help improve his muscle tone and control his weight as well.

Social Development

During elementary school, the child will begin to notice differences between himself and his peers. This is probably the time to inform him about having Down syndrome, if he has not already been told. If he simply feels different, he may also feel inferior. He needs to know clearly what his situation is, what it is called and what his prognosis is—as far as he can cognitively manage the information.

Others may tease or ridicule him because of his appearance or his behavior. It is vital that he be reminded of his strengths and talents as well as his deficits. He should be told that everyone has things they do well and things they can't do (Selikowitz, 1990).

Social interactions with his peers should be encouraged. He can invite a friend over to play, displaying his toys and his expertise in his own environment. This also gives him a chance to practice his social skills in a familiar setting.

Cognitive Development

Some of the important learning that goes on at this age involves the management of daily life. Most people learn skills such as managing time, planning wardrobes, and carrying out household maintenance chores without formal instruction. They are able to make inferences about certain requirements and to generalize from one experience to another. For some children with Down syndrome, transferring information and behavior between situations is difficult. A more formalized approach is needed to ensure that skills needed in daily life are learned and integrated (Sugden, 1990). This may require specific, step-by-step instruction with adequate opportunities for practice and correction. Even if it requires a considerable amount of time and energy, it is important that the child master these expected tasks so he will not find himself in embarrassing situations later. For example, he needs to know how to check to be sure that all his buttons and zippers are properly closed after he uses the bathroom. He also needs to know where his locker is and how to open it. Feeling confident about these supposedly simple matters allows the child to bolster his own self-esteem and his image among his classmates and teachers as well.

Some instruction on tasks of daily living occurs in schools and much of it happens at home. In either setting, the learning will be much easier if the child's particular style of information intake is acknowledged and used. Instructions can be given verbally, then the desired behavior can be demonstrated and time allotted for practicing the new skills (Sugden, 1990). In addition, a poster with pictures of each step in a chore may be helpful. By using verbal, motor, and visual input, the parent or teacher ensures that the child's particular style of learning has been tapped.

During the school years, a child will encounter death and loss. A pet may die, a relative may become sick, or a friend may move away. Sheltering the child from grief is not beneficial. At some time, he will face difficult situations and he needs the opportunity, as do all children, to learn about loss and to learn how to grieve (Selikowitz, 1990).

Summary of Tasks

Exhibit appropriate social skills	Basic social skills are adequate but he may have difficulty in generalizing to other settings.
Demonstrate decision making	Simple, concrete decisions are mastered first, complex decisions later.
Master complex thinking	Concrete thinking is more easily mastered, abstract ideas are more difficult.
Engage in educational activities	Success in sight reading and basic math can be expected.

| Develop sport, hobby, and artistic skills | Talents are emerging and need to be encouraged for current enjoyment and as adult hobbies. |

Visual Impairment

In working with children with visual impairment, it is important to consider the age at onset of blindness. People who are congenitally blind or become blind before about 5 years of age do not have a workable visual imagery (Moore, 1995).

As for all children, educational success is the major goal for a child with visual impairment. He needs to know about personal hygiene, appropriate communications, mobility, and a variety of concepts that will be featured in the books he reads and the lessons he studies. To help him conceptualize the world around him, it will be helpful for people to describe various incidents and settings to him (Finkelstein & French, 1993).

The experiences the child has had in navigating a variety of settings will support his ability to adjust to the school environment. He can be reassured that, just as he has learned to maneuver around his home and his yard, he will soon feel comfortable with his mobility at school as well.

Physical Development

A child with a visual impairment can benefit from increasing his physical activity levels (Skaggs & Hopper, 1996) to help him avoid obesity and to increase his fitness. If he is not involved in physical activities, it may be due to the overprotectiveness of his parents or other caregivers, or he may not have been introduced to games or sports that he enjoyed and felt comfortable doing. Schools may not have appropriate programs or trained personnel for enhancing the physical fitness of children with visual impairment. Activities such as walking, jogging, weight training, swimming, aerobic dance, tumbling, and wrestling can be enjoyed by children with and without visual impairment (Skaggs & Hopper, 1996).

Orientation and mobility are other skills that must be mastered by the child with visual impairment. Orientation involves a person's knowing where he is and how to get to where he wants to go. Mobility refers to moving safely through the environment (Hill & Snook-Hill, 1996). In preparation for these skills, a child needs to know how to walk and use stairs as well as being able to understand instructions used during his mobility training. Some of the words he will need are prepositions such as behind, under, and over. He will also be using all of his senses to be aware of the environment (Hill & Snook-Hill, 1996). He needs to be able to determine the sources of sounds so he can begin to learn to cross streets safely by himself.

For a child with low or no vision, travel requires an enormous amount of concentration. The child who is using a cognitive map to navigate his environment must remember where he is going, be aware of factors such as the change in a hallway from linoleum to carpeting, the location of doors and intersecting hallways, and constantly be prepared for unexpected events such as encounters with the janitor mopping the hallway after a spill. With some assistance and instruction, children are fully capable of negotiating their surroundings and developing a strong sense of self-control and self-confidence.

Social Development

Some children with low or no vision engage in movements such as body rocking and hand slapping (Sugden, 1990). These activities may be distressing to adults or other children and may limit the child's opportunities to engage in social interaction. In some cases, the actions of a child with visual impairments result in his being labeled as autistic. Rather than focusing on the label, it may be more productive for the social worker to determine what benefits the child receives from the behavior and to help him modify it. If he rocks back and forth, he may need more physical activity to use up his excess energy. On the other hand, a child with low vision may withdraw into repetitive behaviors if his environment is too visually complex to comprehend all at once. Adjusting his visual environment may allow the child to perform more appropriately rather than spending his energy on distracting or distressing behaviors (Groenveld, 1993). It is reassuring to parents and teachers to know that most of the child's mannerisms will probably disappear by the time he is an adult. Either he will learn not to engage in these behaviors, or he will indulge in them only when he is alone (Freeman, Goetz, Richards, & Groenveld, 1991).

Low or no vision can also affect social interactions by reducing the amount of information he can gain from observing others' body posture, gestures, and facial expressions. To compensate for this, he can learn to interpret tone of voice and conversational pauses to replace the visual cues he cannot use.

A child who has nystagmus—random, jerky movements of the eye—may tend to tilt his head to reach a point at which the eye movements are reduced or stopped. If a teacher or other adult encourages him to sit up straight and hold his head up, this may negate the successful adaptation he had made to his disability (Groenveld, 1993).

Participation in the routines of his home provides important information for the child. As he helps with laundry, he learns about the smell of soap, where to put dirty and clean clothing, how to sort clothes by touch, and the various complexities of a task that he may originally have thought was accomplished by magic (Hill & Snook-Hill, 1996). Having regular chores that he is expected to complete gives concrete evidence of his importance in the family. In addition, learning to be consistently responsible for his household duties forms a solid base for the behaviors employers will expect of him when he is a teen or adult (Szymanski & Hanley-Maxwell, 1996).

Cognitive Development

In school, the child must have access to the necessary adapted materials and the training to enable him to use these materials skillfully (Brasher & Holbrook, 1996). In addition, he must be included in activities if he is to benefit from them. The presence of a Scout troop or a drama group, for example, will be of little use unless he is involved in them.

During the school hours, in addition to instruction traditionally offered to his sighted classmates, he may receive tutoring in special skills. These may include orientation and mobility, reading and writing in Braille, skills of daily living, communication and listening skills, and adaptive physical education and recreation. Typing is another important skill for a child who uses Braille because it allows direct communication with sighted people either at school, or later in employment settings (Brasher & Holbrook, 1996).

Rather than relying on what he can read on the chalkboard, the child with visual impairment must listen and remember items such as assignments (Brasher & Holbrook, 1996). He may, therefore, require some additional time at the end of class to gather his materials and to ensure that he has all the information necessary to complete any homework.

Literacy is an essential component of daily living because adults and children are constantly reading. This is so much a part of life that a person may forget how many times a day it is necessary to read to get the data needed for a task. This information is found in a huge variety of sources such as telephone books, magazines, menus, newspapers, cookbooks, signs, brochures, and church bulletins. For a child with low or no vision, literacy is just as important as for others. His "reading" may use other formats than the customary printed page. He may, for example, "read" books that have been prerecorded (Brasher & Holbrook, 1996). The book and audiotape combinations that are featured in the children's section of most libraries and bookstores were not necessarily designed for the child with a visual impairment but he can certainly use them.

Another component of cognitive development is decision making. Making, and living with the consequences of, age-appropriate choices gives the child some power in his life and helps him to take responsibility for the outcomes of these choices. If, after choosing pistachio ice cream because he likes the sound of the name, he finds he prefers chocolate, he can either eat the cone he purchased or wait until the next trip to try another flavor. He can be offered the choice to take his bath before or after watching television. Small choices that he can actually make provide him with an understanding of how to choose and how to live with the outcome of those decisions.

Summary of Tasks

Exhibit appropriate social skills	He turns his head toward a speaker, gestures appropriately, and listens for pauses so he can join conversations.
Demonstrate decision making	Choosing clothing or food are precursors to more important decisions.
Master complex thinking	Assistance may be needed in grasping global concepts.
Engage in educational activities	He must have appropriate equipment and supplies along with the chance to participate in activities.
Develop sport, hobby, and artistic skills	Encourage all talents for current enjoyment and as adult hobbies also.

Cerebral Palsy

Most parents have some hesitation about sending their child off to school to be shaped and trained by others. When the parents have spent 5 years working intensely with the child, it may be particularly difficult to turn over his care and guidance to others (Cogher et al., 1992). This may be especially true for the child with cerebral palsy for whom massive amounts of time have been spent on therapy and assistance.

Physical Development

Prior to his entering school, the child needs a thorough examination to determine his strengths and abilities as well as his needs. One facet of his physical examination will be an assessment of orthopedic difficulties that may reduce his mobility. Contracted muscles may pull his hips back or his legs out, preventing him from walking easily. If he is nonambulatory, he will also be checked for scoliosis, which can affect his sitting, balance, and flexibility (Dormans, 1993).

It is essential that the school be prepared for this individual child as well as for other children with disabilities. Information about his energy level and physical abilities over a whole day are important. If he is able to walk but tires fairly easily, this needs to be taken into consideration when planning his routine. Staff should be aware of how to encourage correct posture and how to assist him in moving about or transferring from his wheelchair to his desk or the floor. If they understand why a particular position or activity is important, gaining their compliance may be much easier (Cogher et al., 1992). Any therapy he may require should be included in his IEP as this is mandated by the law (Eicher & Batshaw, 1993).

If the child has expressive speech delays, the use of sign language, communication boards, or computers may support his need to communicate. To be an active member of his class, he must be able to interact with others and let them know what he wants to say.

A child with cerebral palsy should be exposed early to sports and the skills necessary to participate in them. It is vital that each child have areas in which he is successful. If regular sports and activities are not possible, he may be able to participate in modified aquatics, bowling, or adapted dance (Miller & Bachrach, 1995). These activities provide an opportunity to engage in games with his peers during his school years. In later life, these skills form a base for hobbies and recreation that he can enjoy throughout adulthood (Sherrill & Rainbolt, 1986).

Social Development

The beginning of school marks a major transition for a child. If he has been enrolled in preschool programs, he has some experience with peer interactions and with responding to authority figures other than his parents. At "big school," his time will be much more structured and he will have many more rules to follow. It is essential that he learn to manage his behavior or his educational success and his successful social development will both be severely curtailed (Miller & Bachrach, 1995).

During the school years, children become very aware of themselves and any differences between them and their peers. A child who has cerebral palsy may see himself as different and therefore inadequate. His response to this may be to withdraw to avoid being hurt. It is important that his parents be honest with him about his limitations and, at the same time, truly celebrate his successes (Miller & Bachrach, 1995). Parents of other children with cerebral palsy may have excellent suggestions about handling this issue.

A child needs the opportunity to interact with his peers but the effects of cerebral palsy may make this more difficult. His peers may see him as different and be uncomfortable in trying to play with him. His parents may need to set up situations in which he can show off his abilities and talents without their intervention. If he is using a computer, a few classmates might be invited over to play computer games. In this way, he is the "star" in at least one activity and the other children have a reason to want to be around him (Miller & Bachrach, 1995). The book, *Computer Resources for People with Disabilities,* is an excellent source of information about choosing and buying computers and related equipment (Alliance for Technology Access, 1996).

Social success is an important component of a child's development. Involvement in scouting organizations, sports teams, or musical groups provides a scheduled, structured setting in which he can improve his social skills while he helps other children overcome their fears or embarrassment at being around someone who is different (Miller & Bachrach, 1995).

Cognitive Development

A child who has cerebral palsy may be capable of learning material that is presented to him, but he may have difficulty in demonstrating his knowledge because of his motor or language problems. For him, knowing may not equal performing. Teachers, parents, and others will need to work out a system that allows him to show what he has learned (Miller & Bachrach, 1995). A computer may allow him to demonstrate his knowledge if he has limited speech capacities.

In addition to his schoolwork, the youngster is learning to manage other areas of his life. He is becoming more responsible for chores around the home, and he is practicing his skills in money management and decision making. All of these skills are essential to his success as a teen and as an adult, and he needs the opportunity to learn and perfect them.

Summary of Tasks

Exhibit appropriate social skills	Social skills are improving.
Demonstrate decision making	Simple, concrete decisions are mastered first, complex decisions later.
Master complex thinking	Concrete thinking is much easier, abstract ideas are more difficult.
Engage in educational activities	Depending on the level of the disability, success in sight reading and basic math can be expected.
Develop sport, hobby, and artistic skills	Adapted sports and leisure activities can be enjoyed by most children.

Siblings

Ten-year-old Steve has cerebral palsy. He has little understandable speech and uses a wheelchair for ambulation. To maintain flexibility in his joints, his parents must do an hour of exercises with him each night.

Both parents work and Steve's 15-year-old sister, Debbie, is often required to look after him. Until recently, she didn't mind, but now she wants to spend more time with her friends.

The time and energy required to manage Steve's needs greatly restrict the amount of attention his parents can give to Debbie. She feels neglected and is tending to act out her feelings in rebellious ways. Up to this point, her most outrageous activity was to get her hair cut in a very punk look. Her parents are concerned about their ability to manage all of Steve's needs and yet provide time and attention to Debbie.

1. What are some of the normal developmental markers for Debbie's stage of life?
2. What suggestions can you give the parents about dealing with Debbie?
3. What resources are available to help the family provide care for Steve?

Spina Bifida

Throughout his school years, each child should continue to progress toward greater levels of self-control and self-management. His level of social, physical, and cognitive development will affect these efforts. It is, therefore, important to set reasonable, achievable goals and to help him and his family to achieve them.

Parental coping styles may affect the life satisfaction of parents and children (Barakat & Linney, 1995). If the parents are able to emphasize the child's talents and abilities and to assist him in developing coping skills, they will be much more effective in helping him become an independent and self-confident adult (Dallyn & Garrison-Jones, 1990).

Physical Development

Though training about skin care and bladder and bowel management should have begun during the preschool years, it is important that these educational efforts continue. The child's progress toward independence is contingent on being able to care for himself independently and thus be away from parents and other caretakers for extended periods of time.

Shunt malfunction is a continuing possibility. If his school achievement begins to decline, this may indicate the need for evaluation of the shunt to be sure it is performing appropriately (Peterson, Rauen, Brown, & Cole, 1994).

Puberty begins, for most children, during the elementary school years. Though parents are given information and assisted in managing the physical problems of their child who has spina bifida, virtually no one prepares them for dealing with her or his emerging sexuality and concerns such as menstruation and sex education (Edser & Ward, 1991). This is especially problematic because early pubertal changes frequently occur in children with spina bifida. Some girls with spina bifida begin menstruation at 7 or 8 years of age. It is important that they see this change as a positive thing, feeling reassured that they are moving toward maturity. Otherwise, this may be perceived as one more difference between themselves and their peers (Rauen & Aubert, 1992).

Another issue for a child with a disability is that he never really "owns" his body. He is constantly subjected to examinations, therapy, or other interventions, making it difficult for him to take responsibility for his body and his own self-care.

Many children with spina bifida will be ambulatory at some level. It is important, however, for them to also develop skills in using a wheelchair and in transferring in and out of it. If this training is deferred until the child is older and heavier, the skills will be more difficult to master (Hunt & Poulton, 1995). As the ambulatory child encounters new surfaces and settings, he will be required to learn more advanced skills such as stair climbing. Some children who have previously used braces and crutches may find that a lightweight wheelchair is more suitable for some settings such as school buildings or shopping malls (Peterson et al., 1994). Periodic use of the chair can allow him to move about the school at the same speed as his classmates. He may still employ braces, crutches, or both when he is participating in games and other activities. Other skills he will be practicing are dressing, applying and removing his braces, and transferring from the wheelchair to the toilet, car, or desk (Kurtz & Scull, 1993).

A school-age child is entitled to instruction in physical education. This should include work toward development of physical and motor fitness as well as skills in swimming, dance, games, and sports. He should be able to enjoy these activities in the community as well. By law, recreation centers and gymnasiums must be accessible in terms of their physical environment, their equipment, and their activities (Connor-Kuntz, Dummer, & Paciorek, 1995).

Social Development

One demand that is placed on a child with a disability is to be able to explain his condition to others—peers and adults alike. The child and his family are probably quite conversant with his condition and the care required. It is important that they be able to discuss these factors with others both to educate them and to establish relationships that will allow for requesting assistance when it is needed.

A major task for the preteen is to develop a sense of his own sexuality and self-identity, concepts that typically emerge or are refined during interactions with his peers. This can be difficult for a child with a disability because he is often closely supervised. He has little time to sit and talk with his friends, learning the social mores. Instead, he is hurried away after school in a special bus and very possibly spends his afternoons in therapy instead of at the movies or participating in after school sports activities (Edser & Ward, 1991).

At school and in sports or other settings, each child needs to experience competitive success with peers. This may be in the form of games, puzzles, computer knowledge, or other areas. Development of skills and interests in a variety of recreational activities can set the groundwork for a lifetime of leisure enjoyment (Rauen & Aubert, 1992).

Accepting responsibility for his actions and their consequences is an important component of the school-age child's progress. He needs to have regular chores at home; in addition, he must be held accountable for his behavior and for the choices he makes.

Cognitive Development

In most cases, a child who has spina bifida will have normal or near-normal intelligence, therefore he will be placed in mainstream classrooms. His early educational and social experiences, however, may be limited by incontinence, the need for braces or wheelchairs, and by interference from physical therapy sessions, a lack of transportation, and architectural barriers (Lord, Varzos, Behrman, Wicks, & Wicks, 1990). The result can be inadequate development of requisite social skills and academic accomplishments.

The IDEA, formerly known as PL 94-142 (the Education for All Handicapped Children Act), requires that each child receive a free and appropriate education in the least restrictive environment (Albrecht, 1995). The first step in this process is to determine the level at which the child is functioning. A thorough assessment of his strengths and weaknesses in learning is essential. Some children with spina bifida display a lower cognitive ability than their nonhandicapped peers (Dallyn & Garrison-Jones, 1990), but with early identification, any learning difficulties can be addressed. A large number of interventions and learning techniques are available to help compensate for any cognitive deficits. If, however, these difficulties are ignored, the child may begin his school career with negative experiences that can lead him and others to have low expectations for his achievement. To support maximum progress, his assessment should evaluate issues such as perceptual and motor abilities; comprehension; ability to concentrate, memorize, and organize materials; and strengths or weaknesses in sequencing and reasoning (Peterson et al., 1994).

One element of continuing cognitive progress is the awareness of difference and of permanence. At some point during the elementary years, the child will probably comprehend that his disability is permanent and is not going to go away. A period of grieving may accompany this new knowledge (Peterson et al., 1994), and family counseling may be appropriate to assist him in moving through this phase.

Summary of Tasks

Exhibit appropriate social skills	Appropriate discipline and consistent expectations support his progress.
Demonstrate decision making	Decisions become more complex and difficult as he nears his teens.
Master complex thinking	Progress varies with his level of intellectual ability.
Engage in educational activities	Identification of any learning problems allows for suitable intervention to prevent loss of self-esteem.
Develop sport, hobby, and artistic skills	Encourage all talents for current enjoyment and as adult hobbies also.

CHAPTER SUMMARY

During the elementary school years, the child and his surroundings change dramatically. He becomes involved with many other children and adults in settings outside his home. Cognitively, he is developing rapidly. He is learning about himself and his environment as well as the academic subjects he encounters in school.

This developmental period is critical for a successful future. The child learns how to care for himself and his surroundings. He becomes more proficient in understanding his disability and its effects and in explaining his situation to others. He expands his horizons and widens his world from home to school to neighborhood, activity groups, shopping centers, and recreation. In conjunction with his academic instruction, all of this new knowledge and all of his new behaviors provide him with an appropriate and adequate base for the greatest possible success as an adult.

DISCUSSION QUESTIONS

1. Compare the benefits and problems of mainstreaming versus separate educational settings.
2. A child who must spend hours each day on special buses or in therapy misses out on some of the typical experiences of his peers. What suggestions do you have to solve this dilemma?

PART II

Teens and Adults

The second section of the book addresses the developmental tasks of the adolescent and adult. In addition to the four disabilities discussed in the earlier chapters, a person who has a spinal cord injury is added at the young adult stage.

Some of the important issues for the teen and adult life stages revolve around the transition from dependence to interdependence and on moving from reliance on the family to interacting with a wider variety of others. In making this shift, it is important for the young person and the family to assist service providers in focusing on strengths and abilities rather than on deficits and problems. There is a definite tendency for social service and medical personnel to empower people with disabilities to do what the professionals think they should do rather than what the clients themselves would choose (Sobsey, 1994).

In moving toward independence and interdependence, it is likely that the young person will continue to need some resources. While she is still enrolled in school, the Individualized Education Plan can be used to plan for and obtain resources. For example, the IEP can state that assistance will be provided in learning to use the public transportation system or in obtaining a driver's license. Emphasis on tasks needed for independent living can ensure that the young person learns how to manage laundry, hygiene, job preparation, and the appropriate handling of leisure time.

Once the young person has graduated from school or has turned 22, the educational system will no longer be involved in providing or coordinating services. These responsibilities will fall on the young adult and the family, requiring them to locate and qualify for benefits that have previously been automatically available. Finding and accessing suitable housing and transportation are also essential if the young adult is to be successfully employed.

Throughout adulthood, the search for needed benefits and services may continue to be problematic. It is important that all family members have a clear understanding of what benefits and programs are available and what their requirements are. Estate planning, long-term care, and other issues must be addressed by the family members long before they would seem to be needed. Delays in these plans can mean loss of benefits as well as the potential of inappropriate placement if the customary care providers become ill or unable to offer help.

Other issues facing adults with disabilities include the need for affordable and appropriate health care. The influx of managed care and the emphasis on cost management will have direct consequences for this population. The precise effect of these changes is just becoming evident. Advocacy from families, service providers, and medical personnel will continue to be a necessity or the cuts in governmental spending could present severe problems for millions of people with disabilities and other chronic conditions.

STRENGTHS-BASED SERVICES

As mentioned in the Introduction, policies and programs for people with disabilities have been based on several paradigms. There is general agreement among those involved in disability studies that the Social Model of disability is the most reasonable. The focus here is on changing the environment, removing attitudinal and physical barriers to allow and encourage full participation.

Within social work, the strengths-based model has a similar perspective. The idea is that when a person presents a problem, the first target of intervention should be the environment rather than the individual. Only after these efforts have failed should the focus be placed on what needs to be changed within the person (Saleebey, 1992).

If the client has an obvious disability, it may be tempting to assume that any problems emanate from the disability itself. This is an erroneous base for decision making and planning, even though it is very common. It is essential that the service provider assess all the strengths and assets of the person and the family or other support systems. Only then can appropriate, individualized plans be made. It is easy to assume, for example, that any adult with Down syndrome will be a happy, placid person who is satisfied performing routine, repetitive tasks every day rather than being subjected to the stress of learning new skills. Instead, the entire range of possible cognitive abilities, physical capacity, and personal interests must be evaluated. The assumption should be made that the young adult can accomplish any task, until this is proven to be wrong. Listening to Christopher Burke in his role on the television series *Life Goes On,* or reading the comments of Jason Kingsley and Mitchell Levitz (1994) in their book *Count Us In* can serve as distinct reminders that we have not even begun to understand just how far these young people can go.

Adults with disabilities now have life expectancies approaching those of the nondisabled population. It is vital that social workers and other service providers learn about the adult developmental trajectories of these groups and prepare to provide the benefits and programs that will allow them to live successful lives at an appropriate level of independence.

Chapter 5

ADOLESCENCE
Thirteen to Nineteen Years

One of the great joys in Tina's life is her job at the pizza parlor. She enjoys visiting with her coworkers and is very comfortable with her responsibilities. Though there was some initial hesitation about hiring a teen with Down syndrome, her boss now knows that he can rely on Tina to show up for her shift and to stay late if the workload demands. With 5 years of good work behind her, Tina is now one of the long-term employees.

During adolescence, a child experiences changes in every area of her life. The physical changes of puberty are accompanied by qualitative alterations in her ability to comprehend ideas and facts. She is expected to become more independent, monitor her own morality, and be increasingly responsible for her own behavior. In the midst of all this, the major concern from the teen's perspective is to be accepted by her peers; above all, she does not want to be "different" (Davis, Anderson, Linkowski, Berger, & Feinstein, 1991).

PHYSICAL DEVELOPMENT

For a girl, puberty usually begins prior to the teen years. She develops secondary sexual characteristics such as budding breasts, pubic hair, wider hips, and the onset of menstruation. It is not unusual for the growth spurts she experiences to result in her reaching full adult height by the age of 14.

For the young teen boy, sexual development and the changes of puberty may not begin until 14 or 15. This means that he will very likely be shorter than most of the girls in his peer group for a year or more. He may also lag behind his female classmates in developing an interest in dating.

The development of a sense of her own identity and an acceptance of her sexuality are essential for the adolescent. Most teens receive enormous amounts of information about their sexual development and about sexual activity and the possible dangers that can result if they are sexually active. This information may, or may not, have any effect on behavior.

Physical abilities, such as being a sports star or exhibiting outstanding dance skills, can move a child higher in her peers' estimation. Lack of these skills can promote a corresponding drop in her position within the group.

SOCIAL DEVELOPMENT

Peers are a major influence on a teen's sense of self. She continues to perceive herself as the center of attention. If others are gathered in a group, talking quietly, she will very likely assume that they are talking about her. If she has an unsightly pimple, she is sure that everyone will notice because she believes everyone is scrutinizing her intently.

In fact, teens do examine their peers closely, generally looking for some fault. Any difference can single a child out for taunts, shunning, or outright persecution. This is one reason that teens strive to dress exactly alike. If she conscientiously wears the "uniform," speaks the correct slang, and demonstrates the prevailing attitude, she will be "in." The major goal is to prevent others from spotting any differences between herself and her peers. Such differences could be as serious as family problems, or as seemingly innocuous as failure to wear the right clothes, or being too smart or too slow.

In addition to being as similar as possible to her friends, the teen must begin the process of individuating from her family. This often entails at least some period of rebellion against the family's values and ideas. The teen may have little comprehension of who she *is,* but she knows clearly what she *is not:* She is not a clone of her parents.

COGNITIVE DEVELOPMENT

Most teens are in school. They are expected to learn the required material and move successfully through and out of the educational system. They are also learning to fine tune their decision-making skills and to develop the knowledge and ability to proceed into a career. In addition, their skills at money management and household maintenance should be increasing.

During this developmental stage, the teen experiences an enormous advance in her ability to think abstractly, to imagine concepts, and to make judgments. She is unlikely to handle ambiguity well. Things are either positive or negative. People are either right or wrong. She may well become very judgmental about people who are not living up to their promises or fulfilling their responsibilities. From time to time, her parents may be the objects of her derision for their failure to measure up to her standards.

LEISURE AND RECREATION

Social and physical development interact for the teenager as she develops her recreational and leisure skills. She may be active in sports, music, writing, art, photography, or computer games. Her knowledge and abilities in these areas can serve as entry cards to peer groups that otherwise might ignore her.

For future mental and physical health, the recreational skills learned during adolescence form the base for adult participation in various hobbies or groups. Being active and involved are essential to good health, and the foundation for these activities is established in adolescence.

SPIRITUALITY

A child's moral development progresses through a few basic stages, but the major advances occur during adolescence and adulthood. During the early teen years, approval from others is a major key for decisions. Later, she acquires the ability to make decisions based on more objective criteria but may still rely heavily on the word of authority systems. Only later in adulthood, if ever, can most people base their moral sense on internally generated principles (Gilligan, 1982).

Association with a formal religious organization may provide a teenager with an ethical foundation for her decisions and activities. Difficulties can arise, however, when the teen's cognitive development, which has her questioning rules, authority, or the truth about tooth fairies and storks, also has her challenging the tenets of religion. This can be very troublesome for her parents if they regard this type of action as heretical.

CAREER DEVELOPMENT

Most adults will be involved in work settings at some time in their lives. A realistic assessment of her own skills, abilities, and interests are the foundation for the teen's career planning. In preparation for future employment, she may enroll in vocational training or may enter college. She will save herself a great deal of frustration if she has a fairly accurate idea of what she would like to do and what she can do. Becoming involved in volunteer activities can allow her to try out different interest areas and gain valuable experience at the same time. More and more companies are hiring graduates who have participated in internships or other volunteer activities.

The teenager should keep excellent records of all her activities. A shoe box or a file folder is adequate for storing ribbons or awards, complimentary letters or notes from employers or supervisors, and copies of any materials she has developed such as flyers or brochures. She should also have a list of all organizations in which she was involved and the names and addresses of leaders or other adults who can verify her activities. By documenting her participation, her perseverance, and her ability to be responsible, she exhibits the qualities that are important to employers.

SELF-CARE AND
HOUSEHOLD RESPONSIBILITIES

One expectation of adolescence is that the young person prepares for independent living. Parents anticipate that their child will eventually finish school, get a job, and move out. There is often an additional expectation regarding the young person's involvement in intimate relations, possibly culminating in marriage and the production of grand-children.

The teen years are, then, an essential time for mastering the foundation skills necessary for independent living. The teen should learn and become proficient in daily tasks such as doing laundry and preparing meals, including planning, shopping, cooking, and cleaning up. She should also notice when her hair needs cutting and manage that task autonomously. Being aware of the time for annual medical and dental checkups, as well as setting and keeping the appointments are another component of controlling one's own life.

Learning to handle money is a key factor in living independently. The teen needs the opportunity to earn money, plan its expenditure, and manage at least some of her expenses through budgeting. As she approaches adulthood, it is very important that she have a checking account and learn the skills for balancing her accounts so that she can pay her bills and live within her income.

Driving a car is, at least in some parts of the United States, a powerful symbol of the passage to adulthood. The opportunity to use the family car provides the teen with assurance that her family trusts her ability and her judgment.

SUMMARY OF TASKS

- Adjusting her self-image to correlate with the physical changes of puberty
- Developing a sexual identity and acquiring the requisite knowledge and skills to act responsibly
- Establishing a balance between the expectations of peers and adult society
- Preparing for independent living by developing employment, self-care, and leisure skills
- Nurturing a solid spiritual and moral foundation for life

TEENS WITH DISABILITIES

Medical, educational, and architectural advances have removed many barriers that historically prevented teens with disabilities from full participation in their communities. It is now expected that the teen, whether she has a physical or learning disability or a combination of these, will move through the same developmental stages as her nondisabled peers and become self-reliant, to the extent that her disability allows (Nelson, Ruch, Jackson, Bloom, & Part, 1992).

Though some teachers, social workers, and other adults tend to expect that teens with disabilities have a lower self-esteem than their counterparts without disabilities, this expectation is not consistently supported in the literature. Factors such as the psychosocial characteristics and functional level of the family, and parental values and expectations may be more important explanatory factors in a teen's self-esteem than the presence or absence of a disability. If a teen has low self-esteem, it would be wise to consider other factors before automatically dismissing this as a result of having a disability (King, Shulz, Steel, Gilpin, & Cathers, 1993).

For the teen with a disability, a number of factors may make the transition to independence more difficult. The changes of puberty can exacerbate problems such as balance and mobility. If she is not involved in groups with nondisabled peers, she may have limited knowledge and understanding about sexual issues, current speech patterns and fashions, and "good" music. This information gap may decrease her peers' acceptance of her, resulting in a negative effect on her self-esteem.

If special classes, separate transportation systems, therapy sessions or parental protectiveness limit her involvement in extracurricular activities and weekend social or sports events, the teen's integration and acceptance into her peer group may be restricted. This prevents her from learning about dating, sexual activity, and other social necessities from her peers. Though she may receive accurate facts from adults, she is still missing the important components that can only be supplied by members of her own age group.

A primary task for the teen is to learn to deal with her own emerging sexuality in a socially acceptable manner (Bregman & Castles, 1988). Sexuality, sex education, and information about contraceptives are topics that have been largely ignored by parents and professionals who work with teens with disabilities. Historically, society has had difficulty in believing that someone with a physical or mental disability is actually a sexual being or has a right to be sexual (Bregman & Castles, 1988).

The issues surrounding individuation from the family can be especially difficult. If the teen must rely on her parents for assistance in issues as basic as bathing or bowel management, she may feel very uncomfortable challenging the rules of the family.

Another major task for adolescents is preparation for employment. The transition from school to work is not well articulated even though it has been a concern for more than 50 years. To facilitate the progression from school to work, the teen's Individual Educational Program can specify that she be involved in career-oriented activities. She should incorporate the successful acquisition of problem-solving skills, social skills, and strategies for self-monitoring and self-management into her individualized education plan (IEP) (Szymanski & Hanley-Maxwell, 1996). Supported employment programs can also serve as a link between school and job by assisting her as she adapts to the social, interpersonal and work demands of the job site (Goldberg, 1995).

As the young person nears the end of formal schooling, a dramatic change will occur in access to resources. Programs that have been available at school, assessments that have been conducted regularly, and even some resources that are critical to independent functioning will no longer be automatically obtainable (Rauen & Aubert, 1992). A considerable amount of time and energy may be required from the teen and her parents or other caregivers to reestablish services and resources that are necessary. This is an area where the social worker can take the lead as a case manager. For example, the social worker may be able to identify needed resources such as accessible housing and assist the teen and parents in completing the paperwork necessary to obtain them.

Adolescence and the transition to independent adulthood are stressful times for all families. They may be even more so for families when the teen has a disability (Harris, 1987). The literature provides no clear information regarding what adaptations a family might need to make to ensure that their child is properly prepared to make the transition to self-reliant adulthood (Nelson et al., 1992).

To design appropriate strategies for helping, social workers and other professionals must consider the teen's sense of social identity, motivation for developing and changing, her method of functioning and her sense of self-worth. Any proposed interventions will also need to take account of her view of herself, her wishes, and her plans for the future (Appleton et al., 1994).

Down Syndrome

Because much of the data that is currently available regarding young adults with Down syndrome was obtained from people who spent at least part of their lives in institutions, this information may not coincide with the experience of people who have been raised in their own homes. Even for those who have been raised by their families, expectations set at the time of birth have often limited their experience. New techniques for encouraging physical growth and fitness and for promoting language competency are allowing young people with Down syndrome to regularly surpass any expectations placed on them (Fowler, 1995).

During adolescence, the young person with Down syndrome may become much more aware of differences between herself and her peers (Selikowitz, 1990). As difficult as this is for parents, they must be truthful and encourage the teen to talk about her feelings and concerns. If she understands that it is because of the Down syndrome that she has difficulty in learning, this may reduce some doubts about herself as a person (Trueta, 1995). Parents and others should emphasize her strengths and talents and remind her that everyone, including her parents and teachers, has things they cannot do or cannot do well.

Physical Development

Limited information is available in the medical literature on the physical and sexual development of the adolescent who has Down syndrome. In some males, the testes are small or have not descended. Teens may be shorter than their peers and may be overweight as well, but this does not appear to affect the rate of development of secondary and primary sex characteristics (Pueschel, 1988). Females with Down syndrome appear to experience ovulation and some have been reported in the literature as becoming pregnant. The onset of menstruation generally occurs at about 12 years of age but may occur a year later than in other girls. Most young women are capable of managing menses hygiene on their own.

Some physical issues continue to be sources of concern. The teen with Down syndrome tends to have dry skin with rough patches on her elbows and knees. To ensure that her thyroid is functioning properly, she should be checked regularly. Both hypo- and hyperthyroidism can occur and should be treated because adequate thyroid output is necessary for continued intellectual functioning (Hayes & Batshaw, 1993).

Increased weight gain may also be a problem for a teen with Down syndrome. As she becomes heavier, it is less pleasant to engage in exercise, so her weight increases even more. It is important that she learn to manage her food intake and engage in exercise and physical activities to maintain optimum weight levels (Hayes & Batshaw, 1993).

On the positive side, this teenager is continuing to master new tasks and develop her abilities. With some supervision and with adequate medical care, she will emerge from adolescence as a healthy and competent adult.

Social Development

An important aspect of adolescence is interacting with peers. A teen with Down syndrome may have limited language skills, which can reduce her ability to relate to her peers. She may demonstrate competence in understanding conversations and in making appropriate short responses or waiting for her turn to speak. These strengths, however, may not correlate with her ability to express herself verbally (Fowler, 1995). It may be difficult for her to formulate and convey her ideas so that others understand her. During extended discussions, she may appear to be an inept conversationalist because once she has responded to an opening question, she seems to run out of something to say. It is very important that she engage in activities and experiences that can provide substance for her conversations. She needs to listen to the music of her age group and attend concerts if possible. Her clothes should be similar to her peers and she should be included in shopping excursions so she can see what is available. She should also be encouraged to participate in choosing her clothing and accessories. If sports are significant to her, participating on a team, attendance at sporting events, or watching sports on television with family and friends can provide a wealth of conversational material.

Clear enunciation is another issue for teens with Down syndrome. She needs to practice communication in a variety of settings: ordering in a fast food restaurant, talking on the telephone, and conversing with friends. Parents and close friends may understand her speech, but strangers may not. Speech therapy can help her to pronounce words clearly and accurately, essential skills for success in the world outside home and school.

Sexuality and Sex Education. One ethical dilemma that arises for a teen with Down syndrome involves her sexual rights. In the past, segregation of males and females, or even sterilization, were used to prevent inappropriate sexual activity (Hayes & Batshaw, 1993). Today's teen is bombarded with sexually oriented commercials, movies, and songs. She wants to dance, date, dress, and interact just like the models she sees in the media. She may not have sufficient social experience, however, to be able to express her feelings in a socially acceptable manner. It is important that she be involved in programs that will provide appropriate and complete information regarding her sexuality to help her learn what is acceptable behavior and how to protect herself from pregnancy and sexually transmitted diseases as well as from abuse (Bregman & Castles, 1988).

Many teens get most of their knowledge about social and sexual matters through incidental observation and association. In general, the teen who has Down syndrome does not learn well incidentally. She needs concrete learning experiences that allow her to connect a particular situation with the information she needs to be able to decide what her behavior should be (Edwards, 1988). Role play exercises and supervision during group outings can provide opportunities to practice new behaviors and receive feedback on her performance.

Cognitive Development

As mentioned earlier, much of the information that has been available about teens with Down syndrome was based on studies with people who were in institutions for at least part of their lives. New and more useful data are being developed, largely through the efforts of people with Down syndrome and their parents and family members. One research center, The Center on Human Policy at Syracuse University, involves people labeled as mentally retarded as planners and researchers, not simply as subjects of the studies. To ensure that people labeled as mentally retarded are appropriately involved in research, the participants created a program through which they train their peers in deciding whether they want to participate in research studies.

Participation in planning for her own life is another important issue for the teen. Though the IDEA mandates participation of the family and the teen in establishing educational goals, neither teens nor their families consistently experience this involvement as useful or helpful (Morningstar, Turnbull, & Turnbull, 1995). Little attention seems to be paid to planning for a smooth transition from school to work; yet such planning is essential to counteract the teen's difficulties in generalizing concepts she has learned (Masino & Hodapp, 1996).

The cognitive developmental trajectory of a teen who has Down syndrome lags behind her age mates. The ability to process abstract concepts and to deal with complex ideas is generally slower to develop. Consequently, if she is attending mainstream classes she may need extra help in some areas.

A rather difficult issue that should be addressed with a teen is that of coping with loss and death. When she was younger, her parents and caregivers may have sheltered the young person from knowledge of death or from grief related to loss. This is unrealistic and prevents her from learning how to confront loss and deal with it. The death of a pet is frequently a good starting point for discussing dying. In most cases a teen, with or without disabilities, considers herself immortal and feels that death is not an issue she needs to fear. It is important that she be introduced to the idea of death at a level that she can comprehend. She should also be allowed to learn to grieve in her own way (Selikowitz, 1990).

Spiritual Development

For the teen with a disability, participation in formal church activities or in youth groups centered on religious interests may offer further social and intellectual stimulation. Her cognitive developmental level may limit her understanding of the finer points of religion and morality, but participation in a group that provides warmth and support may be beneficial regardless of her ability to comprehend its tenets.

Development of a sense of spirituality may require some assistance in sorting through doctrines or traditions that regard disability as a punishment from God. Parents or others working with the teen will need to provide assistance in understanding the concepts and in relating them to her in a way that builds self-esteem and supports her further development.

Leisure and Recreation

For teens, recreation and leisure activities serve several functions. They are a focus for socializing with peers and thus for learning appropriate, or at least current, jargon, dress, gestures, and ideas. Recreational activities and sports encourage physical activity and may help the teen in controlling her weight. Though school or other educational pursuits occupy much of her time, the teen still needs to learn constructive uses for her discretionary time.

Special Olympics is one outlet for teens. Many parents and professionals who emphasize inclusion feel that Special Olympics separates the teens from their peers. The special hugs and cheers are also seen as infantalizing the athletes. Supporters of Special Olympics, however, focus on the thrill of competition and the sense of belonging that the teen may not experience in other settings. This, like so many other areas, is a decision that the parents and their child need to make.

Inclusive recreational activities are available through many sources. Scouting and Camp Fire, YMCA and YWCA, as well as many sport associations frequently have groups that include teens with Down syndrome. The teen's particular personality traits, energy level, and interests will determine what kinds of activities appeal to her and fit her needs.

Career Development

To function in the work world, every teenager, including those who have Down syndrome, needs to learn appropriate conversational skills. She should be able to contribute to conversations without dominating or interrupting, and she should develop pleasant telephone habits.

Being able to hear, comprehend, and follow instructions are skills that are essential to job success. A teen with Down syndrome tends to be a visual learner. In some cases, she may have difficulty in following verbal commands that encompass a series of steps or topics. It may be much more effective to break an assignment into its various components and give her a series of single commands, possibly accompanying these with a poster or a sheet that presents the commands pictorially. This allows her to rely on her strengths to understand what is expected and may reduce the need to repeat instructions or to repair the results of incorrectly followed orders. Once she is comfortable with the individual components of a task, these can be linked one or two at a time until she is confident in her ability to carry out a series of commands after hearing the request only once. This requires practice and may take time. It is important that the skills involved in listening to and following orders be honed prior to her first job to ensure her success and the consequent strengthening of her self-esteem.

Independent Living Skills

Independence in one's living situation can range from living alone with no assistance to living in a structured setting that supports maximum, appropriate participation in decisions and activities. Progress toward independent living requires that the teen learn to keep her surroundings neat and clean, manage her clothing and laundry, shop for food and cook for herself, and handle her money in a responsible manner. It must be noted that many teens, with and without identified disabilities, prefer to let their parents handle these chores as long as possible.

The teen's unique learning style should be identified and used when helping her to master independent living skills. If she is a visual learner, photos or drawings of each step in a task can help her to manage it. Daily charts may be helpful, allowing her to mark off the various chores she has completed.

She can gradually assume more responsibility for meal preparation and clean up. Accompanying her parents to the grocery store is good training as she learns to select items and control expenditures.

Independent living for people with Down syndrome was not considered a possibility a few years ago. Today, young people who have received early intervention services, stimulating educational training, and social support are breaking new ground and regularly surpassing the expectations of the experts.

Summary of Tasks

Adjust self-image	Wearing fashionable clothing and hairstyles helps her fit in with her peers; using her talents supports her self-image.
Develop sexual identity	She successfully manages hygiene and is learning sexual information.
Manage peer relationships	Her desire to be with friends helps build strong social skills. She continues to develop her conversational abilities.
Prepare for independent living	She handles her household responsibilities and is building money management and decision-making skills.

Visual Impairment

An adolescent with a visual impairment will experience physical developmental changes similar to her peers. Her cognitive development is dependent on the educational program she has attended and on the stimulation and experiential input she has had. Social progress may be the most difficult area because any differences between herself and the larger group can lead to separation or ostracism. Continued development of leisure skills, self-care abilities and career-oriented competencies are important.

Physical Development

The usual growth spurts and development of secondary sexual characteristics affect the teen with visual impairment. As her muscles and bones grow, she may experience changes in her sense of balance, requiring ongoing readjustment in her awareness of her body and her spatial orientation.

Mobility, the ability to travel about in her environment, is a major skill that must be mastered by the teen with a visual impairment. She must maintain an internal, or cognitive, map of the area where she will be. She must also be prepared for unexpected or unfamiliar conditions and adapt as she encounters them. Her limited vision may reduce her ability to anticipate and prepare for incidents such as debris in the path or a large dog wishing to be friendly. All of this concentration can bring about sensory overload and cause her to make mistakes (Sugden, 1990).

Social Development

Peers and their approval are major factors in a teenager's sense of herself. Her primary concern is to be just like her friends and therefore be acceptable to them. To accomplish this goal the teen with low or no vision needs to be comfortable and competent in her personal hygiene, her clothing, and her social behaviors. Appropriate table manners, gestures, and head turning, along with a pleasant conversational style are essential. She must also learn how to ask for assistance when she needs it and how to decline unwanted help without offending the other person (Holbrook, 1996).

A major resource in ensuring the teen's social success is the IEP, which is developed each year through the educational system. When needed, extra help in table manners, mobility, and personal hygiene can be included in the teen's school program. A problem may arise, however, if participating in these specialized activities further segregates her from her peers. A teen who has partial vision may hesitate to use needed visual or mobility aids because she does not want to stand out from her peers (Groenveld, 1993).

Feeling comfortable about her disability can help the teen in making others feel more at ease around her. She may need some special counseling or assistance as she develops explanations that are satisfactory to her and helpful to others.

Sexuality and Sex Education. The teen with a visual impairment has the same desires for intimacy and love and the same hormonal urges as her peers; therefore, she needs the same sex education as they do. One difficulty may arise from the fact that one of her primary sources of information is touch, and touching her genitals or anyone else's may be considered inappropriate. Using anatomically correct dolls or models and allowing her to handle personal hygiene items and birth control devices give her the opportunity to learn through touch the information that others gain through observation.

The teen with visual impairment may not see things around her that stimulate questions about sexually related matters. This does not mean that she isn't interested or does not need the information. It is important that parents or other reliable sources assess her level of knowledge and offer direct input rather than waiting until she raises the issue (Holbrook, 1996).

Cognitive Development

Language deficits, or knowledge gaps from earlier grades, could affect the teen's school experience. With adaptive equipment, Braille materials, and audiotaped books she should be able to manage her classes. Computers with speech output or Braille screens can also be very helpful in completing school work.

Questioning ideas, rules, and even authority is one component of cognitive development. It may be difficult for the teen to challenge her parents or others when she relies on them for basic, everyday assistance. When she rebels, parents should recognize that this is a typical and normal occurrence. Rather than indicating the parents' failure, their teen's actions reflect successful accomplishment of their parenting responsibilities. Someday they will look back and recognize these actions as evidence of the teen's differentiation of herself from her family, rather than her rejection of their values.

Spiritual Development

Involvement in formal religious activities may provide another context for social interactions, in addition to its identified purpose of providing spiritual sustenance. Braille or other adapted materials make it possible for the teen with a visual impairment to participate in singing and in worship.

In conjunction with her growing cognitive abilities, the teen may find involvement in a church or other setting assists her in understanding where she fits in the greater scheme of things. An issue of concern may be, however, the accessibility of the facilities and their materials. Availability of Braille literature and songbooks along with audiotaped books will support or limit the teen's participation. For some religious groups, visual impairment or any other disability is viewed as a punishment from God. If this is the perspective of the group, the teen's involve- ment may bring more pain and distress than support and encouragement.

Leisure and Recreation

Most people learn about sports and recreational activities by watching others at play. The teen with a visual impairment, however, may not be able to observe and imitate others and she may, therefore, be unaware of some of the possibilities. Parents and others need to encourage her, provide instructions in sports or crafts she might enjoy, and model appropriate uses of leisure time. She may enjoy passive activities such as listening to music, watching television, or going to movies. With descriptive video or a companion to describe what is happening, she can participate in many of the same pastimes as her peers. If she is watching a sporting event, it may be helpful to keep a radio tuned to the play-by-play announcer to enable her to follow the action (Holbrook, 1996).

Active leisure involvement is important for physical and mental fitness. Kickball can be made accessible if the person on the base provides sound cues so the teen with visual impairment knows which way to run. Jogging or walking with a sighted friend can offer both exercise and companionship. Groups for blind skiers can provide role models and incredible recreational opportunities for the teen (Holbrook, 1996).

Implementation of the Americans with Disabilities Act requires that community facilities be adapted to allow the participation of people who have disabilities. The teen should be able to choose recreational pursuits that are of interest to her, not merely those that are already available.

Career Development

The academic skills and the social competence that the teen is developing form the foundation for success in employment as well. She needs good personal hygiene and excellent communication skills. It is also helpful if she is aware of her strengths and weaknesses. As for other teens, participation in a variety of organizations and activities will give her a broad base of experience. She can learn about what she does well and what she still needs to learn. She can also demonstrate her abilities in nonacademic settings. All of this helps her to decide what she wants to do, or what she wishes to avoid.

If further education is anticipated, the high school years are the time to apply for acceptance, arrange for financial aid, and set up living arrangements. Advance preparation will give the teen confidence that she is ready for college or training school as well as indicating to the admissions personnel that she is motivated and organized.

Independent Living Skills

In addition to managing her hygiene needs and ensuring that her physical appearance (clothing, hairstyle, and makeup) are acceptable, the teen is expected to develop skills in time management, mobility, and the accomplishment of household chores.

Adaptations are available to assist in handling all of these tasks. Knots can be sewn into the pockets or collars of garments to indicate those that go together. Pieces of tape, notches or Braille labels can be used in the bath, the kitchen, and the shop to ensure that the teen can accomplish tasks independently (Holbrook, 1996). Mobility may be a problem if public transportation is not available, or if it is not acceptable to the teen and her peers. If her group typically travels by car, she may be able to participate by paying some of the expenses in return for having others do the actual driving.

Money management is an essential skill for independent living. The actual physical handling of cash can be simplified with techniques well-known to those with visual impairment. This is another area that is made more manageable by contact with competent, successful adults who have low or no vision.

Summary of Tasks

Adjust self-image	Good self-care skills and physical fitness give her confidence.
Develop sexual identity	Accurate information and self-knowledge support her progress.
Manage peer relationships	Conversational skills and an acceptable appearance are supplemented by special knowledge of computers, sports, or other interest areas.

Prepare for independent living	Mastering techniques for handling daily chores, managing money, and mobility promotes independence.

Cerebral Palsy

The teen who has cerebral palsy experiences the same physical growth, cognitive progress, and hormonal changes that influence the lives of her peers. The limits imposed by her disability may restrict her ability to express herself verbally or to maneuver easily through her environment. By using adaptive equipment and taking advantage of the resources of the educational system, she can learn to successfully manage her life and prepare for an independent adulthood at a level appropriate for her.

Physical Development

In some cases, a child with cerebral palsy will experience precocious pubertal development. She needs to be reassured that this is normal for her; otherwise, she may resent the changes as one more factor setting her apart from her friends. For some teens, on the other hand, menarche may be later than expected. If she has not begun to develop breast buds by age 14, she should be seen by a physician (Miller & Bachrach, 1995).

Changes in height and in muscle density can affect the teen's balance and mobility. Braces or equipment that have served for several years may be quickly outgrown, time after time, as she experiences the growth spurts of puberty.

Social Development

Some research indicates that teens with disabilities do not necessarily have a more distorted body image or worse emotional well-being than other teens, and there is no significant difference in their level of sexual activity (Lamarre, 1994). It is important to remember, however, that most teens, with or without disabilities, have a fairly distorted body image.

Major concerns of teens focus on dating, driving and dressing (Thompson, 1990). A teen with sufficient cognitive ability should be able to drive a vehicle that has the needed adaptations. Grooming, dress, special clothing, and social skills must be addressed and satisfactorily managed if the teen is to be accepted by her peers.

In supporting the teen's progress toward independence, it is essential that the social worker take into consideration the social, cultural, religious, and economic values of her parents. They have spent many years supporting her, helping her to develop to her maximum potential, and advocating for her with a variety of institutions and systems. Being aware of the pitfalls she may encounter, they may not feel confident that their child's self-confidence and decision-making abilities are sufficient to enable her to succeed without their guidance and support.

One of the services the social worker can provide is to ensure that the teen is as prepared as possible for social independence. She should be able to communicate effectively, using gestures, tone of voice, and body language. If her disability limits her interactions, she needs to learn to compensate by using speech boards or other aides. Her hygiene and personal appearance must be impeccable and her clothing, equipment, and makeup should be as up-to-date and colorful as possible. In every way, she should be assisted in fitting in with her peers. A source of assistance in managing social situations may come from an adult with cerebral palsy who can provide coaching and reassurance about the possibility of a "normal" life (Thompson, 1990).

Much of a teen's learning about these social mores comes from observations of, and interactions with, her peers. She would usually develop skills such as self-assertiveness, problem solving, and making friends based on experience with this group. If adults are always present, or if opportunities are limited by equipment or by time shortages, the teen may miss out on some important learning experiences. It is important that, if at all possible, time with her peers be included into her schedule. These peer interactions allow her to learn and practice behaviors, and to receive feedback from her friends about which actions are socially acceptable and which will more likely lead to isolation or exclusion from this all-important group. Without some assistance, it is possible that the teen may learn adequate skills for engaging in work activities but not be prepared for her role as a friend, a girlfriend, or a date (Wadsworth & Harper, 1993).

Sexuality and Sex Education. Typically, the physical changes of puberty are accompanied by an increasing awareness of the adolescent's own sexuality. She is interested in the changes that she is experiencing and in the new, and sometimes frightening, feelings that arise. Many adults, teachers, and parents assume that a teen who has a disability is not capable of, or interested in, sexual activity. The result is a reduced sense of urgency, on the part of adults, about instructing these young people about sexuality and birth control because "people" don't think the issue is pertinent (Lamarre, 1994).

Difficulties can arise when the teen has been protected or barred from information about sexuality and sexual activities, thus reducing her opportunities to prepare for potentially difficult or abusive situations. She needs to know specifically what is socially acceptable and what is not. Otherwise, in attempting to be acceptable to her peers, she may submit to intercourse or other abusive situations without being fully aware of either her right to say "No," or the possible consequences of agreeing to participate.

Cognitive Development

A major task for the teenager is to establish herself as an independent human being with ideas and goals of her own. This generally means that she will reject at least some of the rules and values of her family while she tries out new concepts and behaviors. As she moves from total reliance on her family, she transfers her allegiance to her peer group (Miller & Bachrach, 1995). Though this is a normal component of adolescence, it can be very frightening for her parents.

Contact with parents of other teens who have cerebral palsy, and with adults with cerebral palsy, can provide parents with information about techniques and strategies for dealing with the teen years. Knowing that other families have survived these tumultuous times can be very reassuring.

The teen's cognitive abilities are maturing. She is able to understand more complex concepts and is attempting to integrate this new knowledge with what she has learned in the past. One component of this new knowledge may be the awareness of permanence. As she looks at her peers, she may come to realize that she will not "grow out of" her difference. She needs to understand and accept who she is and then learn to manage her life accordingly.

It is very possible that the teen with cerebral palsy will complete high school and college. These are exciting times, and the assistance she receives in fitting in with her peers and maximizing her abilities will prepare her for future learning and a successful adulthood.

The development of the IEP must focus even more on inclusion of the teen's ideas and goals. Otherwise, peer pressure and a desire to be just like her friends may place a considerable block on her willingness to carry out the activities in the IEP (Thompson, 1990).

Spiritual Development

Participation in church-related activities may provide another source of social and cognitive stimulation and interaction. As part of her preparation for adulthood and her integration of complex new ideas into her personal belief system, involvement in religious-based organizations may give another forum for trying out ideas. She may join a church or synagogue, or she may simply learn what they have to offer and move on.

The tenets of the particular sect or denomination can offer support and a recognition that every human being has value and a purpose. On the other hand, if the group sees disability as a mark from God based on past misbehavior, the teen may need to look elsewhere for spiritual support.

Leisure and Recreation

Though school and family responsibilities occupy much of a teen's time, there are still opportunities for leisure. At this point, the ball handling skills, computer knowledge, or artistic interests that she developed during childhood can serve as a foundation for recreational activities. Though passive recreational pursuits such as watching television or listening to music are normal for teens, she also needs physically active pursuits (Rauen, 1995). Swimming, horseback riding, adapted dance or exercise, and a variety of sports are potential choices for a teen who may use crutches or a wheelchair. Adapted equipment and rules can allow her to join her peers in many activities. Teens need to be encouraged to engage in active and passive recreational activities for their social, mental, and physical well-being and for the lifelong patterns that can be based on these pastimes.

Career Development

During her later high school years, the teen may begin to work in part-time jobs or in volunteer roles. These experiences prepare her for the future as she exercises her skills in arriving promptly, dressing appropriately, and displaying socially acceptable behaviors and mannerisms. Clear, well-enunciated speech and pleasant conversational behaviors are also vital components of employment success.

Involvement in organizations, volunteering to work at school or church, or in some setting such as a nursing home or child care center, are all activities that can demonstrate her skills and build her resume. The characteristics that lead to success as a volunteer are the same ones employers seek when hiring someone. Having documented experience allows the teen to show potential employers what she can do on the basis of what she has already done.

Independent Living

Dressing, self-care, and household responsibilities such as laundry, cooking, and cleaning are all components of independent living. The teen needs to practice these skills and to be assisted in learning to direct others if she will require assistance in completing some of the daily living tasks.

Adapted equipment is available for every imaginable chore around the house. Occupational therapists are skilled in assessing the person's strengths and weaknesses and developing strategies or equipment that allows maximum independent functioning. Shoe strings that can be secured with one hand, scrubber brushes that are attached to the sink for washing glasses, grabber rods that extend the person's reach and specially designed utensils for cooking and eating are just some of the adaptations that allow each person to accomplish as many tasks as possible independently.

Summary of Tasks

Adjust self-image	Her appearance, abilities, and needs are becoming integrated into a sense of self.
Develop sexual identity	Sexual urges are present; she can learn positive ways to manage them.
Manage peer relationships	Her peer groups may include teens with and without disabilities.
Prepare for independent living	Mastering household tasks, mobility expertise, and job skills are building blocks for future success.

Sexuality and Disability

Tina has worked at Pizza Hut for more than a year. She enjoys her job—keeping the silverware stocked and the serving areas tidy.

At school, Tina and Joey have been friends for some time. Now they want to start dating like the other kids at school. They have had classes in sexuality, but because they have never dated, the information didn't seem to apply to them.

The parents of both teens are struggling with what to say to them and how to support their normal interactions and hopes. At the same time, the adults want to prevent any sexual encounters.

1. What are some of the issues the social worker would need to consider?
2. In supporting the client's right to self-determination, who is the client?
3. What resources are available for the teens and for the parents?
4. What are your attitudes about people with mental retardation and their right to express themselves sexually, to marry, and to have children?

Spina Bifida

For years, little attention was focused on the teen and adult phases of people with spina bifida because their survival rate and longevity were severely limited (Rauen & Aubert, 1992). Today's teens are the beneficiaries of medical advances and technological supports that allow them to have increased physical functioning and the full expectation of a long and healthy life (Blum, Resnick, Nelson, & Germaine, 1991). It is important, therefore, that social workers and other professionals be aware of the unique challenges faced by these teens and their families.

During adolescence, significant biological, cognitive, emotional, and social changes occur. The teen must manage to separate from her parents, identify her own self-identity, take increased responsibility for her own care, plan for her future career, and establish relationships that can last for the rest of her life (Dallyn & Garrison-Jones, 1990). The teen with spina bifida must accomplish all of this within whatever limits or adaptations are needed to manage her disability and its effects.

Physical Development

The teenager brings a vast experience of managing the effects of her disability and of understanding her own expectations, strengths, and physical and psychosocial needs. On the other hand, social workers and other professionals may mistakenly assume that the teen's knowledge of the medical aspects of her situation are sufficient. In fact, though she manages herself and her daily life quite adequately, she may lack in-depth knowledge about her condition and her prognosis (Dallyn & Garrison-Jones, 1990).

The teen years are a time of rapid physical growth and changes. The young person must learn to manage her balance and mobility skills during this period when her bones and muscles are growing, and her weight and muscle mass are increasing. For the teen with spina bifida, this may mean using crutches and braces for traveling short distances and a scooter or wheelchair when she needs to keep up with her peers at the mall or the ball game.

Despite the pressures to be just like her friends, she must also become increasingly responsible for her own physical health and care. When she was a child, her parents probably focused on managing her therapeutic regimes to ensure that they were carried out correctly. At her current life stage, however, the teen is more interested in managing these routines so they present minimal interference with her social activities (Blum et al., 1991). She needs training and encouragement to conduct daily checks for skin breakdown or pressure lesions and to pay meticulous attention to hygiene, catheterization and her bowel program (Kurtz & Scull, 1993). The customary high-fat diet of the adolescent can lead to severe digestive problems, compromising the teen's ability to remain continent (Peterson, Rauen, Brown, & Cole, 1994). She must learn to maintain her healthy diet at the same time as she is trying to be just like her friends.

A major goal for the teen's physical development is maintenance of health, mobility, and functioning. For many, a motivator for continued physical involvement is participation in sports, but this may require support and encouragement from parents and others. Athletes tend to be involved in sports when they feel competent and may drop out if this sense is missing (Martin & Mushett, 1996).

Sexuality and Sex Education. Parents and others who work with teens who have spina bifida may wish to ignore issues of sexuality. If a teen lacks sensation and movement below the waist, adults may heave a sigh of relief and assume that sexual interest and activity are not a concern for this person.

In reality, it is essential that the young person with spina bifida be involved in accurate and helpful sex education. Having been subjected to examinations and therapeutic interventions all of her life, she may not have developed clear boundaries regarding her body (Lollar, 1994). Sex education should be presented within the context of respect for self and others, and the knowledge that sexual or physical intimacy are only some of the ways to express caring and love.

Parents, or other adults, may need to take the initiative in raising issues about sexuality. Most teens without disabilities receive at least some of their sex education from their peers. The limited amount of discretionary time available for many teens with spina bifida, however, means that the majority of their information about sexual matters comes from parents and teachers (Blum et al., 1991). The media constantly bombards teens with images that emphasize sexuality. If the teenager doesn't learn about these issues from her friends because of limited extracurricular contact and if her parents and teachers are hoping any sexually oriented thoughts will just go away, this may leave her feeling that something is terribly wrong. An open discussion of her disability and its effect on sexual behavior can help to relieve any fears she might have that her disability is so frightening or horrible that no one is willing to acknowledge and discuss it with her (Johnson, 1988).

One issue for parents or others to consider is that the teen may have limited knowledge of her own body. She may never have looked at or touched her genitalia and may firmly believe that because other parts of her body are different, her genitals are abnormal as well (Edser & Ward, 1991).

Spina bifida does not usually limit a female's fertility. Even though she may have a lack of genital sensation, her sexual functioning is not affected. Depending on the level of his lesion, the male who has spina bifida may not be able to attain an erection. A variety of prostheses and treatments are available to enable him to participate in intercourse (Edser & Ward, 1991).

Social Development

Developing independence from parents is an important task for the adolescent (Davis et al., 1991). Her move toward independence may be tempered, however, by the need to rely on others for some assistance in managing her disability (Johnson, 1988). To develop independence, or interdependence, she must accept the reality of her disability and incorporate it into her sense of self. In addition, she must be able to manage the effects of the disability in accomplishing tasks of daily living.

In one study, 98% of the teens with spina bifida reported that the relationships in their families were good. Some, however, noted that their parents tended to be overprotective—providing excessive assistance, warning them to avoid certain activities, constantly reminding them about self-care, and deferring to the teen more than was appropriate (Blum et al., 1991). In this process toward autonomy and differentiation, the teen and her parents can benefit from contact with successful adults who have spina bifida (Johnson, 1988). These interactions remind the whole family that the teen's goal of successful, independent living is realistic and achievable.

Friends are important for all teens. The teen with a disability may have trouble deciding which peer group is appropriate for her—others with a disability or others the same age (Davis et al., 1991). It is important that she have the opportunity to form friendships in both groups. In one study, teens with spina bifida indicated that their best friends were people they saw at school, on the bus, or at camp. Their activities with these friends centered on passive entertainment such as watching television or playing board games. Few of the teens indicated that they had an active social life. Most of the teens in the study had not dated, though they hoped for marriage and family later in life (Blum et al., 1991).

Key issues for a teen revolve around peer social acceptance. If she has a negative perception of her physical appearance and overall self-worth, her motivation for maintaining appropriate hygiene, nutrition, exercise, and self-care routines can be reduced (Appleton et al., 1994).

Cognitive Development

The expectation for an adult with spina bifida is that she will function within the mainstream world. To be prepared, she needs interactions within the nondisabled community. The school system is the most likely place for this training and acculturation to occur (Lord, Varzos, Behrman, Wicks, & Wicks, 1990).

Mainstreamed educational programs are generally promoted as the best possible option for teens with disabilities. An unanticipated outcome of mainstreaming, however, may be a lowering of the teen's sense of social competence. She will be comparing herself to classmates who are not contending with the effects of a disability and she may feel that she does not measure up (Appleton et al., 1994).

The teen's improving abilities in abstract thinking and in integration of information and ideas lead her to question much of the information and many of the rules she has learned throughout her life. This is an essential component of differentiation from her family but it can be quite distressing to parents. For a teen who must have assistance in some of her daily self-care routines, challenging her family may be too uncomfortable (Blum et al., 1991). If she requires considerable assistance, she may feel that it would be wrong to be anything but grateful and thankful to her parents. Over time, however, she may accumulate feelings of pent-up anger and resentment that can explode (Edser & Ward, 1991).

Teens are expected to begin making their own decisions and gaining a sense of mastery and control in their lives (Patterson, 1988). The realities of the disability, or the presence of protective adults, may make completion of this goal very difficult. Ideally, the teenager has been participating in age-appropriate decisions throughout her life. By her early teens, she should be comfortable with routine choices such as clothing or leisure activities. During adolescence she will be required to make more complex decisions in situations in which the guidelines may be ambiguous. When she is in groups with her peers, these choices must be made without adults to cue her. It is essential that she be encouraged to practice these skills so she will be prepared when her decision-making ability is tested.

Leisure and Recreation

Participation in games, sports, and creative activities allows the teenager to associate with her peers in "normal" experiences, perhaps without the ever-present observation of parents or other adults. She needs to master the physical, cognitive, and social components of a variety of leisure pursuits so that she will have a repertoire of activities to employ as she gets older.

Swimming, adapted aerobic dance, and wheelchair sports such as tennis, track, or basketball are available if the teen is interested. Though the exact movements may differ, teens who use crutches or wheelchairs can certainly participate in dancing.

The mandates of the Americans with Disabilities Act require that facilities and activities be available to those who are interested. This means that the teen need not search for a recreation center or gym that is already accessible. The recreation center or the school must provide the equipment, instruction, and support for the teen to engage in the sport or game of her choice. When she participates in recreation opportunities in the community, the teen can interact with people who have disabilities and those who do not (Rynders & Schleien, 1988).

Spiritual Development

It is likely that the teen with spina bifida is involved in regular classroom activities with her peers and is thus accustomed to dealing with others in her community. Participation in church-related activities may have been ongoing since childhood, if her parents are involved.

Even if she is not active in an institutionalized religious group, the teen will be engaged in her own spiritual search. As she integrates the new information she is acquiring at school, her awareness of herself and her abilities, and the expectations of society, she is refining her ideas about her role in the world. During the next decade, she is likely to do some serious soul searching and it may be helpful if she knows others who have strong moral beliefs that are compatible with her own.

Career Development

Among the many tasks allocated to the teen years is that of choosing a career. The teenager should learn how to manage money, time, and energy without supervision from others. She must also master the techniques and strategies necessary to allow her to arrive at school or any other appointment on time, dressed appropriately and prepared to engage in the assigned activities.

As with any other teen, involvement in volunteer roles and internships offers an opportunity to examine various professions or careers. Consistent participation as a volunteer serves as an excellent resume builder even for the teen who is too young to be employed.

Independent Living Skills

Most of the efforts of educators, health care workers, and vocational experts focus on preparing the teen for employment (Brannan, 1988). The ability to get a job is very important, but there are 16 more hours in the day with concomitant chores and expectations that must be handled. The teen must be comfortable managing all areas of her life. Being able to type or create software programs or design landscapes won't be very much help if she is unable to cope with the daily details of her life. Having a competitive job may not mean that she can successfully manage her independent living situation if she is not comfortable with mundane chores such as cooking, laundry, and house cleaning.

For many teens, an important marker toward adulthood is possession of a driver's license. The availability of vehicle adaptations means that many teens are physically capable of driving. The ability to drive an automobile opens many opportunities, and all but the most severely disabled should be evaluated for driving with special hand controls (Dixon & Rekate, 1990). This is another item that can be included in the teen's IEP as part of her move toward greater independence in adulthood.

Summary of Tasks

Adjust self-image	A growing sense of self accommodates her awareness of the permanence of the disability.
Develop sexual identity	Increasing knowledge about sexual issues provides protection from abuse and supports appropriate interactions.
Manage peer relationships	Self-confidence and appropriate social skills bolster acceptability with peers.
Prepare for independent living	Proficiency in self-care and daily living tasks form the foundation for choices in future living situations.

DISCUSSION QUESTION

The literature consistently suggests supporting teens with disabilities to be as similar to their peers as possible. At what point would you feel a need to draw the line on this kind of encouragement? For example, if the teen wanted to shave his head? Or wanted to have a tattoo on her shoulder? How would you make that determination?

Chapter 6

YOUNG ADULT
Nineteen to Thirty-Five Years

Last year I was going to Toastmasters, the speaker's club. It was such a great opportunity. But I have cerebral palsy, and everybody else in the room was nondisabled. They all kept looking at me like I was some kind of a hero. I get tired of hearing that. I'm a person first. I have the same problems as lots of other people; I just have a visible disability.

The progression from adolescence to young adulthood is characterized by the transition from school to career and from family to independent living (Clark & Hirst, 1989). Most young adults are working, even those enrolled in college or vocational school. They are also involved in recreational and leisure activities. In addition, a large percentage of their energy is consumed by the search for, or the maintenance of, intimate relationships.

The sudden spurts of physical growth associated with the teen years diminish during adulthood. Physical changes are generally smaller and slower. Cognitive development continues but no qualitative transformations are expected. The focus of attention is on integration of one's knowledge, abilities, expectations, and limitations into an acceptable self.

Depending on the young adult's ethnic and racial origins and on his socioeconomic status, the cultural expectations for independent living may vary dramatically. Some families are insistent that, once he has completed school, the young adult should establish his own life and allow his parents to resume theirs. Other families expect the young person to remain at home at least until he is married and possibly for years after that. Even in families whose goal for the young adult was independent living, the "revolving-door syndrome" may have them dealing with returning young adults whose successful launching has been marred by divorce, job loss, or financial problems.

SUMMARY OF TASKS

- Become involved in the work world
- Establish an independent lifestyle
- Initiate appropriate casual and intimate relationships
- Develop a sense of self as an adult

YOUNG ADULTS WITH DISABILITIES

Over the first 18 to 20 years of his life, the parents of the young adult with a disability may have achieved a sense of balance. The parents are able to provide for his needs and to work with the medical, educational, and social service systems to obtain necessary resources. As the young person reaches adulthood, however, his parents may feel that they are losing the sense of control and purpose that they had experienced when he was younger (Schilling, Schinke, & Kirkham, 1988). They must address again the issues of his disability and what that disability means to him, the family, and their futures.

Young adults with disabilities, for the most part, are moving along a developmental trajectory toward autonomy and independent living. Parents and social service personnel are not, however, always prepared with appropriate services to support this progress (Lamarre, 1994). As the young adult leaves the educational system, he may be required to find and enroll in an entirely new continuum of services. Even if the family has anticipated this transition and located potential programs and benefits, these services may have insufficient funding or long waiting lists (Krauss, 1987). As new services and programs are identified and incorporated into the young adult's life, it is important that his capacities and strengths be emphasized at the same time that adaptations or interventions are developed to compensate for his limitations. Without this dual focus on strengths and limitations, it is unlikely that the highest possible quality of life will be available or supported (Weisgerber, 1991).

There are some specific tasks for the period of transition from school to work (Healy, 1982). These include learning to interact with adults; learning about the variety of jobs and careers and how to obtain the training required; trying out a variety of activities to see what he enjoys and can do; developing constructive work-related habits such as being on time, improving his planning, and problem-solving skills; and building a sense of self-confidence and self-control.

As mentioned, many families expect that their young adult children will move out of the home into some type of independent living situation. When this does not happen, even in families in which the children are nondisabled, their continued presence may be stressful because it violates social expectations. Parents of young adults who have disabilities may find themselves in a similar situation (Darling, 1991). Family members may experience mixed feelings as they wish for independence and a "typical" adult life for the person with a disability at the same time as they wish to protect him from harm (Todd & Shearn, 1996).

Even successful transition to independence can encounter some pitfalls. For example, limits based on age or school enrollment may leave the teen ineligible for his parents' health insurance. Independent coverage may be difficult to locate and very expensive, even though discrimination based on handicap has been outlawed by some states (Kaplan & Moore, 1991).

Another concern is preparing for the future. As parents write wills and engage in estate planning, they must be aware of the consequences of these decisions. It is important that consideration be given to the potential loss of benefits that may occur if the young person is designated as the beneficiary of even small amounts of money or property. Bequeathing him a house to ensure that he always has a place to live, for example, could make him ineligible for some benefits and services.

Down Syndrome

Young adults who have Down syndrome can now expect to live a long and healthy life, but this is a fairly recent development. Information about learning styles, health promotion, and other aspects of adulthood is being generated by families of adults with Down syndrome, by the young adults themselves, and by researchers from a variety of disciplines (Nadel & Rosenthal, 1995).

Young adults with Down syndrome and their families need to be encouraged to plan for the future even though this may be an unpleasant thought. Wills, trust funds, estate planning, and permanent care or assisted living arrangements need to be established. A lawyer who is experienced in planning for people in these situations is a necessity. It is possible for the person with Down syndrome to lose benefits because of inappropriate bequests from parents or other relatives.

Social Interactions

A young adult with Down syndrome faces many of the same issues as others his age. He is reaching the end of formal schooling and will be entering the workforce. He is probably interested in dating and hoping to marry and have children someday.

The young adult who is fairly high functioning may face a difficult time as friends and classmates go off to college, start careers, or marry. If he has been involved in mainstream educational and sports activities, the renewed awareness of differences between himself and others may be especially painful. Some of his expectations may not be realistic. It is important, therefore, to plan for activities, goals, and transitions that suit his abilities and wishes—*and* are acceptable to family. This is not the time for the social worker or case manager to invite sabotage by going against what the family wants or believes is possible. The young adult is still a part of this system and will be affected by its support.

Career Development

For most young adults, a major adjustment is required in making the transition from school to job. The educational system has structured tasks and timetables and uses grades to furnish immediate feedback on performance, whereas the job setting requires more self-monitoring and provides feedback only at evaluation time. All of his previously learned skills will be needed to successfully enter the world of work.

He must wake up on time, take care of his personal appearance and clothing, be sure that he has had sufficient breakfast, and arrive promptly ready to work. Throughout the day, he must respond appropriately to supervisors, coworkers, customers, and the public. If he has some problems with speech and articulation, he must be attentive to others to ensure that they understand what he has said. Even if he is frustrated, he must control his temper.

To enhance the likelihood of job success, he will call on knowledge he has gained in previous experiences as a volunteer or as a member of groups such as Scouts or Camp Fire. These prior successes will reinforce his and others' expectations that he does have the skills and knowledge to do well in his job.

If the young adult is still involved in the educational or rehabilitation system, a job coach may be sent to the job site to assist the employer in conducting appropriate and helpful training. An on-the-job mentor or buddy may be assigned to answer questions and provide informal coaching. Assessing and putting to use the young adult's strengths will enhance his success. For example, if he is a visual learner he can use photos or sketches of various steps in a task as cues. If he is a quiet, introverted type, he can be given some time to learn skills before being called on to demonstrate them to others. A little attention at this time can build a strong base of success for the young adult and for his employer and coworkers.

Life Skills Management

As the teen enters adulthood, he needs to continue the refinement of his self-care skills to live independently, to the extent this is reasonable. This means learning how to shop, cook, clean, and manage his money. Getting up on time, arriving at work promptly, and using his leisure time responsibly are other skills he must master.

Mobility, or the ability to get around in his environment, is an important factor. If the young adult will not be able to obtain his driver's license, he will need another form of transportation. Successful programs have trained adults with a variety of limitations to make use of the public transportation system independently. A gradual, hands-on training program can allow the young adult with Down syndrome to learn, practice, integrate, and perfect his mobility skills. He will then be able to travel to work or to leisure activities without always having to wait for someone else to transport him (McInerney & McInerney, 1992).

Leisure activities are especially important to young adults. Even full-time jobs allow some discretionary time. Sports interests and hobbies developed in childhood and adolescence will be important bases for his adult activities. Involvement in these types of activities can help him maintain a balance in his life and provide opportunities to practice his social skills. Interactions, even when the focus is fun, encourage him to develop and maintain his language skills, increase his attention span, and expand his ability to persevere in a task (Lawrence, Brown, Mills, & Estay, 1993).

A variety of barriers may hinder the young adult's development of active leisure pursuits. There may be a lack of suitable recreational facilities and activities—specially in small towns or rural areas. If he is beginning a new sport or activity, he may feel unsure about his competence. In a new setting, he may wonder if others will accept him. A buddy or parent who is willing to accompany him for the first few times may be all that is needed to set the groundwork for the young person's independent involvement.

Another barrier to participation in some recreational events can be the cost of the activity. Concert tickets, for example, are expensive and transportation may be difficult to manage. Pooling money for a cab for several young adults may solve the transportation problem (Lawrence et al., 1993).

The decision about living arrangements is a difficult one for many families. It requires planning and decision making by the parents, the young adult, and any social service providers who may be involved. All of these parties should assess the potential living situation, giving consideration to issues such as, How will this setting facilitate his growth and independence? Who, in the home or somewhere else in his network, will assist him in achieving his goals? (Lawrence et al., 1993). Once a decision about living arrangements is made, the details should be recorded in a straightforward written document approved by the young adult, the parents and family, and any service providers.

Professionals working with parents of young adults with Down syndrome may perceive an attitude of overprotection. In fact, the parents may have a very realistic assessment of their adult child's abilities and wishes as well as a clear understanding of the gaps in services and facilities provided by the outside community (Tingey, 1988). This is a point at which the professionals must align themselves with the family and young adult to provide appropriate transitions in work, social activities, living arrangements, and leisure pursuits. Advocacy may be needed in developing new outlets for young adults who are not comfortable in some settings frequented by other adults. This might mean organizing sports, music groups, theater, or coffee bars so young adults with Down syndrome have places to gather and socialize.

An excellent resource for parents, young adults, social workers, and the community at large is *Count Us In,* written by two young men who have Down syndrome. Jason Kingsley and Mitchell Levitz (1994) are friends and coauthors of this introduction to active, successful adulthood for a population who were not even expected to survive infancy. Both young men have some limitations but they have a far greater number of successes and abilities.

Spirituality

The young adult may be involved in a job and in leisure activities that pique his interest and keep him physically and mentally involved; yet he still needs to pay attention to a wider view of his life. Involvement in a church or in information situations that address spiritual and philosophical issues can fill these gaps in his life.

It might appear that a young adult with cognitive limitations would not need, or be interested in, issues that appear to be abstract and ephemeral. If he was involved in church activities as a child or a teen, however, these activities might provide social contact and intellectual stimulation in addition to their religious value. It is important that he have the opportunity to decide for himself whether he wishes to be involved in these types of activities and organizations. It should not be automatically assumed that he has no interest or that he is unable to participate in a meaningful manner.

Summary of Tasks

Become involved in the work world	Competitive or supported employment provides social contact and financial support.
Establish an independent lifestyle	Living at home or in a supported situation, he can learn to manage his time and money.
Initiate appropriate casual and intimate relationships	Dating, socializing in groups, and marriage may be desired.
Develop a sense of self as an adult	Understanding and acknowledging strengths and limitations, and celebrating successes contribute to positive sense of self.

Visual Impairment

The young adult who has visual impairment faces many of the same tasks as others his age, and he will also encounter some issues related to his disability. With successful mobility training, sufficient technological assistance, and accessible housing and transportation, the expectation is that a young adult with low or no vision can manage his life independently and successfully. He will require some assistance, but by this point in his life he has probably learned how to ask for help when he needs it.

Social Interactions

When he was a teen, the young person with visual impairment may have experienced some difficulties in fitting in with his peers. Their constant search for, and avoidance of, anything "different" may have reduced opportunities for interactions. As an adult, however, his involvement in work, school, church, or leisure activities probably puts him in contact with people in settings in which his disability is not the primary consideration. There is a much higher likelihood that his abilities and strengths will be recognized and his limitations minimized. The presence of a visual impairment will not necessarily restrict his social interactions nor his ability to date, marry, and meet other social obligations common to his life situation.

This is the time in his life when all of the careful training about eye direction, head turning, gesturing, and voice modulation will be of benefit. As he is able to make others feel comfortable, they will find it easier to include him in activities and in friendship groups.

A young adult's sense of self-esteem may depend on at least two factors: feeling similar to his peers and being able to demonstrate competence in some area. If he perceives himself as very different from his peers, this difference may have a negative effect. If, however, he is able to demonstrate to himself and to others that he is competent and successful in some area, his self-esteem may be much improved (Martinez & Sewell, 1996). He may be a whiz at computer games, a math star, an excellent debater or musician. This positive sense of self will be based on the skills and knowledge he has gained throughout his life and his ability to establish himself as being "good" at something.

Career Development

The availability of adaptive equipment for reading print, for producing documents, and for managing daily activities has reduced some of the barriers to employment. A huge range of career opportunities are available though transportation may be an ongoing problem. One solution is to use carpools, supplying money or gasoline in place of taking his turn at driving.

The social skills he has mastered may be the key to obtaining interviews and jobs. A pleasant telephone manner and a strategy for making others feel comfortable can be essential to getting his foot in the door. Once he is in the interview situation, if he has rehearsed well, he should be ready for any questions he may be asked. A carefully prepared portfolio that illustrates his accomplishments can supplement his interviewing skills. By showing letters of commendation and describing accomplishments in earlier jobs or in volunteer settings, the young adult will be able to assure the potential employer that he has the skills and the perseverance to succeed in the position he is seeking.

Life Skills Management

The adaptive equipment that supports successful employment can also benefit the young adult at home. Having the assistance of a mentor can allow him to learn techniques and strategies that make daily tasks such as cooking and laundry much easier.

His prior practice in house cleaning, laundry, cooking, and money management will allow him to live independently and confidently. If, during his teen years, he accepted the responsibility for self-care issues such as setting appointments for physician's visits, dental care, and haircuts, he knows that he is capable of handling these chores.

He will also be responsible for his own mobility. He may use public transportation, mobility aids such as a cane or a guide dog, or the assistance of friends and coworkers as he establishes carpool arrangements

.Spirituality

As with other young adults, the young person with a visual impairment needs to address his spiritual needs as well as his physical, social, and financial concerns. He needs to understand how he fits in the scheme of things and be able to establish his goals with reference to what he considers his moral obligations.

These activities may take place in an established church, through reading and discussion with others, or through meditation or private study. Regardless of the setting, those who are working with the young adult need to help him establish a sense of spirituality that is comfortable to him.

Summary of Tasks

Become involved in the work world	With training and adaptive equipment, competitive employment can be expected.
Establish an independent lifestyle	Adaptations and some assistance allow independent living.
Initiate appropriate casual and intimate relationships	Friendships and dating may be easier in adulthood than for teens.
Develop a sense of self as an adult	Integration of career, social, and spiritual aspects of self leads to sense of wholeness.

Cerebral Palsy

Many people with cerebral palsy live independently as adults. Some services and assistance may be necessary to support this independence, however, and if these programs are unavailable or have a waiting list, family members may be left to fill the gaps. Educational services provided under the IDEA (the Individuals With Disabilities Education Act) must continue until the person is 21 years of age or until he graduates from high school (Kaplan & Moore, 1991).

Social Interactions

In early adulthood, the training and experiences of the young person may affect his success. If, as a teen, he was isolated and unable to be involved in activities with his peers, he may not have had the opportunity to observe others and learn how to engage in age-appropriate interactions (Wadsworth & Harper, 1993). For young adults who have mastered social skills, however, involvement in social situations and in dating may become easier than when they were teens. Contact may now occur in a variety of settings, such as work or leisure activities, in which the disability is not the primary focus of attention. If the young adult's speech is difficult to understand, adaptive equipment may ease his entry into various situations.

Dating and marriage are highly possible for the young adult with cerebral palsy. For a woman, becoming pregnant and bearing children need not be problematic. Good prenatal care will allow her to carry and deliver her child successfully (Winch, Bengtson, McLaughlin, Fitzsimmons, & Budden, 1993).

Career Development

One factor in obtaining a job is the ability to get along with others. A young adult with cerebral palsy who has not been exposed to a range of other adults may have missed opportunities to learn social skills modeled by others (Wadsworth & Harper, 1993). This lack of skills may reverberate through his life, limiting his success in applying for and obtaining jobs, maintaining an independent lifestyle, and feeling socially competent and acceptable.

Vocational Rehabilitation services are designed to prepare people with disabilities for employment. For young adults with severe disabilities, these services are more accessible than in the past, due to recent adjustments in the law. Services are no longer restricted solely to those who will be able to enter competitive employment. Individuals who apply to Vocational Rehabilitation will be evaluated and given an individualized written rehabilitation plan (IWRP), or an individualized habation plan (IHP). These are similar to the individualized education plan (IEP) that was used in the educational system. The IWRP identifies the services that are needed for the person to be able to work productively (Kaplan & Moore, 1991).

A huge range of career possibilities is available to the young adult with cerebral palsy. A few of the many potential choices include being an artist, clinical psychologist, computer programmer, accountant, film producer, mathematician, engineer, writer, college professor, or rehabilitation counselor. In choosing a career, the young person needs to consider his personal interests and aptitudes as well as his educational background and his previous experience (Miller & Bachrach, 1995).

Life Skills Management

Living independently of one's parents is a major goal for many young adults. This is not a transition that will occur automatically as he reaches a certain age; it requires years of preparation that began when he was little more than a toddler. If he has practiced his money management and his decision-making skills, participated regularly in household chores and responsibilities, and learned to get along with peers and adults outside his own family, his chances of successful independent living are greatly enhanced. Even with all of this background, however, if his parents are hesitant to see him move out, their lack of support may be a critical factor. With parental support, even a young adult with severe disabilities can achieve a measure of independence. He may move through a series of settings with gradually decreasing assistance and support until he reaches a situation that is comfortable for him and acceptable to his family (Kokkonen, Saukonen, Timenon, Serlo, & Kinnunen, 1991).

Health insurance is a major issue the family may encounter as the young person enters adulthood. Some states outlaw discrimination based on handicap but insurance is often difficult to obtain as well as being expensive (Kaplan & Moore, 1991).

Many young adults with cerebral palsy are able to pass the driving examination and receive their driver's license (Kaplan & Moore, 1991). Adaptive equipment such as lifts or hand controls may be needed but instruction is available in the use of such adaptations. If the person tends to have seizures, however, a license may be denied due to the potential loss of consciousness during a seizure.

Spirituality

If a young adult with cerebral palsy chooses to be involved in a formal religious institution, he may need to make arrangements for transportation and be sure that the setting is accessible. Some churches may be willing to provide special transport but others may expect him to use public transportation or establish a carpool. If the facilities are not accessible, this may present a problem.

Some religious groups make a policy of soliciting the participation of those who are different from their usual members. Others, however, may feel quite uncomfortable if the prospective member has difficulties with speech or with mobility. It will be up to the young adult to locate a situation that is comfortable and conducive to his spiritual growth. This may be the church his family attended during his childhood or it may be something entirely different. If his family tended toward more traditional religious practices and he is interested in alternative worship groups, this could cause difficulties. This may be a test of his ability to assert his wishes and establish independence, or he may need to accede to the family's wishes and save the confrontation for another issue.

Summary of Tasks

| Become involved in the work world | Social skills, educational training and volunteer experience can lead to full, competitive employment. |

Establish an independent lifestyle	Experience in household chores and self-management, accompanied by adaptive devices as needed, can allow independent living.
Initiate appropriate casual and intimate relationships	Interactions at work, school, church, or play offer opportunities for social contacts that may develop into friendships, dating, or marriage.
Develop a sense of self as an adult	Caring for himself and contributing to his community serve as a base for seeing himself as a competent adult.

Socialization Issues

Mark likes his job as a counselor at the Center for Independent Living. He enjoys working with others who have disabilities. Because he has cerebral palsy, he feels more qualified than a person without disabilities to help the clients see what they may be able to accomplish.

Once work is over, however, the quality of his life drops dramatically. Accessible transportation is not always available so his recreational activities are limited. Some churches he has attended were uncertain about how to respond to him. The members didn't seem willing to get to know him and to take the time to learn to understand his speech. The only social activities he has found are geared toward people with mental retardation—folks with whom he feels he has little in common.

Mark has always attended mainstream schools and worked in competitive jobs. He has seen his peers from work and school begin to date and then to marry. Now he is feeling discouraged about his lack of a social life. He is resentful that others do not have to cope with the daily consequences of having cerebral palsy. He is also concerned about his future. He sees long years alone with nothing but work.

1. What would you identify as Mark's problem?
2. How can his issues be addressed?
3. As a social worker, what is your role in helping to develop some social or recreational outlets that would be available to Mark and his peers?

Spina Bifida

Advances in medical technology, surgical procedures, and educational programs have extended the lifespan of people with spina bifida so that most are now expected to survive into adulthood. This a comparatively new development and the educational and career planning services needed to assist these adults are still sparse (Schriner, Roessler, & Johnson, 1993). Medical knowledge based on long-term follow-up is also incomplete. As the first large wave of teens with myelomeningocele survived into adulthood during the 1980s, they left the traditional children's services and were no longer included in the tracking system. Many were lost to follow-up and the pattern of medical surveillance ceased (Rauen & Aubert, 1992).

Today, most young adults who have spina bifida are able to live independently, be employed, and lead productive, satisfying lives (Rauen & Aubert, 1992). It is up to the individual and his family, however, to assess his strengths, abilities and needs and then to seek out and coordinate whatever services, benefits, adaptations and resources are needed to support maximum independence.

The lack of sensation below the level of his lesion means that the young adult with spina bifida will cope with ambulation, bowel and bladder functioning, skin care, and weight control throughout his life (Schriner et al., 1993). He will always need to be vigilant in preventing secondary disabilities such as obesity, pressure ulcers, kidney failure, and urinary tract infections. Bladder and bowel continence is absolutely essential to social acceptance and this is achievable as long as he maintains his high fiber diet, high fluid intake, and consistent toileting times (Rauen & Aubert, 1992).

A major concern for people with spina bifida is severe allergic reaction to latex. Their health providers must be made aware of the potential dangers of this reaction and take precautions to prevent exposure (Rauen & Aubert, 1992).

An adult who was ambulatory as a child may begin to use a wheelchair. This is not a sign of failure but an accommodation to realities such as weight gain, pain, fractures, and spinal deformities. Manipulating braces and crutches or canes reduces his ability to carry objects and to maneuver in certain situations. It also requires much more energy than wheeling a chair.

If it is necessary for the young adult to use a wheelchair, he must be aware of potential problems such as osteoporosis and repeated fractures, concerns that might make him hesitate about moving around. When at all possible, he should be involved in a program that involves standing erect for some period of time each day. This can help to reduce the potential for fractures while improving range of motion in joints, improving bladder drainage and increasing circulation (Rauen & Aubert, 1992).

Social Interactions

The young adult with spina bifida can draw on all of his experiences as a child and as a teen to assist him in establishing social contacts. He has learned how to care for himself, realizing that good hygiene, acceptable clothing and equipment, and the ability to arrive at the appointed destination in a timely manner are essential to ongoing friendships.

As he leaves school and enters the world of work, he gains even more content for conversations. He can discuss not only the latest movies and music but the joys and woes of interacting with supervisors and co-workers.

Career Development

A major concern for adults with spina bifida is obtaining and retaining health insurance (Schriner et al., 1993), and this can be a factor in decisions about employment. If a potential job does not have health insurance, the person cannot afford to lose the benefits provided by Social Security Disability Insurance or other programs. This is an issue that can be addressed before the young adult leaves the educational system. He and his parents can examine the various benefits and programs for which he might qualify to determine the effects of various choices on the availability of health insurance. A major problem with this strategy, however, is that the rules and regulations regarding programs and benefits are subject to frequent and often incomprehensible change. Involvement in a network of others facing the same situation can enable all parties to share knowledge and information about how to find, qualify for, and enroll in various services and programs.

Life Skills Management

There are various developmental tasks for young adults (Erikson, 1963). Establishing a sense of self-identity, independence, and intimacy are vital for young adults with spina bifida as they are for all young people (Rauen & Aubert, 1992). Some of the skills required for independent living include self-care, housekeeping, meal planning and preparation, and financial management. In addition, a young adult must also feel competent in making and keeping appointments related to his health care needs (Rauen & Aubert, 1992).

To live independently, the young adult must be cognizant of his abilities and skills. He can then be assisted in learning to manage the various tasks of daily life by developing strategies and techniques based on his abilities (Rauen & Aubert, 1992).

It may be left to the young adult and his family to manage the coordination of services and benefits that was previously handled through the educational system. An assessment of available services must be made and this information should be included as the family plans for the future. Any type of estate planning, for example, must include safeguards against loss of future benefits. If the young person is the beneficiary of even small amounts of money or property, he may become ineligible for some programs.

In managing an independent lifestyle, a major concern for adults is transportation. For most, the preferred mode of travel is by private automobile. Vehicle modifications and driver training are available that allow the young adult to be a safe and competent driver, but financial considerations may be a barrier. He must still pay for his driver's license, insurance, and vehicle maintenance. These expenses may be prohibitive for a young person, especially if he is employed part-time or works for minimum wage. These problems may lead to reliance on expensive private transportation companies that must be scheduled in advance and may be unreliable (Rauen & Aubert, 1992). Because of the Americans With Disabilities Act, public transportation systems must be accessible for the person with a disability, but this has not led to a reliable, user-friendly daily service for most people.

Leisure and Recreation

Recreation and leisure activities are a vital part of a normal lifestyle. For the young adult with spina bifida, social participation as a teen may have been less than satisfactory and may not have provided him sufficient experiences to develop a range of social pursuits. He may need some help in becoming informed about activities and programs that are available in the community. He may also need some encouragement to participate, at least initially (Dallyn & Garrison-Jones, 1990).

If transportation, or a social network that supports involvement in activities, is not easily available, the young person may rely on passive entertainment such as television or video games. It is very important that he at least be offered the opportunity to engage in a variety of recreational pursuits, some of which are not sedentary. The physical benefits of these activities are supplemented by the social interactions that can develop when people are engaged in enjoyable pursuits. An important side effect of a recreational program, therefore, is to diminish the incidence of isolation and loneliness (Rauen & Aubert, 1992).

Spirituality

As with other young adults, the person with spina bifida has the opportunity to integrate all of his interpersonal and cognitive skills as he seeks an avenue for addressing his spiritual concerns. He may have a job, a car, friends and family but feel that the spiritual aspect of his life is unfulfilled. For some, reaching out for a spiritual home means following the tradition of their families. For another, the need to address his own concerns, or a need to declare his individuation from his family, may lead him to associate with groups who have very different ideas and practices.

Social workers who are assisting young adults may need to help them explore the reasons for selecting a particular religious or spiritual group. The young adult may also need assistance in locating groups that are physically accessible, and intellectually and emotionally compatible. Support may be needed if the young adult is making choices that are not popular with his family.

Summary of Tasks

Become involved in the work world	Skills, knowledge, and social competence form the base for successful employment.
Establish an independent lifestyle	Self-care, consistent monitoring for health problems, and independent mobility support independence.
Initiate appropriate casual and intimate relationships	Participation in job, leisure, and religious activities provides social contacts.
Develop a sense of self as an adult	Integration of self-knowledge and success in work and friendship supports self-esteem.

Spinal Cord Injury

The young adult period is the one in which a person is most likely to experience spinal cord injury. Approximately 200,000 people in the United States are affected by spinal cord injury. Two thirds of these injuries involve people under the age of 30 and about 75% of them are male. Prior to World War II, spinal cord injury almost inevitably resulted in death. With recent advances in technology and surgery, however, the lifespan of a person with spinal cord injury has increased to about 75 years (Spoltore & O'Brien, 1995).

The level of the spinal cord injury determines the areas of the body that will be affected, and the degree to which the cord is severed determines the severity of the paralysis. If the lesion is complete, sensation below the injury is generally lost. The cervical, or neck, area of the spine (vertebrae C7 and above) controls essential functions such as arm movement and breathing. Injury in this area causes quadriplegia or tetraplegia—paralysis of all the limbs. An injury above C3 often results in death because the person is unable to breathe without a ventilator. If the injury is at C4 or C5, he will have weakness in his diaphragm and limited strength and movement in his arms and hands. With assistance for his daily living activities and the use of a mouth stick or head pad to control his wheelchair and various other mechanical devices, the person with a C4 injury can manage mobility, employment, and social relations quite adequately (Priebe & Rintala, 1995). Many people with C5 injuries can drive a specially modified vehicle. Though an injury at C6 to C7 affects all limbs, some arm and hand function is usually retained. This allows him to operate a wheelchair and, with adaptations and training, to retain the chance for some independence in dressing and eating (Priebe & Rintala, 1995).

Paraplegia refers to paralysis of the legs and lower body and results when the injury is at the thoracic (chest), lumbar (lower back), or sacral (tailbone) level of the spine. Injuries at T1 to T3 affect the lower body and the person's balance. Arm function is intact, however, allowing him to function independently in many aspects of life. The lower thoracic area controls leg movement, but injuries below T4 generally leave the person with full use of his upper arms and his torso. Sacral or lumbar level injuries cause loss of bowel and bladder control, but by using braces, crutches, or both, the individual may be able to walk.

Immediately after the injury, stabilization of the vertebral column is the primary medical concern (Spoltore & O'Brien, 1995). Expert medical care is essential to avoid further injuries and complications (Hammell, 1992). For the first few days after his injury, the injured person may be confined to a Stryker frame that rotates his entire bed. This device is designed to prevent decubitii (pressure sores or ulcers) from developing and to enhance his circulation and muscle tone. The social worker should remind the family that while the injured person is confined to this frame, what he can see of the world is limited to alternating views of the ceiling and floor. In addition, having someone stop by every 2 hours to rotate the bed is hardly conducive to consistent restful sleep (Hammell, 1992). If he also needed a tracheotomy to allow him to breathe, he will not be able to speak until this is reversed. All of these interventions may leave him feeling irritable and somewhat confused. He may be diagnosed as depressed when, in reality, he is simply responding to boredom and loss of sleep.

Many theorists believe that adjustment to a traumatic injury occurs in stages. One perspective holds that the person experiences denial, rage and anger, then bargaining, depression, and finally acceptance (Hammell, 1992). Little objective evidence exists to support the stage theory (Treischmann, 1980) but it seems to make sense for some rehabilitation and medical personnel. Social workers and other professionals may, therefore, expect the injured person to complete the various theoretical stages of adjustment and may watch intently for denial as the first step. If the young adult chooses to focus on his future and on his desire to maximize his potential, the professionals around him may view this approach as denial rather than as positive acceptance of the situation. If he expresses any optimism about his situation, this may be viewed as dysfunctional and inappropriate (Hammell, 1992). The young adult may have some difficulty displaying the exact emotional and cognitive state expected by the medical and rehabilitation professionals who appear to be in charge of his life.

The person with a spinal cord injury must learn to cope with a range of changes in his physical condition. In addition to the paralysis, other physical concerns include pressure ulcers (decubitii) and urinary tract infections (Spoltore & O'Brien, 1995).

The most dangerous physical reaction for people with injuries above the level of T6 (the middle of the chest) is autonomic dysreflexia. It is triggered by a noxious stimulus such as a distended bladder or an impacted bowel, or an infection such as an ingrown toenail. Symptoms include an uncontrolled rise in blood pressure and a decreased pulse rate. He may have a pounding headache, cold sweats, flushing and blotching of the skin (Spoltore & O'Brien, 1995). It is essential that he and others in his household be aware of this potentially fatal problem and call for immediate medical assistance if the symptoms appear. Without treatment, he may die.

It is also vital that all members of the person's family have the same definition of words such as *pressure ulcer* or *bedsore*. These are not small blisters that will go away. They are major medical problems that must be handled before they become more serious. If the injured person cannot feel pain or move about to relieve pressure on his back or buttocks, he can easily develop decubitii or pressure ulcers. Untended, they can quickly become infected causing damage to skin, muscle, and even bone. To avoid this, he is trained to perform frequent pressure releases—shifting in his chair or turning in the bed. He may use a digital watch with a timer to remind him when it is time to do a pressure release maneuver (Spoltore & O'Brien, 1995).

Bladder and bowel management must also be learned. Most people with a spinal cord injury do not have voluntary bladder and bowel control. Loss of sensation below the level of the injury also prevents awareness of fullness in the bladder or bowel. Regular catheterization and the development of a bowel program are essential to progress toward independence (Spoltore & O'Brien, 1995). Successful management of these issues allows many people with spinal cord injury to be fully employed and have active social lives.

Another result of the spinal cord injury is a reduced ability to control the body's temperature. He may not sweat and therefore may not be able to handle heat well. Clothing and environmental temperatures need to be monitored carefully (Spoltore & O'Brien, 1995).

Rehabilitation

Once the injury has been stabilized, the young adult will begin the rehabilitation process. Much of the focus during this period is on assisting him to manage mobility and the activities of daily living, but attention must be given to social and psychosocial issues as well (Gless, 1995). Once he leaves the rehabilitation unit, he will be required to function in a world that is not designed with his needs in mind. Other people may regard him as "different" or as less able than he was before. He may even feel that they regard him as no longer belonging in regular society (Spoltore & O'Brien, 1995). He will need to develop some new mechanisms for meeting others and for making them feel comfortable. These techniques can also enhance his opportunities for jobs. Even if he is qualified for a particular position, it may be necessary to make others feel comfortable in the presence of the chair or other equipment before a potential employer can visualize him in the post he is seeking.

It is important that, during rehabilitation, attention is paid to the physical and psychological changes that typically accompany young adulthood (Bozzacco, 1993). During this life stage, a person is expected to become more independent and autonomous, and to make interpersonal and career commitments. For the person with spinal cord injury, restricted physical ability, increased time needed to accomplish daily tasks, and a perception of social stigmatism may slow his progress toward the independence of adulthood (Blake, 1995). Some of his major concerns may include the lack of transportation, or being required to use a clunky and utilitarian van rather than a jazzy sports car. The goal of living alone, or independent of family, may be more difficult to reach. Accessible housing may not be available where he would choose to live, or his neighbors may be older or limited in their abilities and in their appeal (Blake, 1995).

Women and Spinal Cord Injury

The majority of people with spinal cord injuries are men, and therefore, most services and programs were designed for men. At any given time, there may be only one woman in a spinal cord unit and she may be the first woman they have ever served (Resources for Rehabilitation, 1994). Feeling out of place, she may hesitate to ask questions regarding her health or her home situation. She may not challenge the information or the programs, even if they are not appropriate for her, because they are so institutionalized as to appear unchangeable. This lack of peers and mentors means that she must actively seek other women who can teach her techniques for catheterization, use of tampons, handling various household activities, and even recommendations for managing the intricacies of sexual intercourse.

Because spinal cord injury overwhelmingly affects young adults, issues about sexuality and intimacy are major concerns. This is the period of life when the young person is expected to develop intimate relationships and experiencing a spinal cord injury may make any hope of marriage and children seem farfetched. In reality, the injury will cause some changes and may require adjustments in regard to sexual activity, but it need not be a permanent barrier. Alternative positions and techniques can be used to ensure that sexual intercourse will not just be possible but pleasurable.

Immediately after the injury, a woman's menstruation may stop, but it will probably resume within 6 months. There is no reason for the spinal cord injury to be a barrier to conceiving, bearing, and raising children (Resources for Rehabilitation, 1994). During pregnancy, the woman with a spinal cord injury will need to be extra vigilant about pressure sores, and toward the end of the pregnancy, her added weight and altered balance can make transfers in and out of her wheelchair more difficult. Having completed her pregnancy successfully, it is very likely that she will be able to deliver her baby vaginally.

For many women, maintaining a positive sense of self-esteem requires constant work. After a spinal cord injury, this may be an even greater issue. It will be vital that she become involved with other women in a similar situation to observe their successful adaptation and to learn techniques to make daily living a little easier. When she is ready to return to work, she may face the double minority status of being a woman and having a disability. The interaction of employment barriers facing people who have disabilities and issues confronting women in the workplace leads to drastic underemployment for women who have spinal cord injuries (Resources for Rehabilitation, 1994).

Life Skills Management

In working with a person with spinal cord injury, the social worker needs to assess several areas such as lifestyle prior to the injury, coping mechanisms, interests and goals, and personality style relative to self-managing or self-destructive behaviors (Spoltore & O'Brien, 1995). It is also important to identify his priorities. Though the rehabilitation team may consider it essential that he be able to cook and clean and manage all aspects of his environment, he may prefer to allow someone else to carry out some of these tasks. This, then, allows him to preserve energy for activities such as socializing which he may regard as much more important (Siosteen, Lundqvist, Blomstrand, Sullivan, & Sullivan, 1990).

For a person with a spinal cord injury, successful community integration may have a broad range of meanings. For some, it means living in an independent setting and participating in competitive employment. For others, it may involve volunteer work and home-based activities. It is important that the social worker understand the distinction between the goal of reintegration and the concept of employment; the two are not always linked (DeVivo & Richards, 1992).

Technological advances over the last few decades have resulted in equipment and adaptations that allow many people to live alone or at least within the community. The availability of ramps, widened doorways, slings and lifts for transferring from the chair to the bed or tub, and hand-controlled vans and cars means that a person with very little muscle control can manage many of his daily activities.

A major issue for a person with spinal cord injury who is living alone is the time required for daily personal maintenance activities such as bathing, dressing, and eating (Spoltore & O'Brien, 1995). He may need to remind his friends and family to slow down to accommodate the increased amount of time he needs to accomplish even simple tasks such as getting in and out of a car (Blake, 1995).

Another potentially problematic area is finances. There is a need to know and understand the enormous number of programs and services that may be available. It is essential to be aware of the rules and regulations of all these programs, many of which may be contradictory. A primary concern is maintaining some sort of health insurance coverage (Bozzacco, 1993). A federal program may be the only source of such insurance so the person must be extremely careful not to violate regulations regarding amount of income earned or other limitations. Loss of health coverage may result in months or years with no insurance before being able to qualify again (Bozzacco, 1993).

As mentioned earlier, a person with a high level spinal cord injury will experience limited movement and strength in his arms and upper body. To be able to live in the community, he will need to find an affordable and reliable source of attendant services to assist him with his personal care and with other activities around the house (DeJong & Batavia, 1991). A huge number of issues arise around hiring, supervising, and managing attendants. If a home health service serves as a clearinghouse to screen, train, and hire attendants and then manage the payroll, there may be a lack of clarity as to who gives instructions to the attendant. Paying for attendant care is another concern. For purposes of funding, attendant care falls outside the purview of most service providers. Done correctly, it is not a medical nor a home chore service. Therefore, insurance companies and most benefit programs will not fund attendant care. Without this component, however, the much more expensive alternative of institutionalized care is the only choice (DeJong & Batavia, 1991).

Despite all the difficulties, many people with spinal cord injury see their lives as satisfactory and productive. When they can use appropriate assertiveness to maintain some control in their lives and when they can establish a balance between dependence and independence, they are able to see their lives as valuable and acceptable (Bach & McDaniel, 1993).

Spirituality

Typically during young adulthood, spirituality emerges as a purposefully chosen component of life. At the time of serious injury, however, the beliefs and attitudes that the young person has accepted may be seriously challenged. If he formerly believed in a just world, he must somehow harmonize the dissonance between what he expected life to be and what he is currently experiencing (Lilliston, 1985). This may be very difficult for him and for his family as well.

Leisure and Recreation

Leisure and recreation are increasingly recognized as vital components in rehabilitation. Even in the rehabilitation hospital, a person needs to have a reason to try to get out of bed in the morning (Hammell, 1992). Involvement in wheelchair sports is one potential source of physical activity and motivation for regaining strength and mobility. This type of participation can result in increased stamina, fitness, and mobility, as well as feeling more comfortable using the wheelchair. Participation in physical activities also leads to a better mental outlook, greater acceptance of the disability, an improved self-image, and a more independent attitude (Jackson, 1987).

Summary of Tasks

Become involved in the work world	Adaptive equipment allows participation in many careers.
Establish an independent lifestyle	Accessible housing, accompanied by attendant care if needed, supports independence.
Initiate appropriate casual and intimate relationships	Self-acceptance is a major step in helping others feel comfortable.
Develop a sense of self as an adult	Active participation in work, leisure, religion, and social activities supports a positive sense of self.

DISCUSSION QUESTION

Discuss your ideas about the importance of spirituality and sexuality in the lives of young adults. Now, how do these ideas change when you think of young adults with disabilities?

Chapter 7

MIDDLE ADULT
Thirty-Six to Sixty-Five Years

> I'm just plain vanilla blind, Sue said. At midlife, I don't have
> as much energy and it's not as easy to perform all the daily
> tasks. Sometimes I think, I've done this for so long, seems
> it ought to be somebody else's turn for a while. The one thing
> I wish is that I could put on a pair of high heels and walk
> down the hall real fast the way I hear other women do.

During the middle adult years, the first major signs of aging begin to
appear. Hearing acuity decreases, changes in vision become evident, and
physical strength declines. Most women will experience menopause,
thus ending their childbearing years. Concerns for the future center on
planning for retirement, developing wills and other instruments to
provide for others, and ensuring that children and parents will receive
necessary care. Some of the activities for the midlife adult include
reevaluating her life and dreams, facing her own aging and mortality
and that of her parents, family and friends, and possibly negotiating the
stresses of being sandwiched between her children and her parents
(Power, Hershenson, & Schlossberg, 1991).

Relationships typically undergo changes during this period as well.
Children are becoming adults and desire, or need, to be treated as such.
In most cases, these children will move out of the home and establish
independent lives of their own. During the last few decades, however,
failed marriages, lack of job opportunities, or financial difficulties have
forced many young adults to return to the family home. This revolving

door syndrome can drain the midlife couple of financial resources at a time when they were planning to establish a retirement fund. It may also prevent the older couple from moving away from parenting roles and toward their roles as a couple. In some cases, the midlife couple may become grandparents and thoroughly enjoy this new role. Others, however, must perform the role of parent for these grandchildren if their adult children are unable to manage their responsibilities.

The parents of middle-aged adults are also aging and may need care. This support is often supplied by midlife women who may be providing care to their grandparents and even great grandparents as well. Changes in health insurance that focus on saving money have reduced hospital and rehabilitation stays for many people. Implementation of the diagnostic related groups (DRGs) has resulted in earlier hospital dismissals for people whose health insurance is funded by Medicare. An implied expectation emerging from these cost-saving measures is that someone (usually a middle-aged woman) is available to provide care for people who have been sent home from the hospital with serious medical needs (Glazer, 1993).

The primary psychosocial task for midlife is generativity (Erikson, 1963). Adults are expected to be involved in guiding and assisting the next generation. They are to teach the youngsters and learn from them as well.

For most adults, a major developmental goal is the achievement of a measure of independence. Contrary to popular opinion, however, very few people are actually independent. Each person depends on others for food, electricity, transportation, postal service, and many other components of daily life. A more appropriate goal is that of responsible interdependence (Peterson, Rauen, Brown, & Cole, 1994). In this case, each person does what she does best and negotiates with others for the goods and services she needs to fill the gaps.

SUMMARY OF TASKS

- Prepare for retirement
- Participate in productive pursuits
- Adapt to the effects of aging
- Serve as a liaison between younger and older generations

MIDLIFE ADULTS WITH DISABILITIES

Midlife involves many changes, but researchers do not agree about whether these are crises or transitions (Hunter & Sundel, 1989). In either case, little attention has been paid to midlife for people with disabilities.

As mentioned in the discussion on young adults, the large number of people with disabilities who are moving into adulthood and midlife is a new phenomenon for medical and social service providers. Most of what is being written about preparation for old age and retirement regarding people with disabilities is, therefore, an extrapolation from the experiences of those without disabilities.

By the time a person reaches middle adulthood, she has probably come to terms with her disability. She has learned to make allowances for the time she needs to dress, travel, and manage her daily activities. She also knows her limitations in terms of energy and strength. It is likely that the process of aging, however, will cause her to once more adjust her routines to accommodate the physical changes of midlife. Wear and tear on joints and ligaments, from using crutches or wheeling a chair, may force her to make modifications in her approach to mobility. Decreases in hearing acuity and in tactile sensitivity can affect her if she has visual impairment.

Most midlife adults are employed at least part time. Some of the issues surrounding employment include having benefits such as health insurance, worker's compensation, and funding for retirement. Another work-related issue involves ensuring that there is no wage discrimination strictly because of a person's disability (Turnbull, Turnbull, Bronicki, Summers, & Roeder-Gordon, 1989).

Down Syndrome

Almost half of the people with Down syndrome will live into their 60s and about 14% will live till nearly 70 (Burt et al., 1995). These older adults are part of a new phenomenon for society in general but particularly for social workers and for professionals in medical and rehabilitation settings. Having never dealt with older adults with Down syndrome, these professions have few guidelines or markers about what is to be expected, what is normal, and what constitutes an aberration or a crisis.

For today's midlife adults who have Down syndrome, their survival into middle and late adulthood was not expected and appropriate services and benefits are not always available. When most of this cohort were born, their parents were told to place them in an institution and forget about them. Family, friends, and medical professionals insisted that it would be impossible to raise such a child successfully (Abery, 1996). The families who defied the system kept their children at home and began a wave of advocacy that resulted in massive changes in educational opportunities for children with Down syndrome and other disabilities. Adequate and appropriate educational training, however, was not available when most of today's midlife adults with Down syndrome were in school. In addition, little was known about the physical training and social development necessary to support these young people in reaching their potential. Consequently, some of these midlife adults are not able to live independently. Many are still living with their parents and receiving support and assistance, generally from their mothers. This arrangement has possibly persisted through three, four, or even five decades (Seltzer, Krauss, & Tsunematsu, 1993). As these caregiving parents age, they must make new arrangements for the long term living situations of their sons and daughters (DeJong & Batavia, 1991).

Most of the physical problems that midlife adults with Down syndrome faced as infants and children were corrected. Some problems, however, have a lifelong effect. Heart defects may have gone undetected until midlife; repairs made to fistulas and blockages in the intestines can develop scar tissue and begin to cause problems. Thyroid functioning must be monitored throughout life to prevent loss of cognitive progress. In addition, visual and hearing deficits will probably worsen due to the effects of age-related changes (Sedlak, 1991).

Some research indicates that fitness programs such as aerobic dance or step training can improve the cardiovascular fitness of people with Down syndrome. This may help protect against health risks such as coronary heart disease, orthopedic problems, and hypertension (Dyer, 1994).

The research on aging in adults with Down syndrome has produced conflicting results. Some studies indicate significant neurological and cognitive declines, but longitudinal studies fail to corroborate these findings (Burt et al., 1995). Some of this research may reflect the fact that many adults who are in their 50s or 60s lived in institutional settings at some point in their lives. In addition, they were not the beneficiaries of new information on the physical concomitants of Down syndrome and the procedures to counteract these problems.

By the time she reaches her 50s, an adult with Down syndrome may begin to feel fatigued and wish to talk about retirement or part-time work. If she decides to continue working, she may need assistance in obtaining sufficient rest and recreation. It is important that she maintain a balance between work or volunteer commitments, active recreational pursuits, and passive or sedentary activities, so she does not slow herself down to an unhealthy level (Lawrence, Brown, Mills, & Estay, 1993).

An adult with Down syndrome is generally identified as having some mental retardation. With an IQ of 60, she would be considered to have a mental age of 9 or 10. At this level, and with appropriate training and support, she is probably literate, able to do mathematics, hold a job, and live at least somewhat independently. Though her cognitive abilities may be about equivalent to those of a child, her interests are more adult oriented and she should be treated as an adult (Heller & Factor, 1993).

Leisure and Recreation

Leisure activities can assist the midlife adult with Down syndrome in developing and maintaining her communication abilities, fluency in speech, and social skills in addition to helping increase her attention span and her ability to persevere in a task (Lawrence et al., 1993). Leisure activities also serve a vital function in helping an adult to maintain balance in her life and in ensuring that she is using all her potential and all her abilities to retain and improve her level of functioning.

Planning for leisure should begin with the midlife adult herself. She should be asked to indicate what she likes to do, and this should be added to the activities that she needs to do to maintain her physical and emotional wellness. To ensure that she will thoroughly enjoy her recreational opportunities, she may need some specific instruction in the various activities. In many cases, she may have been taught certain needlework or shop skills when she was in school, but if the lessons were boring and context specific, she may have had no motivation or opportunity to generalize what she learned into other settings (Lawrence et al., 1993).

Though an adult with Down syndrome may begin to exhibit some decline in physical and motor abilities, her social skills may continue to improve (Lawrence et al., 1993). Her recreational and leisure interests should support her social skill progress and her cognitive level while approximating those activities that are "normal" for people of her age in community settings wherever possible (Selikowitz, 1990). Consideration should be given to the fact that, based on her mental age and her life experience, her interests may not be fully congruent with her chronological age peers. On the other hand, if her interests seem a bit childish, parents or social workers should look around the community and determine whether her behavior is actually inappropriate before they intervene. Many adults, with and without disabilities, collect things: dolls, teddy bears, model railroads, or buttons. They may also keep objects from childhood and adolescence that have good memories for them (Selikowitz, 1990).

Independent Living

As an adult with Down syndrome becomes more ensconced in the mainstream of the community, she is exposed to choices and decision making on a daily basis. She may also confront dangers that have not been anticipated because, in the past, she and her peers would have been "safely" managed in institutions. Travel, on foot or by public transportation, may be dangerous in some parts of the community. Banning her from this type of travel, however, may eliminate any chance for her to be involved in interesting jobs and social opportunities. For family and social workers, helping the midlife adult to find a balance between safety and opportunity may be difficult.

Managing social interactions, handling money, and dealing with personal hygiene are adult concerns. The person with Down syndrome should have choices and should experience the consequences of these choices just as other adults do. On the other hand, consideration must be given to whatever limitations she may have. There are no easy answers and each situation must be managed in response to the unique strengths and weaknesses of the individual and her circumstances.

A number of issues must be considered in regard to the living situation of the midlife adult. If she does not reside with her family, she needs to have some input on where she lives and with whom. Historically, when decisions about housing have been made, the focus was on the preferences and time constraints of those who were legally responsible for the adult.

Though being able to understand a situation and to make a suitable decision are important skills, little is known about how to assist an adult with Down syndrome in making appropriate choices. If at all possible, she needs to participate in choosing the location of her new home.

Consideration should be given to its proximity to her job, her family and the sources of leisure activities that she enjoys (Turnbull et al., 1989).

Some other issues that will affect her quality of life are the number of housemates, their gender, interests, and the level of their ability. She should also be allowed some voice in whether she has a roommate. One project used pictures of various situations to supplement interviews about housing choices. For example, the adult was shown a picture of one person brushing her teeth and then of two people in a bathroom with several sinks. She was told that in some homes several people live together, and in others a person has a room and a bathroom of her own. Then she was asked to indicate her preference for sharing a bathroom or having one to herself (Foxx, Faw, Taylor, Davis, & Fulia, 1993).

Planning for the Future

In earlier decades, as mentioned, people with Down syndrome died at a fairly early age; few of them outlived their parents and caretakers. With progress in medical treatment and with inclusion in community living situations, people with Down syndrome are living into their 60s and 70s. This makes the issue of guardianship and long-term care a prime concern. Parents need to learn about the legal implications of wills, estates, and trusts. In many parts of the United States, the Down Syndrome Partnership and the ARC (Association for Retarded Citizens) have information and the names of attorneys or law firms who can assist in designing appropriate instruments (see Appendix A). Done incorrectly, the will or trust that the parents hoped would provide long-term care for their child may instead prohibit her from receiving benefits and services for which she would otherwise qualify (Darling, 1991). These limitations and requirements vary from state to state, but the one consistent admonition is that parents must address this issue and develop written plans and documents to ensure that their wishes and intentions are followed.

Another major ethical dilemma is that of guardianship. For some midlife adults who are labeled as mentally retarded, and sometimes for those with physical disabilities that limit their communication ability, there may be concerns about their competence in personal decision making. Mental competence is assumed to be missing in minors (generally, those under age 18) and to be present in adults. Unless a court has ruled the person incompetent, however, no other adult can make personal or financial decisions for her. If a court does determine that an adult is not capable of making decisions, a guardian will be appointed. A personal guardian assists in making lifestyle decisions whereas a financial guardian oversees that part of the adult's life (Turnbull et al., 1989).

As the current cohort of young adults with Down syndrome enters middle age, consideration needs to be given to the aging process they will experience and to the services, programs, and benefits they will need to support their independence and health.

Summary of Tasks

Prepare for retirement	The adult and her family need to prepare appropriate wills and plan for future living arrangements.
Participate in productive pursuits	A job/workshop may occupy the days, but recreational opportunities may be limited.
Adapt to the effects of aging	Continued physical activities combat weight gain and decreased energy.
Serve as a link between younger and older generations	Caring for children and helping parents and neighbors can support a sense of generativity.

Visual Impairment

Most people with visual impairment, even those labeled as "legally blind," are able to distinguish light and dark. Though total absence of light perception is rare, response to various lighting levels varies. Bright light may make it possible for one person to perceive details whereas another may be virtually blinded in such a situation, requiring low light to use her visual capacities. These variations in visual ability may be confusing to her friends and coworkers. In some settings, she may be unable to discern nonverbal cues in social interaction or to correctly identify facial features (French, 1993). Therefore, if she sees a friend in a brightly lighted room, she may recognize him right away. On the other hand, if she encountered him in a movie theater, she might pass by without seeing him at all. Friends or acquaintances who are not aware of the differential effects of ambient lighting may feel snubbed until they understand what is happening.

A midlife adult who has had a visual impairment for most of her life has probably learned to cope with her abilities and her limitations. It is likely that her friends and coworkers accept her for who she is and that her social situation is satisfactory. If her employment circumstances are acceptable and she has adequate arrangements for transportation and for shopping, she may not feel that her disability has a huge influence on her life. For her, the middle adult years may not seem particularly different than for her peers who do not have visual impairment.

If the midlife adult with visual impairment has children, she will be engaged in supporting them toward responsible, independent adulthood. If she is married, she and her spouse will be planning for their later years. In addition to these activities, the midlife adult may be providing assistance for her aging parents and neighbors.

Leisure and Recreation

A number of board and card games are available in Braille. Computers with speech output and those with Braille screens provide access to current information from worldwide sources. Television programs, and some movies, feature verbal descriptions. A midlife adult who wishes to engage in more active sports might try beep baseball, running, swimming, skiing, and aerobic dance.

Many people with visual impairment regard reading as an important leisure activity. Computerized information can be read on a Braille screen that has raised dots that can be interpreted by touch. Other computers have voice output that translates the material on the screen. Books on tape, featuring current bestseller titles, are available in most libraries and bookstores. Newspapers are also available on-line, providing up-to-date information.

Serving as a volunteer or working in political or religious organizations may occupy her time. She may also be involved as a mentor to younger people with visual impairments; for example, she may serve on the board of directors of the school for the blind.

Independent Living

With adequate public or private transportation, and with some adaptations in her home, the midlife adult with a visual impairment can often manage an independent life at the level she chooses. She may have a spouse, sighted or blind, and children who are reaching adulthood. The chances are very good that she is employed and may have been in this job for many years.

A source of stress for the adult with a visual impairment is the concentration necessary for independent travel in novel situations. She must be aware of where she is, how far she has traveled, and exactly where she needs to go. In addition, she must be prepared to handle any unexpected occurrences while retaining all of this information.

Planning for the Future

A major concern for the midlife person is planning for retirement and old age. If her job has not been highly paid or has few retirement benefits, she may be concerned about having sufficient funds for a comfortable retirement.

Current doubts about the viability of the Social Security system may leave the midlife adult with more questions than answers regarding her future. Retirement planners may be able to provide some information; however, to ensure that whatever assets she has accumulated do not reduce or eliminate potential governmental benefits, it may be helpful to consult with a specialist in retirement and estate planning for people with disabilities.

Summary of Tasks

Prepare for retirement	Plans are being formulated for leisure time use, sufficient financial resources, and adequate health benefits.
Participate in productive pursuits	Job, leisure activities, and volunteer work support feelings of productivity.
Adapt to the effects of aging	Reduced tactile sensitivity and hearing may require changes in daily habits.
Serve as a liaison between younger and older generations	She may provide care for children, spouse/partner, parents, grandparents, and neighbors.

Employment and Disability

Sue has worked for the government for 20 years. She began in data entry, using adaptive equipment that allowed her to maintain the same standards as her peers despite her visual impairment. About 5 years ago, she was promoted to consumer services where her record has been very good.

Recently, a new job position was posted. The person would be responsible for working specifically with applicants who have visual impairments as they apply for benefits. Sue felt that her work record coupled with her own visual impairment made her the ideal candidate for the position. When the announcement was made, however, her close friend was hired instead of Sue.

Sue feels very frustrated, angry, and betrayed. She is strongly considering quitting her job, even though she is just a few years from being able to retire with an excellent pension. She says she could just stay home and collect benefits for the blind rather than working so hard for no recognition or appreciation.

1. What are your feelings about what Sue should do?
2. Would you be able to help her sort out the situation without letting your own opinions interfere?
3. Where would you find information on her pension benefits and on the benefits she could receive because of her visual impairments? What formula would you use to compare these benefits?

Cerebral Palsy

Historically, a person with cerebral palsy was not expected to live to old age. Advances in health care and in technological support have changed that expectation. A recent study in England indicated that, for people with mild or moderate disability from cerebral palsy, 20 year survival rates were no different than for the population at large. Contrary to expectations, a person's birth weight and gestational age were not as helpful in predicting survival rates as functional disability (Hutton, Cooke, & Pharoah, 1994). This is important information in being able to plan for services as adults with disabilities age. Current functional ability, rather than historical factors such as birth weight or prematurity, must be considered when estimating her life expectancy.

Some physical deterioration may become evident during the middle adult period. Years of using a wheelchair or crutches can lead to problems such as tendinitis of the wrist and carpal tunnel syndrome (Miller & Bachrach, 1995). It may be necessary for her to begin using a motorized chair or a scooter for longer trips. Exercises such as swimming and stretching may be recommended to reduce stiffness in muscles and joints.

If the midlife adult with cerebral palsy has children, she may be engaged in activities at the school or with various youth sport organizations. If she is married, she and her spouse are probably beginning to plan for their retirement.

Leisure and Recreation

Physical movement is vital to human performance. When a person can participate in sports and other physical activities, her sense of self-efficacy and self-concept can be greatly enhanced. In addition to a feeling of physical fitness, participation in sports can also improve the perception of social equality (Hutzler & Bar-Eli, 1993). When she is engaged in sports, she is demonstrating her physical abilities and the fact that she is fit and strong. Such a sense goes a long way toward negating the traditional passive role that many expect of a person with a disability.

Interests and abilities in woodworking, painting, sewing, or other crafts can link the midlife adult to others while providing intrinsic enjoyment. Computers with their games or their links to the Internet can also serve as recreational and educational outlets.

Planning for the Future

Many benefits for retirement are based on time in the workforce, earnings, or a combination of these. It is possible that the person with cerebral palsy has not had a lifelong history of full employment at a competitive salary. If so, this may severely limit the benefits she will be entitled to receive at retirement.

In addition to planning for her financial well-being, the midlife adult will need to consider her physical environment. At some point, stairs may present a serious barrier. As she ages, joint stiffness, increased spasticity, and possible tendon damage may limit the amount of time she can spend on crutches or using a cane. Early planning for accessibility may make her later midlife and retirement years much more comfortable.

As with other disabilities, planning is essential if the person is eligible for any kind of benefits. Estates, trusts, and wills should be reviewed by someone experienced in negotiating the various programs and services. Possession of even limited assets may eliminate a person's eligibility for benefits. A thoughtful bequest of cash or property may cause rather than solve problems.

Summary of Tasks

Prepare for retirement	Needed benefits, services, and equipment must be arranged.
Participate in productive pursuits	Employment, leisure, and volunteer activities support a sense of productivity.
Adapt to the effects of aging	Deteriorating joints, reduced flexibility, and lower energy levels require adaptation.
Serve as a liaison between younger and older generations	Mentoring others, providing child care, completing child rearing, and assisting elders demonstrate generativity.

Spina Bifida

Among the physical problems that may affect the adult with spina bifida are Chiari II symptoms: pain at the base of the neck, weakness in her arms, and increased spasticity. These are caused by reduced spinal circulation resulting from swelling of the lower part of the brain down into the spinal column. Other problems may arise from the presence of a tethered cord. In this situation, the spinal cord fails to move freely within the spinal column, leading to spasticity and urinary dysfunction. The person with spina bifida must also be alert to the possibility of secondary disabilities related to loss of sensation in her lower body. Obesity, pressure ulcers, urinary tract infections, kidney failure, and loss of ambulation are potential outcomes of a failure to monitor her health (Rauen & Aubert, 1992). If she has foot deformities, these can cause problems with dressing and may require customized footwear.

Over time and with increased exposure, the potential for latex allergies increases. This is an area in which the adult must be extremely cautious (Lollar, 1994). Engaging in sexual intercourse without using condoms can increase the risk of contracting venereal disease or HIV. On the other hand, use of latex condoms may result in toxic, allergic reactions. To avoid this possibility, use of condoms made from sheep gut are recommended. To protect against HIV transmission, double condoms should be used (Rauen & Aubert, 1992).

Weight control is another concern. As the adult ages, she may be less physically active and thus prone to gaining weight. The added weight complicates ambulation or transferring in and out of a wheelchair, thus creating additional barriers to participation in exercise or sports activities. Sound nutritional advice is essential, as is encouragement to become involved in a fitness regime. To support these efforts, exercise videos specifically for wheelchair users are available (Rauen & Aubert, 1992).

To reduce the likelihood of injury and to support maximal health, adults with spina bifida are encouraged to participate in some form of a standing program. Even if her primary means of mobility is now a wheelchair, regular weight bearing can slow osteoporosis, improve the range of motion in her joints, increase drainage of the urinary system, and increase her circulation (Rauen & Aubert, 1992).

A potentially problematic issue is that of health care. With the advent of managed care, a person may be assigned to a physician group without the ability to select a particular physician or the assurance that she will be seen by the same doctor over time. This results in a need to constantly educate her physician regarding the effects of spina bifida and her own particular health requirements.

Leisure and Recreation

Wheelchair sports may be a suitable choice for the active adult with spina bifida. Tennis, basketball, and track are widely available. Videotapes featuring wheelchair aerobics can also support an exercise regime.

Volunteer activities with youth groups or with religious or political organizations may also be a source of leisure activities. For more sedentary hobbies, traditional choices such as photography, arts and crafts, needlework or woodwork may provide enjoyment.

For most people, it is important to stay active and involved. If joining a group is an incentive for consistent participation, it should not be difficult to locate others who are involved in interesting pursuits.

Independent Living

Though the effects of aging may reduce energy and require reliance on a wheelchair or scooter, the midlife adult with spina bifida is probably living independently. Years of experience have taught her how to manage her time so her catheterization and bowel programs fit smoothly into her daily routine.

If she is using a wheelchair, architectural adaptations may be necessary for her home and office. She may also need to change from a regular car to a van adapted for wheelchairs if she has difficulty in transferring from her chair to the car and then maneuvering the chair into the car as well.

Planning for the Future

Though spina bifida is not a progressive disability, its effects may change over time. Planning for physical accessibility is essential as is establishing a means for obtaining and financing health care.

Plans should also be made for retirement and the activities that will occupy her time when she is no longer working. The hobbies and interests she enjoys at midlife may lead to even greater involvement and pleasure when she has more time to devote to them.

Summary of Tasks

Prepare for retirement	The availability of needed benefits, services, equipment, and financial resources should be addressed.
Participate in productive pursuits	Volunteer activities, job, and recreation support a sense of productivity.
Adapt to the effects of aging	Switching to wheelchair or scooter may increase available energy.
Serve as a liaison between younger and older generations	Mentoring younger people, caring for elders, and completing child-raising tasks support several generations.

Spinal Cord Injury

In recent years, life expectancy has increased for people with spinal cord injury because of advances in medicine and technology (Lee, Brock, Dattilo, & Kleiber, 1993). Despite a satisfactory recovery and adjustment to her injury, however, the midlife adult may encounter symptoms that necessitate ongoing medical care. A disability such as spinal cord injury is associated with a higher risk of developing medical complications such as pressure ulcers (Lyons, Sullivan, & Ritvo, 1995).

As a person with a spinal cord injury grows older, age-related deterioration of muscles and joints may contribute to increased dependency (Shephard, 1993). She may have more difficulty transferring from her chair to a car or bathtub, and carpal tunnel syndrome may limit the distance she is able to push her wheelchair.

Health care is another major concern for a person with a spinal cord injury. The predominance of managed care means that most people are enrolled in a health care group that may not allow for seeing the same physician at each visit. This can be problematic because relatively few primary care providers are familiar with the health care needs of persons with physical disabilities (Heller & Factor, 1993). A recurring complaint among people with spinal cord injury is the need to constantly educate primary care physicians about the impairment and its effects and how these need to be considered when treatment or medications are prescribed (DeJong & Batavia, 1991).

Leisure and Recreation

Over time, propelling a wheelchair can lead to carpal-tunnel syndrome and rotator-cuff problems. Fatigue and discomfort resulting from these problems can reduce interest in participating in leisure and fitness activities, leading to increased risk for cardiovascular problems, urinary tract infections, and pressure sores (Janssen, Van Oers, Van der Woude, & Hollander, 1993).

Even in the presence of physical problems, it is important that the person with a spinal cord injury continue to be physically active. Exercise and fitness can contribute to her well-being and can help in controlling disorders such as osteoporosis and obesity (Compton, Eisenman, & Henderson, 1989). Physical fitness regimes may also help in preventing the start of emotional problems and aid in treating mental health difficulties after they have begun (Campbell & Jones, 1994).

Prevention of further disability and secondary complications is important in the midlife adult. Inactivity is related to increased risk for a variety of cardiovascular and cardiopulmonary difficulties, whereas physical activity provides exercise, cardiopulmonary stimulation, social contacts and, in the case of competitive sports, a sense of competence and excitement (Coyle, Shank, Kinney, & Hutchins, 1993). In one study, self-esteem increased the longer the person participated in the sport, and this increase was not related to the level of success in competition (Campbell & Jones, 1994).

Some barriers to participation in sports and other leisure activities are fear of loss of bladder or bowel control, lack of skills to do the activity, concerns about personal appearance, and difficulty in getting information about the activity (Coyle et al., 1993). If the adult does not see herself as able to learn and participate in the sport or activity, she will probably choose not to become involved. This perception may keep her from even seeking opportunities to participate because she thinks she could not play even if she knew where to go and had the means to get there (Caldwell & Weissinger, 1994).

Very little is known about the leisure experience or desires of women who use wheelchairs. Recreation (participating in activities such as sports or dancing) may be differentiated from leisure (doing what I want, relaxing, or doing nothing) by some women. A woman may participate in the same recreational activities she did before her disability but generally must allow more time and sometimes do things differently. She may also require some assistance (Henderson, Bedini, & Hecht, 1994).

A woman with a spinal cord injury faces additional difficulties in engaging in recreational activities. She knows she must allow sufficient time to travel to the facility and to make needed transfers to and from her car or van. In addition, she must carefully allocate her time during the day to have sufficient stamina to participate in the activities. Like other women, she has only limited amounts of energy and may often use all of it in carrying out family and work obligations. In planning her recreational activities, she must also consider safety, availability of activities for women, and finding a companion with whom to play. Access, choices, and opportunity must all fall into place if a woman with a disability is to engage in leisure activities (Henderson, Bedini, Hecht, & Schuler, 1995).

Independent Living

Once physical accessibility has been ensured, a person with lower level spinal cord injury can probably manage her life quite satisfactorily. If she has a higher level injury, she may require assistance in daily activities. In this case, retaining a qualified and appropriate attendant may occupy a good deal of her time and energy.

A concern for a person with a spinal cord injury, as for other people with disabilities, is obtaining and financing health care. When she is employed, she may have access to health care, but this may not be the case if she is not working or does not have a full-time job.

Planning for the Future

Though her physical health may decline somewhat due to age, the effects of the injury are probably constant over time. Once the midlife adult has arranged for physical accessibility, she can manage her life quite comfortably. She may have concerns, however, about having sufficient financial resources for her retirement.

It will be important for her to stay in contact with advocacy or support groups who have information on various programs and benefits and the qualifications for receiving them. As laws and policies change, she needs to be aware of the effect of these alterations on her life.

Summary of Tasks

Prepare for retirement	Access to necessary benefits, equipment, and adaptations should be considered.
Participate in productive pursuits	Employment, volunteer, and leisure activities are important.
Adapt to the effects of aging	Reduced flexibility and strength may slow accomplishment of daily activities.
Serve as a liaison between younger and older generations	Caring for parents, grandparents, spouse/partner, and children demonstrates successful adaptation and builds self-esteem.

DISCUSSION QUESTIONS

1. Design a plan to determine whether there are sufficient accessible recreational facilities in your community to accommodate adults with disabilities.
2. Identify some of the components of the Americans With Disabilities Act (ADA) that will concern you in your role as a professional social worker.

Chapter 8

OLDER ADULT
Sixty-Six Years and Older

> At the ceremony, his friends and family cheered wildly. Jack
> was one of 15 recipients of awards to senior citizens for their
> outstanding accomplishments. He was the only one who had
> a spinal cord injury and used a wheelchair. He was also the
> only one who had established an agency that trains people
> with severe disabilities in computer skills, allowing them to
> obtain competitive jobs in the corporate community.

According to Erikson (1963), the psychosocial task of old age is the
integration of all of life's experiences into a sense of the whole self and
a feeling that life has, indeed, been worthwhile. Without this sense of
wholeness and success, a feeling of despair can emerge (Kivnick, 1991).

Physical changes related to old age include thinning skin, reduced
visual and auditory acuity, decreased respiration, fragile bones, and less
flexibility and dexterity. Loss of spouse and friends can reduce social
contacts and diminished access to transportation may further limit
social interaction.

Despite reductions in his physical, social, and adaptive capacities,
the older adult is expected to continue performing certain roles. To
mediate these potentially conflicting areas in his life, he may need to
reduce some of his activities, retaining those that are most meaningful
and provide the most pleasure (Sullivan, 1994).

When the older person is able to accommodate the changes and losses
in his life and maintain an active lifestyle, this appears to have a

favorable effect on his health. In addition, ongoing physical activity can help to control obesity (Pescatello & DiPietro, 1993), thus reducing stress on bones and joints and helping to regulate blood pressure.

A consistent fear for an older adult is that he will become a burden on others. He does not want to be seen as useless and unproductive (Kopito & Greenberg, 1995). At the same time, many companies and agencies expect their employees to retire at 65, thus further restricting the person's opportunities and motivation for involvement. Many people prefer to continue to work even if this is not an economic necessity. The employment setting provides social contacts and status as well as contributing to a sense of identify and self-esteem (Falvo & Lundervold, 1995).

SUMMARY OF TASKS

- Integrate life experiences into a positive sense of self
- Maintain active involved lifestyle
- Adjust to physical and cognitive changes

OLDER ADULTS WITH DISABILITIES

In some ways, an adult with a disability who has reached old age is more similar to his nondisabled peers than at any other time in his life (Edgerton, 1994). Reductions in visual acuity, joint flexibility, strength, and endurance affect many people as they progress through old age. If the adult with lifelong disabilities and his advocates have been success-ful in demanding ramped curbs, accessible buildings, and transportation systems, and alternative formats for needed information, his nondis-abled peers may owe him an ongoing debt of gratitude.

As mentioned in the discussion on middle adulthood, the cohort of people with disabilities who are entering old age represent a new phe-nomenon for the social work, medical, and rehabilitation professions. In past decades, individuals with developmental disabilities such as Down syndrome or cerebral palsy generally succumbed to infections or other illnesses before reaching middle age. The technology that allows computer speech output, speech boards and electronically controlled homes was not available 30 years ago, nor were medical and surgical techniques to prevent death from spinal cord injury.

Literature on older people with disabilities is just beginning to appear. One difficulty is that many of these studies were conducted with people who had spent at least some part of their lives in institutional settings (Edgerton, 1994). Their experiences and their needs may, or may not, be representative of people who were raised in family settings within the community and who benefited from mainstreamed educational experiences. Given the possibility that current literature may not be applicable, other sources of information must be employed in developing programs and plans. To provide useful service, it is vital that the social worker or other professional discuss proposed actions and available programs and benefits with the person who has the disability and with his family or significant others; he and they know what his abilities and needs are and how he can best be served.

The normal changes of aging occur in a person with disabilities just as they do in other segments of the population. A person who has managed his life with a disability acquired in childhood may now be faced with secondary complications resulting from the disability (Seelman & Sweeney, 1996). Throughout his life, it is likely that some body systems compensated for lost function in other parts of his body. These overused systems may begin to show decline, thus reducing the residual functioning that remains (Falvo & Lundervold, 1995).

For older adults without disabilities, employment can be a source of social contact and personal identity. People with disabilities often have difficulty finding employment even at younger ages. This means that the option of using work as a social and an economic resource is unlikely (Falvo & Lundervold, 1995).

Even though changes due to aging may cause some problems, with rehabilitation training and the use of some adaptations, many older adults with disabilities could continue to function at home and at work. Resources for rehabilitation, however, are extremely limited and have traditionally been focused on younger people. Rather than being enrolled in rehabilitation programs, older adults are left to manage on their own despite the fact that small expenditures on rehabilitation services would allow them to preserve their functional capacity, maintain their independence, and lower the chances of medical complications that can result in institutionalization (Falvo & Lundervold, 1995).

Because the possibility of being involved in an employment setting decreases dramatically with age, recreation and leisure activities emerge as critical components of an active lifestyle. Involvement and participation in physically and cognitively stimulating pursuits can provide older adults with a reason to get up in the morning (Giordano & D'Alonzo, 1996).

Religious groups and institutions may be a source of assistance to older adults with disabilities. Some people may receive concrete help in the form of meals and visitation. Others may benefit from spiritual activities, gaining a sense of peace from meditation or prayer. The social interaction at worship services and the social support of the religious community may meet the needs of other older adults (McFadden, 1995).

For the social worker or other professional who is searching for resources to assist a client, the formal and informal religious community may be an important contact. It is important, however, to examine the practices and the expectations of each church or group to determine what their perspective is regarding older adults and what their views are toward disability. Each congregation, even within a particular denomination, will have its own ideas and these can affect their willingness to assist people with disabilities and their comfort level toward involving these adults in the church (McFadden, 1995).

Down Syndrome

A person with Down syndrome who is now beginning to enter old age may have lived in institutions at some point in his life. Despite the conditions in some of those institutions, he may have established a social network there that was difficult to replace once he moved out into the community (Kropf, 1996). It is possible that he was never able to form the kind of social contacts that other people developed as they grew up in a neighborhood, thus leaving him with a constricted social system.

Psychosocial issues of later life, such as dealing with grief and loss, are often overlooked when working with a person who has Down syndrome. The perception of the professionals is that, because his mental age is only 9 or 10 years, he will not experience the same issues as his chronological age peers. Family and service providers may tend to shield him from topics such as death. He may not have the opportunity to grieve the loss of a family member or a friend through attendance at social rituals such as funerals (Kropf, 1996).

A major concern for older adults with Down syndrome is planning for the future. In many cases, the family may have provided care for most of his life and may have relied little on formal service providers (Parkinson & Howard, 1996). As the parents age, however, plans must be made for the time when they are unable to provide care or for when they die. It may be difficult for the family to address such concerns.

They may assume that a sibling will accept caretaking responsibilities, but formal arrangements may not have been established.

If a long-term care plan is not established, a crisis such as a parent's sudden illness or death can leave the older adult with Down syndrome in a precarious situation. He may be forced to enter an institution that does not meet the family's expectations or his needs because nothing else is available on short notice. This may result in the adult's being moved in and out of several settings before satisfactory arrangements are finalized. The stress and trauma of the moves, added to the loss of a parent, can be very traumatic (Gibson, Rabkin, & Munson, 1992).

Summary of Tasks

Integrate life experiences into a positive sense of self	Social skills can compensate for cognitive deficiencies; fit with peers may be at the highest level of his life.
Maintain active involved lifestyle	Satisfying leisure or volunteer activities can encourage involvement through senior centers, church, or other settings.
Adjust to physical and cognitive changes	Establishing a balance between work and rest is important.

Visual Impairment

The segment of the population with low or no vision increases dramatically at older ages (Kleinschmidt, 1996). In addition to those who have lifelong vision loss, a large number of the elderly experience reduction in visual acuity sufficient to impair their ability to accomplish tasks of daily living. These adults may feel that the loss of vision is simply one more insult in a series of difficulties. A major concern expressed by these adults is the loss of control over their lives and the need to be dependent on others (Orr, 1991).

The older adult with visual impairment will experience the same physical changes as his peers. Joint flexibility and muscle strength will probably decrease and the danger of osteoporosis increases. Reduced hearing acuity, decreased sense of taste, and diminished tactile sensitivity can affect mobility and the ability to accomplish tasks.

There is generally not an expectation that an older adult with visual impairment would want to work, though when asked, many answer, Yes. In reality, because of the way that Social Security benefits are managed, the loss of benefits due to working may be much greater than the increased income (Miller, 1991).

After retirement, it is important that the older adult remain involved in some activities that can stimulate his interests and encourage social interactions at the level he chooses. If adequate transportation is available, he may participate in the Senior Citizens Centers, church groups, political or social action organizations, or groups focused on arts and crafts. Aerobic dance classes or swimming may provide physical exercise.

If he has been married or had children, family duties may even increase as work responsibilities decrease. He may be asked to care for older relatives or for grandchildren. He may also be able to provide assistance as his peers experience reduced vision and request his suggestions on techniques and strategies he has perfected.

Involvement in religious institutions or groups may provide companionship and a sense of comfort for some older adults with vision loss. For others, this loss of vision may be viewed as punishment from God for some ill doing. Such a view may limit the options the elder is willing to consider, feeling that he must simply bear this burden as God wills (Orr, 1991).

In assisting adults who are involved in religious groups, the social worker must be aware of the views of that group regarding disability. It may be helpful to consult with a clergyperson to gain some understanding of that group's beliefs and to develop strategies that can encourage the elder to accept assistance, participate in rehabilitation and training, and become involved in employment or volunteer activities.

Developing living wills and Directives to Physicians, as well as planning for the disposition of his estate, are important tasks for the older adult. He needs to examine current benefit programs and their requirements and limitations to determine his eligibility. Involvement in the American Association of Retired Persons (AARP), or in support groups for those with visual impairment can allow him to keep up with current legislation and with changing rules and regulations for various benefits and services.

Summary of Tasks

Integrate life experiences into a positive sense of self	Examining the influence of historical, technical, and medical changes may give a sense of pride.

| Maintain active involved lifestyle | Family, church, and volunteer activities offer chances for involvement. |
| Adjust to physical and cognitive changes | New adaptations and strategies may be needed to compensate for losses in hearing and touch. |

Cerebral Palsy

For the older adult with cerebral palsy, the physical changes of aging may necessitate adaptations in his daily life. He may need to use a scooter or wheelchair in place of crutches or canes (Overeynder, Janicki, & Turk, 1994). Reduced joint flexibility may make dressing or putting on braces more difficult and time consuming.

Changes in the vestibular system typically affect balance as a person ages. For an older adult with cerebral palsy, this deterioration may occur at an earlier age, increasing the risk for falls and bone fractures. Another concern is increased difficulty in swallowing, which can cause the person to take longer in eating. If these problems result in reduced food intake, his nutritional status and, as a result, his ability to function may be compromised (Seltzer & Luchterhand, 1994).

Specific problems tend to arise when the older adult is required to interact with medical professionals. He may have difficulty in making himself understood, and the physician may have little experience with older adults who have cerebral palsy. It can be problematic to make the distinction between changes related to the cerebral palsy and those brought on by age. One woman was told for several years that the difficulties she was experiencing were indications of the onset of multiple sclerosis. After 5 years of aggressive treatment for multiple sclerosis, she went to another medical center and learned that her symptoms were a result of the interactions of aging and cerebral palsy; the diagnosis of multiple sclerosis was completely erroneous (Overeynder et al., 1994).

If transportation is a problem, the older adult may have some difficulty in maintaining an active lifestyle. Getting to meetings or social gatherings may require considerable planning and coordination.

Worries about the future are common because few older adults with cerebral palsy have role models who have had similar experiences. There are also concerns about the loss of relationships, job, health insurance, and independent living situations (Overeynder et al., 1994).

Computers and modems may allow participation in some groups and can offer connections to vast sources of information. Books on tape can provide enjoyment even if holding a book or turning pages is problematic.

Summary of Tasks

Integrate life experiences into a positive sense of self	Satisfactory involvement with peers and mentoring younger people can support a sense of self.
Maintain active involved lifestyle	Participation in a variety of groups can reduce isolation and loneliness.
Adjust to physical and cognitive changes	Dressing and household tasks may require more time, and some adaptations may be needed to maintain independence.

Spina Bifida

As mentioned in the chapter on middle adulthood, this cohort of adults with spina bifida is the first to reach middle and later life. The literature says nothing about their experiences nor about what might be expected for them.

Based on knowledge about people who are aging with spinal cord injury and cerebral palsy, some extrapolations might be made. It is likely that years of using crutches or wheelchairs will have led to deterioration of some joints and tendons. Carpal tunnel syndrome and rotator cuff problems are likely to interfere with mobility. Weight gain, reduced muscle tone, and lowered activity levels can affect balance and therefore the ability to transfer from wheelchair to automobile, chair, or bathtub. Limited range of motion and reduced joint flexibility may make some activities of daily living more difficult to accomplish.

Reduction in deaths due to infections and respiratory disorders mean that older adults with spina bifida are likely to be seen in the caseloads of social workers and other professionals in the near future. These older individuals should be studied carefully because their experiences, at least until the literature catches up with current practice, will be the base for knowledge of people aging with spina bifida.

Summary of Tasks

Integrate life experiences into a positive sense of self	Assessing one's own accomplishments and mentoring others can leave a positive sense of attainment.

| Maintain active involved lifestyle | Participation in social, charitable, or religious activities supports ongoing involvement. |
| Adjust to physical and cognitive changes | Greater amounts of assistance may be needed to maintain independence. |

Spinal Cord Injury

Because of advances in medical technology and adaptive equipment, the life expectancy of a person with a spinal cord injury is similar to that of the general population (DeJong & Batavia, 1991). The anticipation of early death is no longer applicable; yet little is known about the lives and future expectations of older adults with spinal cord injury because the first cohort of long-term spinal cord injured persons is just now entering old age (Cushman & Hassett, 1992). There is, however, another group of older adults with spinal cord injury—those whose injury occurs in later years as a result of falls or other accidents (Roth, Lovell, Heinemann, Lee, & Yarkony, 1992).

People with spinal cord injury experience some changes as they age. Thinning skin may result in pressure ulcers. Osteoporosis can lead to fragile bones that break more easily even in activities such as transferring from chair to bed. Constant chair pushing, or even transferring from chair to car or bath, can lead to numbness in the hands due to carpal tunnel syndrome (Priebe & Rintala, 1995). In addition, the presence of arthritis in his fingers may reduce his dexterity (DeJong & Batavia, 1991). Renal failure, respiratory disease, skin breakdown, and genitourinary disease have been identified as causes of illness specific to people with spinal cord injury (Whiteneck et al., 1992).

One study of older adults with spinal cord injury found that, though they mentioned some unmet needs such as having children, helping others, and being involved in civic work, they expressed satisfaction with their ability to be involved in activities such as reading, observing sporting events, and listening to music. Overall, the respondents in the study indicated that they were relatively happy with the quality of their lives (Whiteneck et al., 1992).

A major concern of older adults with spinal cord injury, as for many elderly, is loss of control in their lives. As the ability to manage daily activities becomes more limited because of reduced mobility or increased pain, the elder may be forced to depend more on others for assistance. The balance the adult had been able to maintain between independence and dependence may be threatened by the changes of aging (Rodgers & Marini, 1994). It will be very important, therefore, for the social worker to provide adaptive equipment and assistance to maximize the older adult's sense of control and independence. Because psychological factors such as attitude and motivation appear to be almost as important in promoting independence as were the physical adaptations (Cushman & Hassett, 1992), therapeutic interventions to prevent depression and support social involvement may also be indicated.

Though little information is available about the interaction of old age and spinal cord injury, the data that do exist support the idea that a satisfactory quality of life is definitely achievable. Physical adaptations can make the home and other settings accessible, enabling the person to be involved with family and in the community. Careful monitoring and early intervention can reduce the consequences of health problems such as decubitii, genito-urinary disease, renal failure, and respiratory difficulties. The use of therapeutic interventions can support optimal functioning and ameliorate the effects of depression or other side effects of the consequences of aging.

Summary of Tasks

Integrate life experiences into a positive sense of self	An emphasis on enjoyable and accessible activities counteracts a sense of loss for what was not accomplished.
Maintain active involved lifestyle	Technology may allow participation even for those with limited mobility.
Adjust to physical and cognitive changes	Careful monitoring of physical condition can reduce illness.

Life Planning

At 66, Jack is just entering old age. Twenty-five years of coping with the effects of a spinal cord injury, however, have left him feeling much older.

As a C-4 quadriplegic, Jack is unable to dress or feed himself or transfer from his wheelchair to his bed. To meet his physical needs, he is completely dependent on his attendant, Terry, who has been with him for more than 20 years. Terry is almost 70, and his health is beginning to fail.

Both Jack and Terry know that their situation is becoming more difficult. They are so concerned about each other's feelings, however, that they have never discussed what each will do when the other either dies or becomes incapacitated. Terry has no family, but Jack has children and grandchildren in the area.

1. Should Jack and Terry be pushed to address their future situation?
2. How would you identify the issues that must be addressed?
3. What resources are available for Jack and for Terry?
4. Would you as a social worker involve Jack's family in encouraging him to make some arrangements for himself and Terry?

DISCUSSION QUESTION

What would you identify as critical quality of life issues for people with disabilities? How could you confirm that your ideas were congruent with the ideas of your clients or their families?

APPENDIX A: RESOURCES

NATIONAL ORGANIZATIONS

American Foundation for the Blind
11 Penn Plaza, Suite 300
New York, NY 10001

ARC (Association for Retarded Citizens)
500 E. Border Street
Arlington, TX 76010

National Down Syndrome Congress
1605 Chantilly Drive, Suite 250
Atlanta, GA 30324

National Easter Seal Society
230 W. Monroe Street, Suite 1800
Chicago, IL 60606

National Information Center for Children & Youth
   with Disabilities (NICHCY)
P. O. Box 1492
Washington, DC 20013

National Spinal Cord Injury Foundation
600 W. Cummings Park, Suite 2000
Woburn, MA 01801

Spina Bifida Association of America
4590 MacArthur Blvd. NW, Suite 250
Washington, DC 20007-4226

United Cerebral Palsy Association
1522 K Street NW, Suite 1112
Washington, DC 20005

STATE AND LOCAL ORGANIZATIONS

State Mental Health Mental Retardation Agency
State Commission for the Blind
Mental Health Association
Family Service Association
Child Guidance Centers

NEWSLETTERS AND JOURNALS

American Rehabilitation
P. O. Box 371954
Pittsburgh, PA 15150-7954

Published by the Department of Education
Superintendent of Documents

Brimstone Bulletin
P. O. Box 21304
Eugene, OR 97402

A newsletter confronting disability issues
with combustible humor and sentiment. Published by The Mothers from Hell

Down Syndrome News
1605 Chantilly Drive,
   Suite 250
Atlanta, GA 30324

Newsletter of the National Down Syndrome
Congress

Exceptional Parent
P.O. Box 3000 Dept. EP
Denville, NJ 07834-9919

HEATH
One Dupont Circle,
   Suite 800
Washington, DC 20036-1193

National Clearinghouse on Postsecondary
Education for Individuals with Disabilities

The Rural Exchange
52 Corbin Hall
The University of Montana
Missoula, MT 59812

Published by Montana University Affiliated
Rural Institute on Disabilities

Social Security Bulletin
Social Security Administration
Office of Research, Evaluation, and Statistics
4301 Connecticut Avenue, NW, Suite 209
Washington, DC 20008

BOOKS

Access for Technology Association. (1996). *Computer resources for people with disabilities.* Alameda, CA: Hunter House.

Access for Technology Association (ATA) has published information for people with disabilities about choosing a computer. This book provides excellent information about what computers can do and what steps can be taken to ensure that the appropriate computer is chosen.

Albrecht, D. G. (1995). *Raising a child who has a physical disability.* New York: John Wiley.

For parents who are attempting to negotiate the many systems designed to serve their children, this book is an excellent resource. It describes the child's rights, the obligations of schools and other institutions, and some strategies for obtaining what the child needs. The information in Appendix B, regarding files that families should maintain, came from this book.

Batshaw, M. L., & Perret, Y. M. (1992). *Children with disabilities: A medical primer* (3rd ed.). Baltimore: Brookes.

To understand various medical terms and the conditions or remedies they describe, this book is an excellent reference for social workers and other professionals and for parents.

Geralis, E. (1991). *Children with cerebral palsy: A parents' guide.* Rockville, MD: Woodbine House.

This is one of a series of books from Woodbine that give parents and others a good view of a particular disability.

Gettings, R. M., Carson, S. A., & Croston, M. A. (1992). *Summary of existing legislation affecting people with disabilities.* Alexandria, VA: Office of Special Education and Rehabilitative Services.

Though several important pieces of legislation have been passed and implemented since this book was published, its description of some of the seminal laws and policies serves as an excellent base in understanding disability policy.

Holbrook, M. C. (1996). *Children with visual impairments.* Bethesda, MD: Woodbine House.

This is a gentle and helpful book on visual impairment.

Stray-Gunderson, K. (1986). *Babies with Down syndrome.* Rockville, MD: Woodbine.

This is another excellent Woodbine book. It is often distributed to new parents of infants who have Down syndrome.

APPENDIX B:
PERSONAL INFORMATION FILE

Each family should have a secure and organized file of information related to the child. Among other things, this file should contain:

- A certified copy of the birth certificate (the original should be in a safety deposit box)
- Medical records, including letters from physicians supporting requests for special education or other services, immunization records, medication records, and notations about allergies
- Evaluations of the child's need for physical, occupational, speech or other therapy, or any other special testing that may have been conducted
- School records, including results of IEPs and diagnostic tests, report cards, and any letters to and from the school district. In addition, dated notes about telephone conversations to any service providers should be kept
- Communication records such as notes to and from teachers regarding daily activities
- Social service agency information, including the name, telephone number and address of the agency, the contact person, and any services that were provided
- Future reference materials, possibly including information about camps, schools, equipment, books, or sources of assistance
- Medical equipment suppliers, listed with their telephone numbers and addresses and the contact person or sales person. The type of equipment, date of purchase or lease, and a copy of the purchase order should be included. In case of breakage, this information will be available so that parts can be ordered or repairs made. Having dated information may mean being able to document that the item is still under warranty
- Bragging rights—the good things such as ribbons, awards, notes about good conduct, and examples of art and craft work, reminding parents of their child's progress

These excellent ideas came from Albrecht (1995).

APPENDIX C:
SUMMARY OF SELECTED LEGISLATION

EDUCATION OF ALL
HANDICAPPED (1975) PL-94-142

This was the first law to guarantee a free and appropriate public education to all children with disabilities.

INDIVIDUALS WITH DISABILITIES
EDUCATION ACT (IDEA) PL-101-476

The purpose of the IDEA is to ensure the provision of a free and appropriate public education for all children with disabilities. These children should be integrated into regular classrooms to the maximum extent possible (Gettings, Carson, & Croston, 1992).

Part H of the IDEA provides for early intervention programs for infants and toddlers. The family, along with any professionals appropriate for the child's needs, formulates the individual family service plan (IFSP), which lists the goals the family has set for the child and describes services to be provided and persons responsible for these services.

Part C of the IDEA establishes Early Childhood Education services that are to be provided to children from birth through age 8.

SOCIAL SECURITY AMENDMENTS PL-89-97

Social Security. Several programs are available under the auspices of the Social Security Administration. Some are entitlement programs, accessible to anyone who meets the criteria of age or disability. Other programs rely on an assessment of the person's financial need to determine eligibility. Among the entitlement programs are Old Age, Survivors and Disability Insurance (OASDI) and Social Security Disability Insurance (SSDI); Supplemental Security Income (SSI) is based on demonstrated financial need.

Title II—Social Security Disability Insurance (SSDI) provides monthly cash benefits that are paid directly to eligible people with disabilities. The amount of the payment is based on the person's earnings history and length of employment as well as on the age at which the disability was incurred. The law places no restrictions on the use of these payments. To qualify for SSDI, a person must have paid Social Security taxes for approximately half the years since turning 21, be unemployed or earning less than the "substantial gainful activity" level, and have a medical disability certified by the state's Disability Determination Service (Gettings et al., 1992). This means that the person must be unable to engage in any substantial gainful activity because of a physical or mental disability that has persisted, or is expected to persist, for at least 12 months, or to result in death (Albrecht, 1995).

Title XVI Supplemental Security Income (SSI) is a federally administered cash benefits program for those who have disabilities and can demonstrate financial need. SSI benefits are paid from general revenues appropriated by Congress, whereas SSDI benefits come from a special trust fund financed through Social Security taxes (Gettings et al., 1992).

Title XVIII Medicare programs were authorized under the Social Security Act to provide health insurance benefits for people who qualify for Social Security and for those with disabilities (Gettings et al., 1992).

Part A establishes a mechanism for paying for the hospitalization costs.

Part B provides supplemental medical insurance.

Title XIX Medicaid provides for the medical expenses of categorically or medically needy people. These state-funded programs are needs-based with federal matching funds available through an established formula (Gettings et al., 1992).

VOCATIONAL REHABILITATION ACT OF 1973

The goal of this act is to assist people with disabilities to regain work skills.

Section 504 prohibits discrimination against persons with disabilities in any organization that receives federal funds.

Title VII is designed to assist persons with disabilities to achieve and maintain independence. Services provided could include occupational therapy, physical therapy, recreational therapy, attendant care, and prostheses.

Title VII Part A: Centers for Independent Living offer advocacy, attendant training, and referrals for housing (Gettings et al., 1992).

THE AMERICANS WITH DISABILITIES ACT OF 1990 (ADA)

The ADA protects people with disabilities from discrimination in the areas of employment, public utilities (e.g., stores, theaters, hotels), transportation, and telecommunication (Gettings et al., 1992).

APPENDIX D:
EARLY INTERVENTION PROGRAMS

For children with certain diagnoses, federal legislation mandates programming designed to minimize the long-term effects of disability and maximize the child's opportunities for successful functioning. Assessment of the child's physical, social, and cognitive abilities is a major factor in qualification for participation in early intervention programs (Brown & Brown, 1993). Children are eligible if they meet one of three criteria:

1. Having an established condition.
2. Demonstrating developmental delay.
3. Being identified as at risk for becoming substantially developmentally delayed without the provision of early intervention services. The exact definitions of these terms are specified by each state.

Some of the so-called established conditions are as follows: chromosomal anomalies such as Down syndrome; congenital malformations, including spina bifida; blindness, hearing loss or other sensory disorders; and neurological disorders such as cerebral palsy (Brown & Brown, 1993)

"Developmental delays" constitute another diagnostic criteria that can qualify a child for early intervention. This term was first used in special education legislation in 1986 with PL 99-457 (Amendments to the Education for All Handicapped Children Act). Contrary to common usage, developmental delay is not synonymous with mental retardation. In fact, the category was developed to prevent the application of labels that might be harmful or incorrect later in life, while still allowing the child to qualify for needed services. Developmental delays are identified prior to age two and may occur in five areas: physical, cognitive, communicative, social or emotional, and adaptive. A number of tests are available to screen for developmental delays, but parental concern about the child's progress is one of the most reliable early indicators (Brown & Brown, 1993).

The term *at risk* refers to children who have the potential to encounter delays due to biological or environmental factors in the family history or in the environment. These may include parental drug abuse, a history of prior child abuse, or the child's low birth weight or respiratory distress at birth.

EVALUATION AND ASSESSMENT

To plan accurately, the early intervention professionals must assess the abilities and weaknesses of the child and the family. The assessment involves a three part process: medical and developmental history, a physical and neurologic examination, and a developmental screening (Levy & Hyman, 1993). A number of professionals may be involved in the evaluation process. One person must serve as the contact person for the parents to provide interpretation of test results, therapeutic plans, and schedules that inevitably result from team planning. A social worker who serves as a case manager is the ideal in this type of situation.

It is vital to consider the child in the context of the family. The family's strengths, weaknesses, needs, and concerns must be addressed. The geographic location, socioeconomic factors, racial or ethnic characteristics, and educational level of the family will play a part in the success of the interventions.

The child will be tested in five different areas of development: cognitive, communicative, motor, social and emotional, and adaptive (McLean & McCormick, 1993).

For cognitive assessment, some choices are the Bayley Scales of Infant Development—Mental Scales, or the Battelle Developmental Inventory—Cognitive Domain, or the Griffiths Mental Development Scales—Performance Scale.

Communicative development levels may be assessed by utilizing the Sequenced Inventory of Communicative Development (SICD), or the Receptive Expressive Emergent Language (REEL).

The Peabody Developmental Motor Scales (PDMS) or the motor development scales of the Bayley, Battelle, and Griffiths assessments focus on motor skills.

Battelle, Bayley, and Griffiths' scales can be used in measuring social and emotional development, and the Vineland Adaptive Behavior Scales give information on adaptation (McLean & McCormick, 1993).

The purpose of such a thorough assessment is to provide adequate information for setting goals that are appropriate and suitable for the child and the family. Family participation is mandated, important, and relevant. It is also a learned skill. Even highly educated parents can be overwhelmed when considering the outcomes of all the assessments and the huge range of possible goals that can be set for the child. With some guidance from the social worker and other team members, the family can learn the skills of goal setting. Over time, the goals established by the family will become focused and reachable. This is a learning process and a very important one. It serves as a practice time for the goal setting that will be vital when the child enters formal school situations.

The members of the early intervention team may include a psychologist, speech therapist, occupational therapist, physical therapist, social worker, and educators (Levy & Hyman, 1993). It is essential that information from all these sources be coordinated and disseminated by some member of the professional team. In the face of all of this information, the family may feel overwhelmed by the number of professionals, the endless meetings, and the alphabet soup of acronyms for programs, tests, treatments, and benefits

SOCIAL WORK ROLES

One of the roles of a social worker is as case manager or team member for the early intervention team. Because of the enormous amount of information given to the parents, it is essential that at least one team member consistently provide interpretation and coherence for the family. One problem that may arise is that the parents, in attempting to carry out all the tasks and therapeutic assignments, may lose sight of their parental roles. They may feel that they are constantly being evaluated, and that their success as parents depends on the child's "successful" demonstration of the desired behavior or activity (Cogher, Savage, & Smith, 1992).

Sometimes parents become so focused on performing the activities correctly and properly recording the child's progress for the therapists that the fun of the game or exercise is lost. It is important that parents and child alike enjoy at least some of the assignments or the probability of adherence to the therapists' suggestions is not very high.

Early intervention professionals must also be careful to ask parents about any difficulties they are having in carrying out the various assignments. Parents who do not follow through on suggestions may not be resistant but may not fully understand the exercises or activities and the reasons for doing them. Early intervention team members could use a learning styles assessment to assist them in understanding the optimal format for presenting information to each parent: printed information, videos, observing others, or actual hands-on participation and practice.

REFERENCES

Abery, B. H. (1996). Family adjustment and adaptation. In J. E. Rynders & J. M. Horrobin (Eds.), *Down syndrome: Birth to adulthood* (pp. 120-159). Denver, CO: Love Publishing.

Albrecht, D. G. (1995). *Raising a child who has a physical disability.* New York: John Wiley.

Alliance for Technology Access. (1996). *Computer resources for people with disabilities.* Alameda, CA: Hunter House.

Alston, R. J., & Turner, W. L. (1994). A family strengths model of adjustment to disability for African American clients. *Journal of Counseling and Development, 72*(4), 378-383.

Anderson, S. (1991). Daily care. In E. Geralis (Ed.), *Children with cerebral palsy: A parents' guide* (pp. 91-130). Rockville, MD: Woodbine House.

Appleton, P. L., Minchom, P. E., Ellis, N. C., Elliott, C. E., Boll, V., & Jones, P. (1994). The self-concept of young people with spina bifida: A population-based study. *Developmental Medicine and Child Neurology, 36,* 198-215.

Atkinson, D. R., & Hackett, G. (1995). *Counseling diverse populations.* Madison, WI: Brown & Benchmark.

Bach, C. A., & McDaniel, R. W. (1993). Quality of life in quadriplegic adults: A focus group study. *Rehabilitation Nursing, 18*(6), 364-367.

Bailey, D. B., Blasco, P. M., & Simeonsson, R. J. (1992). Needs expressed by mothers and fathers of young children with disabilities. *American Journal on Mental Retardation, 97*(1), 1-10.

Balkman, K., & Smith, T. E. C. (1995). Legal issues. In M. C. Holbrook (Ed.), *Children with visual impairments* (pp. 205-226). Bethesda, MD: Woodbine House.

Barakat, L. P., & Linney, J. A. (1995). Optimism, appraisals, and coping in the adjustment of mothers and their children with spina bifida. *Journal of Child and Family Studies, 4*(3), 303-320.

Batshaw, M. L. (1993). Mental retardation. *Pediatric Clinics of North America, 40*(3), 507-521.

Batshaw, M. L., & Perret, Y. M. (1992). *Children with disabilities: A medical primer* (3rd ed.). Baltimore: Brookes.

Berkowitz, E. (1987). *Disabled policy.* New York: Cambridge.

Blake, K. (1995). The social isolation of young men with quadriplegia. *Rehabilitation Nursing, 20*(1), 17-22.

Blum, R. W., Resnick, M. D., Nelson, R., & Germaine, A. S. (1991). Family and peer issues among adolescents with spina bifida and cerebral palsy. *Pediatrics, 88*(2), 280-285.

Bozzacco, V. (1993). Long-term psychosocial effects of spinal cord injury. *Rehabilitation Nursing, 18*(2), 82-87.

Brannan, S. A. (1988). Leisure education for handicapped students. In S. M. Pueschel (Ed.), *The young person with Down syndrome* (pp. 93-108). Baltimore: Brookes.

Brasher, B., & Holbrook, M. C. (1996). Early intervention and special education. In M. C. Holbrook (Ed.), *Children with visual impairments* (pp. 175-204). Bethesda, MD: Woodbine House.

Bregman, S., & Castles, E. E. (1988). Insights and intervention into the sexual needs of the disabled adolescent. In P. W. Power, A. E. Dell Orto, & M. B. Gibbons (Eds.), *Family interventions throughout chronic illness and disability* (pp. 184-200). New York: Springer.

Brown, W., & Brown, C. (1993). Defining eligibility for early intervention. In W. Brown, S. K. Thurman, & L. F. Pearl (Eds.), *Family-centered early intervention with infants and toddlers* (pp. 21-42). Baltimore: P. H. Brookes.

Buckley, S. (1995). Teaching children with Down syndrome to read and write. In L. Nadel & D. Rosenthal (Eds.), *Down syndrome: Living and learning in the community* (pp. 158-169). New York: Wiley-Liss.

Burke, R. (1991). Adjusting to your child's disability. In E. Geralis (Ed.), *Children with cerebral palsy: A parents' guide* (pp. 33-56). Rockville, MD: Woodbine House.

Burt, D. B., Loveland, K. A., Chen, Y.-W., Chuang, A., Lewis, K. R., & Cherry, L. (1995). Aging in adults with Down syndrome: Report from a longitudinal study. *American Journal on Mental Retardation, 100*(3), 262-270.

Buscaglia, L. (1983). *The disabled and their parents: A counseling challenge.* Thorofare, NJ: Slack Incorporated.

Caldwell, L. L., & Weissinger, E. (1994). Factors influencing free time boredom in a sample of persons with spinal cord injuries. *Therapeutic Recreation Journal, 28*(1), 18-24.

Campbell, E., & Jones, G. (1994). Psychological well-being in wheelchair sport participants and nonparticipants. *Adapted Physical Activity Quarterly, 11,* 404-415.

Charney, E. B. (1992). Neural tube defects: Spina bifida and myelomeningocele. In M. L. Batshaw & Y. M. Perret (Eds.), *Children with disabilities: A medical primer* (pp. 471-488). Baltimore: Brookes.

Clark, A., & Hirst, M. (1989). Disability in adulthood: Ten-year follow-up of young people with disabilities. *Disability, Handicap & Society, 4*(3), 271-283.

Cogher, L., Savage, E., & Smith, M. F. (1992). *Cerebral palsy: The child and young person.* London: Chapman & Hall Medical.

Coley, I. L., & Procter, S. A. (1989). Self-maintenance activities. In P. N. Pratt & A. S. Allen (Eds.), *Occupational therapy for children* (2nd ed., pp. 260-294). St. Louis: C. V. Mosby.

Compton, D. M., Eisenman, P. A., & Henderson, H. L. (1989). Exercise and fitness for persons with disabilities. *Sports Medicine, 7,* 150-162.

Congress, E. P., & Lyons, B. P. (1992). Cultural differences in health beliefs: Implications for social work practice in health care settings. *Social Work in Health Care, 17*(3), 81-96.

Connor-Kuntz, F. J., Dummer, G. M., & Paciorek, M. J. (1995). Physical education and sport participation of children and youth with spina bifida myelomeningocele. *Adapted Physical Activity Quarterly, 12,* 228-238.

Cowan, N. S. (1991). Family life and self-esteem. In E. Geralis (Ed.), *Children with cerebral palsy: A parents' guide* (pp. 133-174). Rockville, MD: Woodbine House.

Coyle, C. P., Shank, J. W., Kinney, W. T., & Hutchins, D. A. (1993). Psychosocial functioning and changes in leisure lifestyle among individuals with chronic secondary health problems related to spinal cord injury. *Therapeutic Recreation Journal, 27*(4), 239-252.

Crnic, K. A. (1990). Families of children with Down syndrome: Ecological contexts and characteristics. In D. Cicchetti & M. Beeghly (Eds.), *Children with Down syndrome: A developmental perspective* (pp. 399-423). Cambridge, MA: Cambridge University Press.

Cushman, L. A., & Hassett, J. (1992). Spinal cord injury: 10 and 15 years after. *Paraplegia, 30,* 690-696.

Dallyn, L., & Garrison-Jones, C. (1990). Reaching adulthood: The long-term psychosocial adjustment of children with spina bifida. In H. L. Rekate (Ed.), *Comprehensive management of spina bifida* (pp. 216-237). Boca Raton, FL: CRC.

Darling, R. B. (1991). Initial and continuing adaptation to the birth of a disabled child. In M. Seligman (Ed.), *The family with a handicapped child* (pp. 55-90). Boston: Allyn & Bacon.

Davis, B. H. (1987). Disability and grief. *Social Casework, 68,* 352-357.

Davis, S. E., Anderson, C., Linkowski, D. C., Berger, K., & Feinstein, C. F. (1991). Developmental tasks and transitions of adolescents with chronic illnesses and disabilities. In R. P. Marinelli & A. E. Dell Orto (Eds.), *The psychological and social impact of disability* (3rd ed., pp. 70-80). New York: Springer.

DeJong, G., & Batavia, A. I. (1991). Toward a health services research capacity in spinal cord injury. *Paraplegia, 19,* 373-389.

DeVivo, M. J., & Richards, J. S. (1992). Community reintegration and quality of life following spinal cord injury. *Paraplegia, 20,* 108-112.

Dixon, M. S., & Rekate, H. L. (1990). Pediatric management of children with myelodysplasia. In H. L. Rekate (Ed.), *Comprehensive management of spina bifida* (pp. 50-65). Boca Raton, FL: CRC.

Dormans, J. P. (1993). Orthopedic management of children with cerebral palsy. *Pediatric Clinics of North America, 40*(3), 645-657.

Dunlea, A. (1989). *Vision and the emergence of meaning.* New York: Cambridge.

Dyer, S. M. (1994). Physiological effects of a 13-week physical fitness program on Down syndrome subjects. *Pediatric Exercise Science, 6,* 88-100.

Edgerton, R. B. (1994). Quality of life issues: Some people know how to be old. In M. M. Seltzer, M. W. Krauss, & M. P. Janicki (Eds.), *Life course perspectives on adulthood and old age* (pp. 53-66). Washington, DC: American Association on Mental Retardation.

Edser, P., & Ward, G. (1991). Sexuality, sex and spina bifida. In C. M. Bannister & B. Tew (Eds.), *Current concepts in spina bifida and hydrocephalus* (pp. 202-211). London: MacKeith.

Edwards, J. (1988). Sexuality, marriage, and parenting for persons with Down syndrome. In S. M. Pueschel (Ed.), *The young person with Down syndrome* (pp. 187-204). Baltimore: Brookes.

Eicher, P. S., & Batshaw, M. L. (1993). Cerebral palsy. *Pediatric Clinics of North America, 40*(3), 537-551.

Elkind, D. (1978). *A sympathetic understanding of the child.* Boston: Allyn & Bacon.

Erikson, E. H. (1963). *Childhood and society* (2nd ed.). New York: Norton.

Falvo, D. R., & Lundervold, D. A. (1995). Aging. In A. E. Dell Orto & R. P. Marinelli (Eds.), *Encyclopedia of disability and rehabilitation* (pp. 27-34). New York: Simon & Schuster.

Featherstone, H. (1971). *A difference in the family.* New York: Basic.

Ferrell, K. A. (1984). *Parenting preschoolers: Suggestions for raising young blind and visually impaired children.* New York: American Foundation for the Blind.

Fewell, R. R. (1986). A handicapped child in the family. In R. R. Fewell & P. F. Vadasy (Eds.), *Families of handicapped children: Needs and supports across the life span* (pp. 3-94). Austin, TX: Pro-ed.

Finkelstein, V. (1991). Disability: A social challenge or an administrative responsibility? In J. Swain, V. Finkelstein, & M. Oliver (Eds.), *Disabling barriers: Enabling environments* (pp. 34-43). London: Sage.

Finkelstein, V., & French, S. (1993). Towards a psychology of disability. In J. Swain, V. Finkelstein, & M. Oliver (Eds.), *Disabling barriers: Enabling environments* (pp. 26-33). London: Sage.

Fowler, A. E. (1995). Linguistic variability in persons with Down syndrome: Research and implications. In L. Nagel & D. Rosenthal (Eds.), *Down Syndrome: Living and learning in the community* (pp. 121-131). New York: Wiley-Liss.

Foxx, R. M., Faw, G. D., Taylor, S., Davis, P. K., & Fulia, R. (1993). "Would I be able to . . ."? Teaching clients to assess the availability of their community living life style preferences. *American Journal on Mental Retardation, 98*(2), 235-248.

Freeman, R. D., Goetz, E., Richards, D. P., & Groenveld, M. (1991). Defiers of negative predictions: A 14 year follow-up study of legally blind children. *Journal of Visual Impairment and Blindness, 85,* 365-370.

French, S. (1993). Disability, impairment or something in between? In J. Swain, V. Finkelstein, S. French, & M. Oliver (Eds.), *Disabling barriers: Enabling environments* (pp. 17-25). London: Sage.

Funk, R. (Ed.). (1987). *Disability rights: From caste to class in the context of civil rights.* New York: Praeger.

Gartner, A., & Joe, T. (1987). *Images of the disabled: Disabling images.* New York: Praeger.

Geralis, E. (1991). *Children with cerebral palsy: A parents' guide.* Rockville, MD: Woodbine House.

Gersh, E. (1991). What is cerebral palsy? In E. Geralis (Ed.), *Children with cerebral palsy: A parents' guide* (pp. 1-32). Rockville, MD: Woodbine House.

Gettings, R. M., Carson, S. A., & Croston, M. A. (1992). *Summary of existing legislation affecting people with disabilities.* Alexandria, VA: Office of Special Education and Rehabilitative Services.

Gibson, J. W., Rabkin, J., & Munson, R. (1992). Critical issues in serving the developmentally disabled elderly. *Journal of Gerontological Social Work, 19*(1), 35-49.

Gilligan, C. (1982). *In a different voice.* Cambridge, MA: Harvard University Press.

Giordano, G., & D'Alonzo, B. J. (1996). Challenge and progress in rehabilitation: A review of the past 25 years and a preview of the future. *American Rehabilitation, 21*(3), 14-21.

Glazer, N. Y. (1993). *Women's paid and unpaid labor.* Philadelphia: Temple University Press.

Gless, P. A. (1995). Applying the Roy Adaptation Model to the care of clients with quadriplegia. *Rehabilitation Nursing, 20*(1), 11-16.

Glidden, L. M. (1995). What we do NOT know about families with children who have developmental disabilities: Questionnaire on resources and stress as a case study. *American Journal on Mental Retardation, 97*(5), 481-495.

Goldberg, R. T. (1995). Rehabilitation of adolescents. In A. E. Dell Orto & R. P. Marinelli (Eds.), *Encyclopedia of disability and rehabilitation* (pp. 12-17+). New York: Simon & Schuster.

Groenveld, M. (1993). Effects of visual disability on behaviour and the family. In A. R. Fielder, A. B. Best, & M. C. O. Bax (Eds.), *The management of visual impairment in childhood* (pp. 64-77). London: MacKeith.

Hammell, K. R. W. (1992). Psychological and sociological theories concerning adjustment to traumatic spinal cord injury: The implications for rehabilitation. *Paraplegia, 30,* 317-326.

Harris, S. L. (1987). The family crisis: Diagnosis of a severely disabled child. *Marriage and Family Review, 11*(1/2), 107-118.

Hayes, A., & Batshaw, M. L. (1993). Down syndrome. *Pediatric Clinics of North America, 40*(3), 523-539.

Healy, C. C. (1982). *Career development: Counseling through the life stages.* Boston: Allyn & Bacon.

Heller, T., & Factor, A. (1993). Aging family caregivers: Support resources and changes in burden and placement desire. *American Journal on Mental Retardation, 98*(3), 417-426.

Henderson, K. A., Bedini, L. A., & Hecht, L. (1994). "Not just a wheelchair, not just a woman": Self-identity and leisure. *Therapeutic Recreation Journal, 28*(2), 73-86.

Henderson, K., Bedini, L. A., Hecht, L., & Schuler, R. (1995). Women with physical disabilities and the negotiation of leisure constraints. *Leisure Studies, 14,* 17-31.

Hill, E. W., & Snook-Hill, M.-M. (1996). Orientation and mobility. In M. C. Holbrook (Ed.), *Children with visual impairments* (pp. 259-286). Bethesda, MD: Woodbine.

Hobdell, E. F. (1995). Perceptual accuracy and gender-related differences in parents of children with myelomeningocele. *Journal of Neuroscience Nursing, 27*(4), 240-244.

Hodapp, R. M., & Zigler, E. (1990). Applying the developmental perspective to individuals with Down syndrome. In D. Cicchetti & M. Beeghly (Eds.), *Children with Down syndrome: A developmental perspective* (pp. 1-28). Cambridge, MA: Cambridge University Press.

Holbrook, M. C. (1996). *Children with visual impairments.* Bethesda, MD: Woodbine House.

Humes, C. W., Szymanski, E. M., & Hohenshil, T. H. (1995). Roles of counseling in enabling persons with disabilities. In D. R. Atkinson & G. Hackett (Eds.), *Counseling diverse populations* (pp. 155-166). Madison, WI: Brown & Benchmark.

Hunt, G. M., & Poulton, A. (1995). Open spina bifida: A complete cohort reviewed 25 years after closure. *Developmental Medicine and Child Neurology, 37,* 19-29.

Hunter, S., & Sundel, M. (1989). *Midlife myths.* Newbury Park, CA: Sage.

Hutton, J. L., Cooke, T., & Pharoah, P. (1994). Life expectancy in children with cerebral palsy. *British Medical Journal (International), 390,* 431-435.

Hutzler, Y., & Bar-Eli, M. (1993). Psychological benefits of sports for disabled people: A review. *Scandinavian Journal of Medicine & Science in Sports, 3,* 217-228.

Jackson, R. W. (1987). Sport for the spinal paralysed person. *Paraplegia, 25,* 301-304.

Janssen, T. W. J., Van Oers, C. A. J. M., Van der Woude, L. H. V., & Hollander, A. P. (1993). Physical strain in daily life of wheelchair users with spinal cord injuries. *Medicine and Science in Sports and Exercise, 25,* 661-670.

Johnson, A. F. (1988). Challenged adolescents with spina bifida. In P. W. Power, A. E. Dell Orto, & M. B. Gibbons (Eds.), *Family interventions throughout chronic illness and disability* (pp. 164-183). New York: Springer.

Kagawa-Singer, M. (1994). Cross-cultural views of disability. *Rehabilitation Nursing, 19*(6), 362-365.

Kaplan, D. M. (1982). Interventions for disorder of change. *Social Work, 27,* 404-410.

Kaplan, J. E., & Moore, R. J. (1991). Legal rights and hurdles. In E. Geralis (Ed.), *Children with cerebral palsy: A parents' guide* (pp. 297-332). Rockville, MD: Woodbine House.

Kearney, P. (1993, November/December). *Listening to the parents of children with developmental disabilities.* Paper presented at the proceedings of Quality and Equality —29th Association for the Scientific Study of Intellectual Disability National Conference, University of Newcastle, Australia.

King, G. A., Shulz, I. Z., Steel, K., Gilpin, M., & Cathers, T. (1993). Self-evaluation and self-concept of adolescents with physical disabilities. *American Journal of Occupational Therapy, 47*(2), 132-140.

Kingsley, J., & Levitz, M. (1994). *Count us in: Growing up with Down syndrome.* New York: Harcourt Brace.

Kivnick, H. Q. (1991). Disability and psychosocial development in old age. In R. P. Marinelli & A. E. Dell Orto (Eds.), *The psychological and social impact of disability* (pp. 92-101). New York: Springer.

Kleinschmidt, J. J. (1996). An orientation to vision loss program: Meeting the needs of newly visually impaired older adults. *The Gerontologist, 36*(4), 534-538.

Koenning, G. M., Benjamin, J. E., Todaro, A. W., Warren, R. W., & Burns, M. L. (1995). Bridging the "med-ed gap" for students with special health care needs: A model school liaison program. *Journal of School Health, 65*(6), 207-212.

Kokkonen, J., Saukonen, A. L., Timenon, E., Serlo, W., & Kinnunen, P. (1991). Social outcome of handicapped children as adults. *Developmental Medicine and Child Neurology, 33,* 1095-1100.

Kopito, A., & Greenberg, S. (1995). Reframing dependence in old age: A positive transition for families. *Social Work, 40*(3), 382-390.

Kozma, C. (1986). Medical concerns and treatments. In K. Stray-Gunderson (Ed.), *Babies with Down syndrome* (pp. 47-65). Rockville, MD: Woodbine House.

Krauss, M. W. (1987). Services to families during three stages of a handicapped person's life. *Marriage and Family Review, 11*(1/2), 213-229.

Kropf, N. P. (1996). Infusing content on older people with developmental disabilities into the curriculum. *Journal of Social Work Education, 32*(2), 215-226.

Kuehn, M. D. (1995). An agenda for professional practice in the 1990s. In D. R. Atkinson & G. Hackett (Eds.), *Counseling diverse populations* (pp. 167-186). Madison, WI: Brown & Benchmark.

Kurtz, L. (1992). Cerebral palsy. In M. L. Batshaw & Y. Perret (Eds.), *Children with disabilities: A medical primer* (pp. 441-469). Baltimore: Brookes.

Kurtz, L. A., & Scull, S. A. (1993). Rehabilitation for developmental disabilities. *Pediatric Clinics of North America, 40*(3), 629-643.

Lamarre, D. (1994). Youth connections. *Exceptional Parent, 24*(7), 53-56.

Lawrence, P. L., Brown, R. I., Mills, J., & Estay, I. (1993). *Adults with Down syndrome: Together we can do it.* N. York Ontario: Captus.

Leck, I. (1994). Structural birth defects. In I. B. Pless (Ed.), *The epidemiology of childhood disorders* (pp. 66-117). New York: Oxford University Press.

Lee, Y., Brock, S., Dattilo, J., & Kleiber, D. (1993). Leisure and adjustment to spinal cord injury: Conceptual and methodological suggestions. *Therapeutic Recreation Journal, 27*(3), 200-211.

Levy, S. E., & Hyman, S. L. (1993). Pediatric assessment of the child with developmental delay. *Pediatric Clinics of North America, 40*(2), 465-477.

Lewis, V. (1987). *Development and handicap.* Oxford, UK: Basil Blackwell.

Leyser, Y. (1994). Stress and adaptation in orthodox Jewish families with a disabled child. *American Journal of Orthopsychiatry, 64*(3), 376-385.

Lilliston, B. A. (1985). Psychosocial responses to traumatic physical disability. *Social Work in Health Care, 10*(4), 1-13.

Lollar, D. J. (1994). *Social development and the person with spina bifida.* Washington, DC: Spina Bifida Association of America.

Lord, J., Varzos, N., Behrman, B., Wicks, J., & Wicks, D. (1990). Implications of mainstream classrooms for adolescents with spina bifida. *Developmental Medicine and Child Neurology, 32,* 20-29.

Lyons, R. F., Sullivan, M. J. L., & Ritvo, P. G. (1995). *Relationships in chronic illness and disability.* Thousand Oaks, CA: Sage.

Martin, J. J., & Mushett, C. A. (1996). Social support mechanisms among athletes with disabilities. *Adapted Physical Activity Quarterly, 13,* 74-83.

Martinez, R., & Sewell, K. W. (1996). Self-concept of adults with visual impairments. *Journal of Rehabilitation, 62*(2), 55-58.

Masino, L. L., & Hodapp, R. M. (1996). Parental educational expectations for adolescents with disabilities. *Exceptional Children, 62*(6), 515-523.

May, J. E. (1991). *Fathers of children with special needs: New horizons.* Bethesda, MD: Association for the Care of Children's Health.

Mayfield, J. K. (1990). Comprehensive orthopedic management in myelomeningocele. In H. L. Rekate (Ed.), *Comprehensive management of spina bifida* (pp. 114-159). Boca Raton, FL: CRC.

McFadden, S. H. (1995). Religion and well-being in aging persons in an aging society. *Journal of Social Issues, 51*(2), 161-175.

McInerney, C. A., & McInerney, M. (1992). A mobility skills training program for adults with developmental disabilities. *American Journal of Occupational Therapy, 46,* 233-239.

McLean, M., & McCormick, K. (1993). Assessment and evaluation in early intervention. In W. Brown, S. K. Thurman, & L. F. Pearl (Eds.), *Family-centered early intervention with infants and toddlers* (pp. 43-79). Baltimore, MD: Brookes.

Menacker, S. J. (1993). Visual function in children with developmental disabilities. *Pediatric Clinics of North America, 40*(3), 659-674.

Miller, F., & Bachrach, S. J. (1995). *Cerebral palsy: A complete guide for caregiving.* Baltimore: Johns Hopkins University Press.

Miller, G. (1991). Don't burn my work boots without my permission. *Journal of Gerontological Social Work, 17*(3/4), 57-68.

Miller, J. F., Leddy, M., Miolo, G., & Sedey, A. (1995). The development of early language skills in children with Down syndrome. In L. Nadel & D. Rosenthal (Eds.), *Down syndrome: Living and learning in the community* (pp. 115-120). New York: Wiley-Liss.

Moore, J. E. (1995). Blindness and vision disorders. In A. E. Dell Orto & R. P. Marinelli (Eds.), *Encyclopedia of disability and rehabilitation* (pp. 115-120). New York: Simon & Schuster.

Morningstar, M. E., Turnbull, A. P., & Turnbull, M. R. (1995). What do students with disabilities tell us about the importance of family involvement in the transition from school to adult life? *Exceptional Children, 62*(3), 249-260.

Nadel, L., & Rosenthal, D. (1995). *Down syndrome: Living and learning in the community.* New York: Wiley-Liss.

Nelson, M., Ruch, S., Jackson, Z., Bloom, L., & Part, R. (1992). Towards an understanding of families with physically disabled adolescents. *Social Work in Health Care, 17*(4), 1-25.

Oelwein, P. L. (1995). *Teaching reading to children with Down syndrome.* Bethesda, MD: Woodbine House.

Olshansky, S. (1962). Chronic sorrow: A response to having a mentally retarded child. *Social Casework, 43,* 190-193.

Orr, A. L. (1991). The psychosocial aspects of aging and vision loss. *Journal of Gerontological Social Work, 17*(3/4), 1-14.

Overeynder, J. C., Janicki, M. P., & Turk, M. A. (1994). *Aging and cerebral palsy: Pathways to successful aging.* Albany: New York State Developmental Disabilities Planning Council.

Owen, M. J. (1985). A view of disability in current social work literature. *American Behavioral Scientist, 20*(3), 397-403.

Palkovitz, R., & Wolfe, C. B. (1987). Rights of children born with disabilities: Issues, inconsistencies, and recommendations for advocacy. *Marriage and Family Review, 11*(1/2), 83-103.

Parkinson, C. B., & Howard, M. (1996). Older persons with mental retardation/developmental disabilities. *Journal of Gerontological Social Work, 25*(1/2), 91-103.

Parsons, T. (1951). *The social system.* New York: Free Press.

Parsons, T. (1958). Definitions of health and illness in the light of American values and social structure. In E. G. Jacoe (Ed.), *Patients, physicians and illness.* Glencoe, IL: Free Press.

Patterson, J. M. (1988). Chronic illness in children and the impact on the family. In C. S. Chilman, F. M. Cox, & E. W. Nunnally (Eds.), *Chronic illness and disability* (pp. 69-107). Newbury Park, CA: Sage.

Pescatello, L. S., & DiPietro, L. (1993). Physical activity in older adults: An overview of health benefits. *Sports Medicine, 14*(6), 353-364.

Peterson, P. M., Rauen, K. K., Brown, J., & Cole, J. (1994). Spina bifida: The transition into adulthood begins in infancy. *Rehabilitation Nursing, 19*(4), 229-238.

Piaget, J., & Inhelder, B. (1969). *The psychology of the child.* New York: Basic Books.

Pomatto, R. C. (1990). The use of orthotics in the treatment of myelomeningocele. In H. L. Rekate (Ed.), *Comprehensive management of spina bifida* (pp. 167-813). Boca Raton, FL: CRC.

Power, P. W., Hershenson, D. B., & Schlossberg, N. K. (1991). *Midlife transition and disability.* In R. P. Marinelli & A. E. Dell Orto (Eds.), The psychological and social impact of disability (pp. 81-91). New York: Springer.

Powers, L. E. (1993). Disability and grief: From tragedy to challenge. In G. H. S. Singer & L. E. Powers (Eds.), *Families, disability, and empowerment: Active coping skills and strategies for family interventions* (pp. 119-149). Baltimore: Brookes.

Pratt, P. N. (1989). Play and recreational activities. In P. N. Pratt & A. S. Allen (Eds.), *Occupational therapy for children* (2nd ed., pp. 295-310). St. Louis: C. V. Mosby.

Priebe, M. M., & Rintala, D. H. (1995). Spinal cord injury. In A. E. Dell Orto & R. P. Marinelli (Eds.), *Encyclopedia of disability and rehabilitation* (pp. 688-695). New York: Simon & Schuster.

Pueschel, S. M. (1988). The biology of the maturing person with Down syndrome. In S. M. Pueschel (Ed.), *The young person with Down syndrome: Transition from adolescence to adulthood* (pp. 23-34). Baltimore: P. H. Brookes.

Quinn, P. (1995). Social work and disability management policy: Yesterday, today, and tomorrow. *Social Work in Health Care, 20*(3), 67-82.

Quinn, P. (1996). Identifying gendered outcomes of gender-neutral policies: Supplemental questions for policy analysis. *Affilia, 11*(2), 195-206.

Rauen, K. (1995). *Guidelines for spina bifida: Health care services throughout life.* Washington, DC: Spina Bifida Association of America.

Rauen, K. K., & Aubert, E. J. (1992). A brighter future for adults who have myelomeningocele: One form of spina bifida. *Orthopaedic Nursing, 11*(3), 16-25.

Reilly, P. R. (1992). Ethical issues in the use of human growth hormone treatments in Down's syndrome. In S. Castells & K. E. Wisniewski (Eds.), *Growth hormone treatment in Down's syndrome* (pp. 233-245). New York: Wiley.

Rekate, H. L. (1990a). *Comprehensive management of spina bifida.* Boca Raton, FL: CRC.

Rekate, H. L. (1990b). Neurosurgical management of the newborn with spina bifida. In H. L. Rekate (Ed.), *Comprehensive management of spina bifida* (pp. 2-26). Boca Raton, FL: CRC.

Rekate, H. L. (1990c). Neurosurgical management of the child with spina bifida. In H. L. Rekate (Ed.), *Comprehensive management of the child with spina bifida* (pp. 94-110). Boca Raton, FL: CRC.

Resources for Rehabilitation. (1994). *A woman's guide to coping with disability.* Lexington, MA: Author.

Rodgers, S. L., & Marini, I. (1994). Physiological and psychological aspects of aging with spinal cord injury. *SCI Psychosocial Process, 7*(3), 98-103.

Roth, E. J., Lovell, L., Heinemann, A. W., Lee, M. Y., & Yarkony, G. M. (1992). The older adult with a spinal cord injury. *Paraplegia, 30,* 520-526.

Rowley, D. I., & Rose, G. (1991). Walking aids. In C. M. Bannister & B. Tew (Eds.), *Current concepts in spina bifida and hydrocephalus* (pp. 104-118). London: MacKeith.

Rubenfeld, P., & Schwartz, A. (1996). Early onset of a disability: Its impact on development and adult outcomes. *SCI Psychosocial Process, 9*(2/3), 60-63.

Russell, P. (1991). Working with children with physical disabilities and their families: The social work role. In M. Oliver (Ed.), *Social work: Disabled people and disabling environments* (pp. 113-137). London: Kingsley.

Rynders, J. E., & Horrobin, J. M. (1996). *Down syndrome: Birth to adulthood.* Denver, CO: Love Publishing.

Rynders, J. E., & Schleien, S. J. (1988). Recreation: A promising vehicle for promoting the community integration of young adults with Down syndrome. In C. Tingey (Ed.), *Down syndrome: A resource handbook* (pp. 181-198). Boston: College Hill.

Saleebey, D. (1992). *The strength perspective in social work practice.* New York: Longman.

Salsgiver, R. O. (1996). Perspectives on families with children with disabilities. *SCI Psychosocial Process, 9*(1), 18-23.

Sameroff, A. J., & Fiese, B. H. (1990). Transactional regulation and early intervention. In S. J. Meisels & J. P. Shonkoff (Eds.), *Handbook of early childhood intervention* (pp. 119-149). Cambridge, MA: Cambridge University Press.

Scheer, J., & Groce, N. (1988). Impairment as a human constant: Cross-cultural and historical perspectives on variation. *Journal of Social Issues, 44*(1), 23-37.

Scherzer, A. L. (1990). *Early diagnosis and therapy in cerebral palsy: A primer on infant developmental problems.* New York: M. Dekker.

Schilling, R. F. (1988). Helping families with developmentally disabled members. In C. S. Chilman, F. M. Cox, & E. W. Nunnally (Eds.), *Chronic illness and disability* (pp. 171-192). Newbury Park, CA: Sage.

Schilling, R. F., Schinke, S. P., & Kirkham, M. A. (1988). The impact of developmental disabilities and other learning deficits on families. In C. S. Chilman, F. M. Cox, & E. W. Nunnally (Eds.), *Chronic illness and disability* (pp. 156-170). Newbury Park, CA: Sage.

Schriner, K. F., Roessler, R. T., & Johnson, P. (1993). Identifying the employment concerns of people with spina bifida. *Journal of Applied Rehabilitation Counseling, 24*(2), 32-37.

Sedlak, C. A. (1991). Assessment of the surgical adult orthopaedic client with Down syndrome. *Orthopaedic Nursing, 10*(5), 27-34.

Seelman, K., & Sweeney, S. (1996). The changing universe of disability. *American Rehabilitation, 21*(3), 2-13.

Selikowitz, M. (1990). *Down syndrome: The facts.* Oxford, UK: Oxford University Press.

Seltzer, G. B., & Luchterhand, C. (1994). Health and well-being of older persons with developmental disabilities: A clinical review. In M. M. Seltzer, M. W. Krauss, & M. P. Janicki (Eds.), *Life course perspectives on adulthood and old age* (pp. 109-142). Washington, DC: American Association on Mental Retardation.

Seltzer, M. M., Krauss, M. W., & Tsunematsu, N. (1993). Adults with Down syndrome and their aging mothers: Diagnostic group differences. *American Journal on Mental Retardation, 97*(3), 496-508.

Serafica, F. C. (1990). Peer relations of children with Down syndrome. In D. Cicchetti & M. Beeghly (Eds.), *Children with Down syndrome: A developmental perspective* (pp. 369-398). Cambridge, MA: Cambridge University Press.

Shephard, R. J. (1993). Research including persons with disabilities: Practical issues and contributions to knowledge of exercise physiology. *Adapted Physical Activity Quarterly, 10,* 336-345.

Sherrill, C., & Rainbolt, W. J. (1986). Sociological perspectives of cerebral palsy sports. *Palaestra*, pp. 21-26.

Shurtleff, D. B., Luchy, D. A., Nyberg, D. A., Benedetti, T. J., & Mack, L. A. (1994). Meningomyelocele: Management in utero and post natum. In Ciba Foundation (Ed.), *Neural tube defects* (pp. 270-280). Chichester, UK: John Wiley.

Singer, G. H. S., Irvin, L. K., Irvine, B., Hawkins, N. E., Gegreness, J., & Jackson, R. (1993). Helping families adapt positively to disability. In G. H. S. Singer & L. E. Powers (Eds.), *Families, disability, and empowerment: Active coping skills and strategies for family interventions* (pp. 67-83). Baltimore: Brookes.

Siosteen, A., Lundqvist, C., Blomstrand, C., Sullivan, L., & Sullivan, M. (1990). The quality of life of three functional spinal cord injury subgroups in a Swedish community. *Paraplegia, 28,* 476-488.

Skaggs, S., & Hopper, C. (1996). Individuals with visual impairments: A review of psychomotor behavior. *Adapted Physical Activity Quarterly, 13,* 16-26.

Smart, J. F., & Smart, D. W. (1995). The rehabilitation of Hispanics with disabilities: Sociocultural constraints. *Rehabilitation Education, 7,* 167-184.

Smith, N. J., & Smith, H. C. (1991). *Physical disability and handicap.* Melbourne, Australia: Longman Cheshire.

Sobsey, D. (1994). *Violence and abuse in the lives of people with disabilities: The end of silent acceptance.* Baltimore: P. H. Brookes.

Spiker, D. (1990). Early intervention from a developmental perspective. In D. Cicchetti & M. Beeghly (Eds.), *Children with Down syndrome: A developmental perspective* (pp. 424-448). Cambridge: MA: Cambridge University Press.

Spoltore, T. A., & O'Brien, A. M. (1995). Rehabilitation of the spinal cord injured patient. *Orthopaedic Nursing, 14*(3), 7-14.

Stanley, F. J., & Blair, E. (1994). Cerebral palsy. In I. B. Pless (Ed.), *The epidemiology of childhood disorders* (pp. 473-497). New York: Oxford University Press.

Steadham, C. I. (1994). Health maintenance and promotion: Infancy through adolescence. In S. P. Roth & J. S. Morse (Eds.), *A life-span approach to nursing care for individuals with developmental disabilities* (pp. 147-169). Baltimore: P. H. Brookes.

Steffens, M. L., Oller, D. K., Lynch, M., & Urbano, R. C. (1992). Vocal development in infants with Down syndrome and infants who are developing normally. *American Journal on Mental Retardation, 97*(2), 235-246.

Stephens, L. C., & Pratt, P. N. (1989). School work tasks and vocational readiness. In P. N. Pratt & A. S. Allen (Eds.), *Occupational therapy for children* (2nd ed.) (pp. 311-334). St. Louis, MO: C. V. Mosby.

Stray-Gunderson, K. (1986). *Babies with Down syndrome.* Rockville, MD: Woodbine.

Sugden, D. A. (1990). *Problems in movement skill development.* Columbia: University of South Carolina Press.

Sullivan, W. P. (1994). Intervening for success: Strengths-based case management and successful aging. *Journal of Gerontological Social Work, 22*(1/2), 61-74.

Sutkin, L. C. (1984). Introduction. In M. G. Eisenberg, L. C. Sutkin, & M. A. Jansen (Eds.), *Chronic illness and disability through the lifespan: Effects on self and family.* New York: Springer.

Swain, J., Finkelstein, V., French, S., & Oliver, M. C. (1993). *Disabling barriers: Enabling environments.* London: Sage.

Szymanski, E. M., & Hanley-Maxwell, C. (1996). Career development of people with developmental disabilities: An ecological model. *Journal of Rehabilitation, 62*(1), 48-55.

Tarby, T. J. (1990). A clinical view of the embryology of myelomeningocele. In H. L. Rekate (Ed.), *Comprehensive management of spina bifida* (pp. 29-48). Boca Raton, FL: CRC.

Taylor, F. (1993). Cerebral palsy: Hope through research. Bethesda, MD: U.S. Department of Health and Human Services.

Thompson, C. E. (1990). Transition of the disabled adolescent to adulthood. *Pediatrician, 17,* 308-313.

Tingey, C. (1988). Cutting the umbilical cord: Parental perspectives. In S. M. Pueschel (Ed.), *The young person with Down syndrome: Transition from adolescence to adulthood* (pp. 5-22). Baltimore: P. H. Brookes.

Todd, S., & Shearn, J. (1996). Struggles with time: The careers of parents with adult sons and daughters with learning disabilities. *Disability & Society, 11*(3), 379-401.

Treischmann, R. (1980). *Spinal cord injuries.* Oxford, UK: Pergamon.

Trueta, M. (1995). Fostering independence from early childhood. In L. Nadel & D. Rosenthal (Eds.), *Down syndrome: living and learning in the community* (pp. 15-17). New York: Wiley-Liss.

Turnbull, H. R., Turnbull, A. P., Bronicki, G. J., Summers, J. A., & Roeder-Gordon, C. (1989). *Disability and the family.* Baltimore: Brookes.

Ventura, S. J., Martin, J. A., Mathews, T. J., & Clarke, S. C. (1996). Advance report of final natality statistics, 1994. *Monthly Vital Statistics Report, 44*(11), p. 79.

Vygotsky, L. S. (1962). *Thought and language* (E. Hanfmann & G. Vakar, Trans.). Cambridge: MIT Press.

Wadsworth, J. S., & Harper, D. C. (1993). The social needs of adolescents with cerebral palsy. *Developmental Medicine and Child Neurology, 35*(11), 1019-1022.

Weisgerber, R. A. (1991). *Quality of life for persons with disabilities.* Gaithersburg, MD: Aspen.

Werner, E. E. (1990). Protective factors and individual resilience. In S. J. Meisels & J. P. Shonkoff (Eds.), *Handbook of early childhood intervention* (pp. 97-116). Cambridge: Cambridge University Press.

White, B. L. (1975). The first three years of life. New York: Avon.

White, G. (1955). Social casework in relation to cerebral palsy. In W. M. Cruickshank & G. M. Raus (Eds.), *Cerebral palsy: Its individual and community problems* (pp. 462-500). Syracuse, NY: Syracuse University Press.

Whiteneck, G. G., Charlifue, S. W., Frankel, H. L., Fraser, M. H., Gardner, B. P., Gerhart, K. A., Krishnan, K. R., Menter, R. R., Nuseibeh, I., Short, D. J., & Silver, J. R. (1992). Mortality, morbidity, and psychosocial outcomes of persons spinal cord injured more than 20 years ago. *Paraplegia, 30,* 617-630.

Winch, R., Bengtson, L., McLaughlin, J., Fitzsimmons, J., & Budden, S. (1993). Women with cerebral palsy: Obstetric experience and neonatal outcome. *Developmental Medicine and Child Neurology, 35,* 974-982.

Yura, M. T. (1987). Family subsystem functions and disabled children: Some conceptual issues. *Marriage and Family Review, 11*(1/2), 135-151.

NAME INDEX

Abery, B. H., 162
Albrecht, D. G., 59, 85-87, 191, 193
Anderson, C., 106
Anderson, S., 46, 47, 57, 70
Appleton, P. L., 112, 131
Atkinson, D. R., xviii
Aubert, E. J., 98, 100, 112, 128, 148-151,
    171, 172

Bach, C. A., 157
Bachrach, S. J., 22, 71, 73, 95, 96, 123,
    125, 145, 169
Bailey, D. B., 5
Balkman, K., 61
Barakat, L. P., 98
Bar-Eli, M., 170
Batavia, A. I., 157, 162, 174, 185, 191
Batshaw, M. L., 8, 11, 14, 15, 16, 18, 20,
    22, 23, 69, 89, 95, 113, 114
Bedini, L. A., 175
Behrman, B., 100, 131
Benedetti, T. J., 26
Bengtson, L., 144
Benjamin, J. E., 87
Berger, K., 106
Berkowitz, E., xxi
Blair, E., 22
Blake, K., 155, 157

Blasco, P. M., 5
Blomstrand, C., 156
Bloom, L., 111, 112
Blum, R. W., 82, 128-131
Boll, V., 112, 131
Bozzacco, V., 154, 157
Brannan, S. A., 133
Brasher, B., 93, 94
Bregman, S., 111, 115
Brock, S., 173
Bronicki, G. J., 161, 165, 166
Brown, C., 197
Brown, J., 28, 29, 74-76, 98-101,
    129-131, 160
Brown, R. I., 140, 163
Brown, W., 197
Buckley, S., 63
Budden, S., 144
Burke, C., 105
Burke, R., 57
Burns, M. L., 87
Burt, D. B., 161, 162
Buscaglia, L., 3, 4, 13, 38, 39

Caldwell, L. L., 174
Campbell, E., 174
Carson, S. A., 191, 194-196
Castles, E. E., 111, 115

SUBJECT INDEX

ABOUT THE AUTHOR

Peggy Quinn is Associate Professor of Social Work at the University of Texas at Arlington where she has taught in the bachelor's, master's, and doctoral programs for 7 years. She has a bachelor's degree in sociology with a special emphasis in social work, a master's of science in social work, and a PhD in family studies.

For the past 10 years, she has written in the area of disability policy, with special emphasis on the effects these policies have on women. Her work with people who have disabilities has included serving on the Board of Directors of the Center for Computer Assistance to the Disabled in Dallas, Texas, and the Center for Independent Living in Niagara Falls, New York.

In addition to a chapter on gender interactions in families in *Research and Theory in Family Science,* she has published several articles in *Affilia* that focused on women and disabilities. Other research interests include teaching techniques and the use of various strategies that tap students' particular strengths and abilities.